WORKING WITH PEOPLE:

Human Resource Management
in Action

Donald B. Miller

WORKING WITH PEOPLE

Human Resource Management
in Action

CBI Publishing Company, Inc.

51 Sleeper Street, Boston, Massachusetts 02210.

Printed in the United States of America

Printing (last digit): 9 8 7 6 5 4 3 2 1

Library of Congress Cataloging in Publication Data

Miller, Donald Britton.
    Working with people.
    1. Personnel management.   I. Title.
HF5549.M474   658.3   79-16914
ISBN 0-8436-0776-9

*To the many creative managers who strive
to make work interesting, challenging,
growth oriented, and satisfying.*

Contents

Preface

The measure of a manager in the eighties will be the quality of his or her ability to lead, counsel, and manage people. Gone is the time when a poor manager can slip by. Why? Simply, for the future we have outrun the effectiveness of capital and technological improvements without parallel improvements in human resource management. Organizations must increasingly rely on human adaptability. Yet, employees more and more are and will be choosing work and location of work not so much on the salary or benefits as on the quality of the work and the work environment. It is in this turbulant social environment that managers face a real challenge.

Should I pay attention to the results, the work process, or the people? How do I conduct an interview effectively? How do I appraise the employee's work performance? Which style of management is most effective, and when? What theory of motivation do I believe? Or should I believe in any theory? How am I measured? How do I challenge my employees? Do they want challenge? What is a good reward? These are the many questions facing managers. This tersely written book, which has grown from real management experiences blended with behavioral science, will address these kinds of human resource questions for the manager.

I believe that now is the time for a people management book geared to managers for the following reasons

- societal and cultural change — changing values about measures of success and the quality of life
- change in work values — the search for a work ethic
- technological change — its value and the direction in which it should be pushed

- evidence that past management principles and techniques seem not to work as we would like
- increasing complexity of the manager's job
- emerging and usable new understandings from behavioral science
- books designed for human resource professionals don't seem to meet the needs of the line manager.

This book is written from the perspective that the organization through the nature of its business, its beliefs, and its climate establishes the human resource strategy. To manage, one must assess and understand that strategy even though it may not be explicitly described and/or documented. Therefore, Part I opens with an overview of where we are in human resource understanding. Next it helps the individual to assess the climate, understand work motivations, and how the work, the manager, and the organization can impact the development of people. Chapters two through five provide both thought provoking questions and suggested actions. Review of these questions should reinforce and expand on the major points of the chapter. Because the primary purpose of the questions is to enhance learning and because "right" answers are discernable only in context, scoring is left up to you, the reader. The action lists should start you thinking about what you can do.

Part II covers most of the classical H/R (human relations — a convenient abbreviation) functions of the manager. At the end of each chapter there is a questionnaire so the manager may assess how he or she is doing. In addition there are suggestions for action, a check list that should stimulate experiment and improvement in that functional area.

The third and final part covers what types of support the manager should expect from professionals in the H/R function. It then provides a framework for your development in leadership, managing change, career management, developing your own managerial strategy and style, and closes with a discussion of vitality. Again in this section chapters end with some probing questions and a check list to stimulate change and experiment.

This book should provide a basis for managerial self study. It can also be used as a text for management development in industry and should be useful in graduate management programs where the student has managerial experience. That is, it is written to be most helpful to someone who is currently managing other people, not for someone who is studying management in theory, and lacks management experience.

The organization of this book and my approach to the subject have been shaped by more than thirty years in industry and education and my study of the behavioral sciences and management. I owe much of my positive thinking about the enhancement of people through work to my many years as a manager with IBM. My experiences have included extensive opportunity to manage people directly and the opportunity to review the management successes and failures of others. One of my functions over the years was to review and recommend action where the employee and management were at odds. What is written here, therefore, is what I believe based on these experiences and I take full personal responsibility for both the quality and quantity of material.

As I write this book I am fresh from teaching human resource management to over forty students in a Master's program in Engineering Management at the University of Santa Clara. These working engineers and engineering managers pelted me with questions, argued my theses, and forced me to shape up. Therefore, they are responsible for some of the freshness of the approach. My struggle with their gutsy questions should benefit you, the reader.

No preface would be complete without my expression of thanks to the many associates who have helped me shape the ideas presented here. First I wish to acknowledge the learning and inspiration that comes from my consulting clients — since I established my consulting practice they have accelerated my learning about organizations and human resource issues. Special thanks go to Professor Albert Cherns of Loughborough University in England who read and commented on drafts of this book and the organization of material. Paul H. Chaddock, Director, Organization Planning and Development of Dayton-Hudson, read an early version and made many suggestions that I used to improve the book, and I thank him sincerely for that assistance. My wife Alice and my editor Norman Stanton should also share in the success this book achieves. Alice not only corrects my thoughts, my writing style, and types manuscript drafts, but also proofreads to catch those many gremlins of publishing. Norm is the one who spurs me on and creates deadlines, which assure that the product gets published. To all my supporters go my sincere thanks.

Donald B. Miller

PART
I

The Base on Which You Build

Your management approach is built on your image of management, your experiences, education, knowledge, and skills. Your outlook, your strategy, and your style grow and develop in an organization in response to, and nurtured by, the philosophies, policies, and climate of that organization. This part should help clarify the basis for your management outlook — who you are and what influences you.

CHAPTER
1

History
Today
Functions
Fun

Human Resources Overview

We are living in an age of change. In fact for many, change is the only constant. The social environment is the most turbulent of the many environments faced by managers. Therefore, even as this page is written the human resource picture it is trying to create and communicate is changing. Not only is how people relate to each other in organizations changing, but how they look at work and how they are managed is changing in the broad sense. The change differs from organization to organization, from one geographic area to another, and for a specific person it even differs from day to day. So the task of this chapter, to transmit a global picture of the subject, is difficult. However, effective communication and the effectiveness of this book require that we have a shared context into which we can put our understandings. This chapter is intended to develop that shared perspective.

Human resource management is the process of finding, organizing, and utilizing people for the purpose of achieving organizational goals. Some aspects of the activity are clearly separable from other aspects of management. For example, the instruction of a person in the duties of a job is normally a person-to-person transaction. Other human resource management actions are not as clearly definable. For example, is ordering a piece of capital equipment part of human resource management? It is if the type of equipment can change the skill and knowledge needs for the persons involved in the process. A manager choosing to invest in capital equipment may be clearly and consciously choosing not to invest in people. However, for the purposes of this book, we will normally take the narrower view. For you and me, human resource management will generally be things you do which directly affect people, their effectiveness, their growth, and their satisfaction.

History

The act of managing people, getting them to work singly and together for a group purpose or value, began in the tribe. As soon as people grouped together for greater safety, for survival against a common enemy, and to build, we had organizations. In early organizations each human being was utilized for his or her skill. The best hunter was assigned hunting tasks and was used to lead and train others in hunting. By contrast, humans were used at low skill levels as convenient forms of energy. Men drawing a cart were used, not for their skill, but for their power to pull. Both these extremes exist today. The model maker is skilled with his hands and tools, and the stevedore has the ability to lift and to tote.

As society became more organized and especially since the industrial revolution, human beings have been used in organizations in another way. They have been used to do the variable tasks, the adaptive tasks, the tasks requiring the use of human senses in conjunction with machines and systems. Thus, humans filled in the gap between mechanized pieces of equipment. We developed a whole new range of human skills having to do with the person-machine interface. The operator of an interactive graphics terminal attached to a computer is probably one of the most advanced examples of this type.

Last, growing out of philosophical debate, early scholarship, and scientific research and experiment, humans have found useful tasks in adding to and finding use for the body of knowledge. Knowledge was probably a much smaller part of the hunter's skill than was ability with the spear or bow. True, a hunter needed to understand the haunts, behavior, and psychology of the animal being hunted. However, today we have many jobs in organizations where physical coordination or dexterity, or even person-machine interface skills, are a very small or almost nonexistent part of the capabilities being utilized. In our complex society, we have people who are employed primarily for their knowledge, the body of information they bring to the job. Such is the case of the physicist, for example, who works with mathematical formulas and concepts.

Managing, applying people to the work, shares some elements with the past but differs in many activities and relationships. To attract the skilled hunter to support the tribe's needs took leadership. Even in tribal times I suspect this required selling the hunter on the goals and motivating the hunter by offering some reward. This aspect of management is not much different today, though more complex, when we try to get the employee of whatever skill to buy organization goals and work for our

5

organization. But I suspect that few managers today have the position of power of the tribal chieftain. We work with a much more highly educated group of people. We deal with sophisticated and complex processes and huge organizations. We don't have the ultimate tools of banishment and death, nor would we want them on most days.

Today

We live in a world of diversity and variety. We have simple organizations today, where the product and process are easily understood. We also have many organizations in today's world that are complex and utilize humans in a broad and diverse range of activities. Planning for your people needs, hiring appropriately prepared people or hiring people and training them, and organizing and managing the activities of these people are basic human resource functions. They exist in the three-person service organization. They exist in the multinational high-technology organization. Yet there are many special attributes of these functions that reflect the mission and type of organization. Examining one variable will make the point. Organizations may consist of many more people and many more functions than in the past. Sheer numbers of people, varieties of skills needed, and task variety have required increased emphasis on people management. Handling large numbers cannot be done in the way it is done with ones and twos. We need systems and policies to assure fairness and equality. Thus, size alone has increased the demand for training, theories, policies, programs, and systems. In addition, managing the highly trained scientist may differ from managing the skilled carpenter, and managing the fast-food salesperson may differ from managing high school teachers. The sophistication of knowledge and skills utilized can affect management practice. Differences in emphasis and style are suggested by these skill and knowledge ranges, if not differences in basic management principles. The first factor, therefore, is diversity and the need for a variety of styles, concepts, and systems.

A second factor that differentiates the management of people today from the human resource function in the past is the movement away from autocratic management toward participative, or democratic, styles. In the early days of industry and mass production people were placed in slots. The general assumption, usually unstated, was that the person should adapt to the system, to the technical requirements of the job. In fact, early industrial engineering emphasized finding the best way and then requiring the person to do it that way. Sometimes the requirement was in the design of the work station and sometimes in rewards or threats. In fact, mismanagement, the poor quality of the work environment, the lack of thought of and for the people, and the long hours and low pay led to unionization. The employee needed someone to stand up for his or her needs because human resources were treated like capital resources. People were a commodity. Some managements did not treat their people as well as their machines. Machines were maintained. People were used. Today, the majority of people are free to choose employment based on the quality of the work and its environment. One element of the human resource management scene that is clearly different is the need for greater care for the employee, the need to provide the opportunity for the employee to help shape the work and work environment. This is not a change built on the milk of human kindness. It is a change built on business needs and profit motives. Sometimes it is built on legal requirements. The government has joined the cause of the employee through such laws as the Occupational Health and Safety Act, which sets safety standards for work environments.

A third factor on the human resource management scene today is the increased education of the employee and the consequently higher expectations the employee brings to work. The extension of public education to higher levels means that the employee brings desires to work that have been generated in the educational process. These are represented by changed desires about work quality, the sense of satisfaction one expects from the work itself, and desires for higher standards of living, all of which put pressure on the organization for higher pay and benefits. In the positive sense this means that the manager has a more highly trained and skilled employee with more interests to work with. Yet the manager may feel negative about the loss of authority and the apparent decline in blind loyalty and commitment to work. Higher educational levels mean more individualized, more complex relationships between people and work.

Another element of the human resource scene is the changing demographics. Because of a change in birth rates, the extension of life through better health, and more recently the striking down of arbitrary retirement at age sixty-five, the work force is growing older. Contrary to the myths and some current beliefs about aging, this does not mean we have or need to have a lot of obsolete, slow, or inadequate employees. It does mean, though, that the effective management style and system to motivate someone in their fifties is probably different from that which motivates people in their twenties. It means that managers must overcome age prejudices and learn new skills of iteratively matching people and work over a longer time span. It means that managers must learn more about the values and goals of the employee as they change throughout life.

Still another element is the increase in specialist services and support for the manger. Where the manager of the past was expected to do all human resource functions more or less alone, today's medium and large organizations support the manager with personnel specialists. This is both good and bad. For example, it is often too easy for the manager to abdicate responsibility for salary administration and let the salary specialist do it. Or it is easy for the manager to feel he or she has little or no responsibility for training when there is an education and training department. These are examples of the bad aspects. However, because the organization and its functions are complex, it is possible through specialists to provide higher quality services. By employing human resource professionals with special technical training or understandings of the complexities of motivational psychology, for example, we can enhance the manager's capability. We have the potential of forming a new partnership of manager and human resource professional and thus the opportunity for some breakthroughs in human resource management.

One of the elements of the human resource scene that motivates me to write this book and probably motivates you, the manager, to read it is that we are demanding more adaptability out of people. Rapid technological change, fast-changing business characteristics, and social change mean changes in our organizations. The energy and capability for managing change is a human component. People make organizations vital. People do the things which make one organization succeed and another fail. Yet human adaptability has costs. On the negative side are the problems described by Alvin Tofler in *Future Shock*. One of these we are seeing more of is negative adaptation to stress caused by work. On the positive side is enhanced vitality and improvement in human satisfaction made possible through the growth and learning that takes place when we adapt. Here is an area where the quality of management can make a real difference.

I could go on listing and describing many of the special features or trends in today's human resource management field. Others might include increasing need to emphasize and understand systems, multicultural challenges in the multinational organization, or the development of special languages (jargon) in businesses, or the management fads, or the problems of the conglomerate. However, these examples should serve to set the scene. The management of people in organizations has and is changing. The need for and importance of good management is growing. In fact the difference between a good place to work and a poor place to work is more and more the difference in the quality of people management. Right now in the San Francisco Bay Area where organization people needs are going unmet, recruiting has become highly competitive. Advertisements for professional engineers and technicians on the radio during commuting times are stressing the freedom to grow and change, to manage one's own career. They are stressing the *quality* of the work environment.

Functions

Both the brief historical view and the foregoing insight into a few aspects of today's people management scene have included some introduction to functions. An overview is needed, however, to define the field more specifically. The following lists of planning and implementing functions include both those generally the responsibility of the individual manager and those generally the responsibility of the human resource, or personnel, manager. Where these functions are handled will vary from organization to organization. The wording of the list is in terms of the organization, in contrast to the chapters of the book which define the individual manager's functions. The list includes most of the major functions, although specific organizations may have others that reflect the unique character of the business.

Planning

· Creation and maintenance of record systems about people and people needs. This means developing an information system including all categories of people for planning purposes. It must include ways of identifying mission-specific people (that is, carpenters for construction, teachers for education) and general groups such as secretaries, model makers, salespeople, and engineering professionals. It must contain data about people today and in the future.
· Projection of future staff requirements by quantity, type, and skill level required because of any change in the character, size, or technology of the business.
· Replacement planning for those who will be lost through turnover. Creation of career and individual development plans for all employees including especially professional, administrative, and management personnel.

- Projection of the need for and objectives for all types of training and educational programs which are necessary to provide personal, technical, professional, and managerial development.
- Planning for organizational changes (that is, new locations, new divisions, new product lines) and preparing the necessary management change, action, and training strategies.
- Conducting and analyzing opinion (attitude and morale) surveys and performance measures for evidence of problems which may indicate a need for new organizations, new or additional training, and management practice changes.
- Establishing meaningful policies, strategies, goals, and objectives for human resources and proposing new programs where necessary. Examples include recruiting and turnover goals, promotion and salary objectives, and changes in benefits policies.
- Integrating the human resource strategies and plans with all other planning activities, including financial and budget planning.

Implementing

- Establishing a recruiting organization, recruiting, selecting, and hiring the necessary numbers with the right qualifications from local, national, and university sources.
- Matching the newly hired employees with the proper openings for initial introduction to the organization and effective use of their skills toward the productive objectives of the organization.
- Providing the necessary initial indoctrination and education as well as continuing education and training for all employees.
- Appraisal and evaluation of the performance with appropriate counseling for growth and improvement or weeding out of hiring errors and those who fail to perform and thrive in the organization.
- Career counsel for long-term individual development of capabilities and early identification of those with significant potential to grow to higher levels of responsibility or to change to other fields or specialties in response to organization needs.
- Promoting both to fill openings and to provide accelerated growth for those with outstanding potential. In a technical-professional organization, promotions also occur in response to increased professional competence, not just as a result of higher-level openings.
- Managing attrition and turnover, both internal and external, to assure challenge and growth and to help retain those of outstand-

ing potential and to provide sufficient change in the organization to maintain and assure vitality. This may mean that as much attention is given to rotation and outplacement as is normally given to recruiting.

· Managing the salary programs to assure that compensation for merit and performance is equivalent or better than that in other organizations in order to keep quality employees.

· Devising such policies and programs as are necessary to assist and to motivate managers and professionals to combat obsolescence and maintain and enhance the vitality and effectiveness of humans in the organization.

· Engaging in organization development and job and assignment design to assure that personal development is stimulated and enhanced by challenging and meaningful assignments. This probably involves the elimination of poor jobs, the creation of temporary task forces, and new kinds of assignments on an overall basis, as well as within the confines of a function. It may call for real innovation in the design of work organizations.

· Devising and selling to management such new and innovative human resource experiments and programs as are necessary to maintain leadership and the health of the organization.

· Creating and monitoring measurement programs to sample attitudes and climate, as well as human resource program accomplishments and the overall productivity of the organization.

· Negotiating with and establishing the most open and positive relation possible with the union where one exists.

Because the foregoing listed human resource functions from the overall organizational perspective, it necessarily used some specialized terms. The book, however, primarily emphasizes what you and I do as managers and will be relatively free of jargon. Wherever possible, specialized terms will be avoided.

Fun

No overview of the management of people would be complete without talking about the fact that it is one of the most challenging, stimulating, and satisfying experiences a person can have. True, some don't want and don't thrive on this exciting task, but successful managers do. Through my

11

interviews of managers and from comments overheard in the hall or at social events, I hear them talking of the rewards of managing. The psychic income is high. It is rewarding to feel you have helped someone else to achieve a higher level of accomplishment and satisfaction. It is exciting to have a role which requires interacting and communicating with changing, growing, creative, and stimulating people. It is fun to try a different way, to try to differentiate your relations to reflect the differences in people. It is exciting to get the feedback which tells you that you make a difference. It is fun to play a game that excels in variety and lack of predictability. It is fun to contribute through the process of turning others on to a better work life.

SUMMARY

Human resource management includes attracting to the organization the people necessary for the organization to pursue its function. It includes matching the individual's needs and capabilities with those of the organization—working to create the most productive and satisfying work environment possible. It includes measuring performance, coaching and training, even weeding out the inadequate. It also includes reward of good performance and increased individual capability.

Good management of people results in an output that is greater, because of the combination of the organization and the individual, than either could produce alone. Good management of people increasingly means adjusting the organization to the people as well as helping the individual to adapt to the organization. Good management of people is tougher today than it has ever been before. It is an exciting occupation, one with increasing challenge and increasing importance because of complexity and change. Change means a need for human adaptation. How you manage can aid and abet adaptation or can make it stressful and costly in lost human capability.

Human resource management is in transition. Good human resource management is becoming increasingly important for the survival of the organizatiion. In fact, there are already signs that we are differentiating between good and poor organizations on the quality of human resource management. This can affect the organization's ability to attract and hold talented people. This means good management of people and organizational success are inextricably tied together. The manager is key to organization success since he or she operates at the interface between the organization and the individual—where the real difference can be made.

CHAPTER
2

Assessing An Organization's Human Resource Climate

Kinds of Human Resource Climates

How Climates Get Established

How Climates Are Changed

Organization Climate and Policies

Every organization has a climate, an environment, created by its purpose or mission, its goals, strategies, and policies, and shaped by management personality and the ways in which responsible people direct the operation. Thus an inventor-founder of a small electronics firm imprints the organization with his or her beliefs, fears, energy, and personality. Despite its growth, Polaroid is still such an organization where Edwin Land's imprint is clearly visible. The nature of the business also shapes the environment and impacts the human resource management theme. For example, in a raw-materials industry such as coal mining, the nature of the work shapes the environment. Climates are also shaped by beliefs and policies. For example, one of IBM's beliefs, supported by policy and management practice, is respect for the individual. The many things that flow from that belief make the IBM work environment humanistic. Yet, that is not the only element of the IBM environment, for it is a high-technology organization, highly competitive, with a sales-experienced top management which is highly profit motivated. All these aspects and more make up the work environment.

As individual managers, our outlook, our style, and the range of our options in dealing with the people we manage are established in part by the organization environment. Thus if we work in an organization that has policies, goals, and practices that support treating employees as adults it is easier for us as managers to do so. If we work for an organization that treats people as machines we will tend to do so. I am not suggesting that we as managers should use the organization as an excuse for not doing better at people management. I am suggesting we need to analyze and understand the climate before we can work at improving our human resource management.

Assessing an Organization's Human Resource Climate

How does one measure the human resource climate of an organization? Certainly one way is to look at and listen to the people. Do their expressions transmit a feeling that this is a good place to work? Do their comments lead you to feel they believe they are respected for who they are and what they can contribute? Do you get a sense of a fair environment where rewards bear a meaningful relationship to accomplishment? In short, is this an organization of good morale? Good morale is neither the only reflection of a positive H/R environment nor an absolute representation of a good H/R environment. Morale could be good under a respected tyrant and poor under a democratic manager who is unable to supply meaning and goals. This lack of clear unquestionable measures is characteristic of the challenge in assessing a climate. It is usually variable and inconsistent. It will not look the same from different perspectives or at different times. Individuals, managers, and groups may represent special cases and fail to reflect the norm.

Another way of measuring the H/R environment is to look for documentation. This means looking at policy manuals, benefit programs, hiring practices, promotion and pay, and other concrete evidences. For example, high turnover rates, higher than for other organizations in that type of business, could be a signal that the H/R environment is poor. People choose to leave an organization because, for a variety of reasons, it is not right for them. Prolonged and difficult union negotiations might also reflect H/R problems. By contrast, low turnover, evidence that the organization has no difficulty attracting new employees, good and well-documented policies, and high relative pay might be concrete evidence of a good H/R environment.

At the end of this chapter there is an organization climate and H/R environment checkup. Now might be a good time to try to fill it out for your organization. Doing so will provide you with increased understanding of the things to look for and may help you understand the way that your organization's climate may be affecting you and your employees.

Kinds of Human Resource Climates

Organizations fall into four basic H/R strategy categories. Each of these tends to create a type of climate. Probably no organization is pure; that is, most organizations are inconsistent. Sometimes the management seems to believe in one of these concepts but acts in accord with another. What we need to look for is the central tendency or most consistent pattern of belief, strategy and practice. The four are:

1. *Humans are disposable.*   An organization adhering to this belief and operating on this basic premise will hire and use people for

the organization's good and when they are no longer needed fire them or lay them off. The general belief is that people are like throw-away batteries. You hire people in charged condition and use them and the charge up, and then dispose of them. Financially this organization sees people as an expense.

2. *Humans are renewable.* In this H/R climate, as in the disposable case, people have a value to the organization and are used up in the process of work. But it differs in its feeling that people can be restored to nearly original value with the right treatment and retraining. This organization takes some responsibility for repair and refurbishment, much as it would care for a piece of equipment or machinery. Financially this organization looks at people as a capital investment that can be kept in working order for a long time but that eventually wears out.

3. *Humans are recyclable.* In this H/R environment the organization treats the employee similarly to a raw material. In the first cycle the organization uses them as they are. When the business changes and needs change, this organization supports adaptation, retraining, and change in the individual to meet new needs. However, the underlying feeling is that in the second or later cycles the individual will never be quite as productive, as capable,

as when used in the original form. Financially this organization views people as a capital investment but believes in a longer useful life than the organization espousing concept two.

4. *Humans are enhanceable.*   An organization adhering to this concept believes in human development and growth. Here we might liken the fresh recruit to a seed. If the organization nurtures these persons, challenges them, and provides opportunities for their development, it is possible that they will achieve value way beyond that which they represented on entrance. This H/R environment is one in which the inevitability of decline and aging is simply not accepted. Financially this organization sees people as an investment with long-term growth and income potential.

These samples of strategies or concepts should forcibly demonstrate the affect of an environment on you as a manager. Even if you started with the belief that people can grow and develop if you live in a type one organization, you are not rewarded or supported in this belief. In fact your desire to help the employee grow is probably viewed as counterproductive. By contrast, if you adhere to the feeling, prevalent in our culture, that people decline in motivation and ability with increasing age, you will be out of tune in a type four environment. Your effectiveness as a manager depends on your being basically in tune with the organization's H/R environment. If the organizational environment is significantly divergent from your own beliefs, values, and desires then this conflict will undoubtedly create stress reactions in you. These reactions may vary all the way from vague uneasiness to actual illness. You may respond by staying in the organization and suffering, staying in the organization and changing your beliefs and values or those of the organization, or leaving the organization for a more compatible climate.

How Climates Get Established

In the beginning of this chapter, founders of organizations were given credit for imprinting their image on the climate of the organization. Some of this is done consciously and as a direct reflection of the goals and personality of the individual. Some of this is done unconsciously as the result of negative experiences or fears. That is, there is active shaping and there is shaping by the absence of action or a position. In this case climates are established by the people of the organization because of an inherent human need to have a rule or limit. The rules that are established may either represent a guess at what the leader wants or an imprinting by middle and lower management. Incidentally, this need for rules or norms can be seen in the games people play. If you set up a game with limited and simple rules, the players will make up rules; so too in organizations. Climates are built by the intentional desire of the leader or leaders to make this organization different. Climates are also established by practices that develop in the absence of a statement of intent or policy.

Climates are also established by events both external and internal to the organization. For example, a work accident which results in injury will often be the cause for creating new safety rules and work practices, sometimes even making design changes. Or the dismissal of an employee for a legitimate reason, poorly communicated, can set up a climate of increased anxiety about holding jobs among other employees. This aspect of climate is often not a reflection of real rules but a perception or belief based on an observable event. External events like economic cycles, natural disasters, and competitive announcements can affect the work climate. Announcement by a competitor of a superior service or product at lower cost immediately increases the pressure for improvement in the vital and responsive organization. If improvement is not forthcoming the loss of business may later set up a climate which supports fear of loss of income or job. Again, climate may be established by intent, sometimes just by the prevailing interpretation of an event, or even in the absence of intent.

The technology, the design of the process and the equipment used by the organization, shapes the H/R climate. An organization whose activity is based on highly complex equipment sets a high value on the skills necessary to use and repair that equipment. The equipment also determines the range and type of activities of the people and influences the beliefs and behavior norms. A group working on an equipment-dependent process where the equipment is unreliable or insufficient will develop attitudes about management's lack of support that will affect their commitment, their work patterns, the energy they use on the job and their sense of what is a fair day's work. One day when I observed cigarette manufacturing I experienced this. Each complex machine was operated by a team of three or four. The noise, the working space, and the idiosyncracies of the particular machine influenced the outlook and behavior of the teams in discernable ways.

The personality of the top management and of each layer imprint the H/R climate. A top manager with a hair-trigger temper, for example, will, over time, probably shorten everyone's tolerance for error or malfunction and establish the style of reaction to that condition. Thus in such an organization, tirades, shouting, and desk pounding are apt to become part of everyone's interpersonal style.

Climates are established in many ways. There is no single source of design, creation, or reinforcement of an H/R environment. It is both the sum of a large number of separate events and management actions and the interaction of these on each other. Climates vary with business mood and time. Yet work climates can be analyzed, and central patterns or thrusts can be identified. Analyzing the climate is an important first step in developing your H/R management outlook. Understanding the events and beliefs that created an aspect of the work climate may be the second step. Your decision about whether these climate norms are beneficial affects both your outlook and style and your ability to enlist others in change and improvement.

How Climates Are Changed

Organizational climates become candidates for change when either management or employees identify a hurt and trace it to work climate. Like people, organizations change when feedback tells them that they are hurting or being less successful than they should be or need to be. They may also change in response to outside forces that they analyze as representing a threat. Typical organizational problems are loss of market, loss of profit, increased employee absences and illnesses, increased turnover of people, lowered morale, and an increase in grievances. Sometimes the first noticeable event is the surprisingly good reception given to an outside group attempting to organize employees into a union. These are but some of the problems traceable to the H/R environment. Each organization has its own hot buttons. These reflect management's views of goals. Some organizations are much more sensitive to H/R disturbances than others. This in itself is a climate difference.

Generally after identification of the problem comes a study of the causes. When management believes that the price of change is more desirable than the continued cost of the identified causes, it initiates action. Here are some typical management actions aimed at improving the H/R climate:

1. Reevaluation of job positions (salary levels) and establishment of new, higher (more competitive) and more output-responsive salary plans and programs.

19

2. Reevaluation of benefits and improvement of the support of the employee in medical costs, holidays, vacations, retirement, savings programs, stock purchase, and so on.

3. Implementation of attitude surveys or interview programs to listen to employee complaints and address them with changes and improvements.

4. Reorganization into new, usually smaller, entities and groups, often accompanied by the selection of new leaders who are believed capable of being more responsive to people's needs and the quality of the work environment.

5. Implementation of organization development activities (OD is a term applied to a broad range of organizational improvements), proactive change implementation programs, which range from providing groups with process consultants (people who help you improve how, not what, you do) to training programs in team development (teaching work groups how they can solve problems and learn as a group) and other group processes designed to improve interpersonal effectiveness.

6. Implementation of new management development and employee development programs in the hopes that education will change values and practices and thus improve the climate.*

7. Establishment of new policies designed to enhance the status, freedoms, and even rights of the employee in relation to the organization.

8. Changing the context in which the work environment is viewed. This usually means significantly increased communication about organizational and individual goals and values and opening up to information about the outside world (other organizations) to enhance the comparative value of the organizational environment.**

---

* As I write this I am consulting with one of my clients on exactly this issue. It occurred to me that an example might help. In this case the organization determined that they had an increase in career frustrations, employees who believed they were not or could not grow in the organization. The question was what could be done to improve the perception of the organization's interest in and support of individual development. Out of a broad range of activities they chose a training program for managers. Oversimplified, this program has two objectives: (1) to encourage the manger to have career-oriented discussions with the employee, and (2) to assist the manager in becoming more comfortable in career-oriented discussions (interviews) with the employee.

** One organization with which I've been acquainted was experiencing a change in the character of the growth of its business. That is, it was becoming possible to increase the size and income of the business without adding more employees. The employees viewed the change as one from a growing organization where personal growth was virtually assured as new people came in below to a stable organization. This organization undertook an extensive program of selling the bright future of the organization and trying to change the view of personal growth from moving up to increased capability.

Which action plans are chosen will also be dependent on the climate, the past experiences, and the values of the organization. Thus an organization that has been paternalistic will more often opt for programs or changes which follow the practice of giving the employee (child) new benefits. An organization with a tendency toward frank, open, adult communication will most often opt for a program that pushes further in that direction by employing items three and five in the above list. Often these actions are taken in combination, and the vigor with which they are pursued will be in proportion to management's judgment about the seriousness of the problem. The duration of the program, how long the new thrust lasts, is sometimes determined by measured change and improvement but often by diversion of management's attention to another pain.

SUMMARY

Organizational climates are created both by the personality of the management and their resulting personal imprint and by the deliberate design of policies and goals. The climate is also shaped by the nature of the business and is often influenced by the absence of specific action. It is possible to assess a climate by asking questions, looking, and listening.

A healthy organization can be created by a management that is clear about the type of H/R climate they wish to establish. But to create a good climate also requires being in touch with the climate you have created. Once the desired climate is defined, it should be reinforced by policy and practice and communciated openly. In other words, talking about it sets up feedback about it which allows you to measure success or failure. One broad way in which organizations differ is in their overall human resource concept. Four concepts were discussed: humans are disposable, humans are renewable, humans are recyclable, and humans are enhanceable.

Your effectiveness as a manager is highly dependent on the congruence between your beliefs and values and the climate of the organization. Thus, it is important to assess the environment and to understand your beliefs. If there is a dichotomy you should work to improve the climate of the organization or modify your beliefs, or find one you can support. Your health, your effectiveness, and your ability to develop an authentic style and role are dependent on this congruence. If you try to manage in an organization with which you are incompatible, you will not be rewarded and you will undoubtedly show signs of stress. In accepting the need for congruence, however, you should not expect absolute agreement. Both you and the organization are living, changing, evolving organisms.

Organization Climate and H/R Environment Checkup

1. List five descriptive terms or phrases that you would use to describe the organization in which you work with special emphasis on characteristics affecting people. You may wish to test their general acceptance and validity by discussing them with others who work with you. Try to find the most important characteristics, the ones which differentiate your organization from others. Typical characteristics might be high person-to-person competition, competitive pay scales, responsiveness to human differences and needs, slow-to-improve benefits and work conditions, in turmoil, a stormy place to work, autocratic, many top-down orders, wandering apparently without clear goals and objectives.

Characteristic   **What is Your Evidence for It?**

_____   _____
_____   _____
_____   _____
_____   _____
_____   _____

2. List five norms of behavior (unwritten, often unexpressed, but generally accepted rules) in your work organization. Examples might be behaviors expected in meetings, types of responses to certain executives, topics that are avoided, dress codes, standardized ways of looking at some aspect of the operation.

Norms   **Your Evidence that the Norm Exists**

_____   _____
_____   _____
_____   _____
_____   _____
_____   _____

3. Indicate whether the following statements describe your work environment as you see it and experience it. The statements are in pairs. Look for deeper understanding in those pairs where there seems to be a significant difference between what you feel the organization does and what you are doing. Then ask yourself what would be the desirable or ideal answer to each question.

	Definitely Yes	Probably Yes	?	Probably No	Definitely No
a. Your manager is open, supportive, and considerate.	( )	( )	( )	( )	( )
b. You are open, supportive, and considerate of those you manage.	( )	( )	( )	( )	( )

		Definitely Yes	Probably Yes	?	Definitely No	Probably No
c.	Jobs and tasks are characterized by variety and challenge, and are meaningful and satisfying.	( )	( )	( )	( )	( )
d.	Your tendency is to consider the likes and dislikes as well as the skills of your employees in making assignments.	( )	( )	( )	( )	( )
e.	In general the organization supports the concept that rewards should be based on performance.	( )	( )	( )	( )	( )
f.	As a manager you pay, reward, and promote on the basis of performance and accomplishment.	( )	( )	( )	( )	( )
g.	Your comanagers, those above you, those at your level, and those below you, despite differences in tasks and objectives, are trusting, supportive, friendly, and cooperative.	( )	( )	( )	( )	( )
h.	You look for and take opportunities to step beyond your prescribed role and help your fellow managers.	( )	( )	( )	( )	( )
i.	Generally people in the organization are concerned with quality of work output.	( )	( )	( )	( )	( )
j.	You are highly concerned by the quality of output and the quality of work and work conditions necessary to produce that output.	( )	( )	( )	( )	( )
k.	The organization does not skimp in supporting employees with up-to-date and high-quality efficient equipment, physical facilities, and services.	( )	( )	( )	( )	( )
l.	You have been successful in improving the equipment space and support so that your employees' capabilities are enhanced and used effectively.	( )	( )	( )	( )	( )

		Definitely Yes	Probably Yes	?	Definitely No	Probably No
m.	The organization provides good education and training to enhance the employees' capabilities and assist in career and personal growth.	( )	( )	( )	( )	( )
n.	You counsel and support your employees in gaining additional training and education even at some loss of work time and effort in the short run.	( )	( )	( )	( )	( )
o.	People in the organization at all levels are generally well prepared in knowledge and skill for their jobs, and these capabilities are utilized.	( )	( )	( )	( )	( )
p.	Your employees are well prepared in knowledge and skill for their jobs, and you work to utilize these capabilities in their assignments.	( )	( )	( )	( )	( )
q.	You are consulted and participate in decisions on goals and ways of doing things in the organization.	( )	( )	( )	( )	( )
r.	You involve your employees in decision making in your group.	( )	( )	( )	( )	( )
s.	Generally the organization sets up a positive but not excessive demand for people to be committed and produce.	( )	( )	( )	( )	( )
t.	You work to motivate your employees in the way which is most effective for each individual but do not demand excessive time or output performance.	( )	( )	( )	( )	( )
u.	The organization is open to change and encourages people to suggest ways of improving both work quality and effectiveness.	( )	( )	( )	( )	( )
v.	You actively solicit and reward suggestions from your group for changes and improvements.	( )	( )	( )	( )	( )

4. What do you believe is the generally held image of the organization's tomorrow? Is there a sense or image of a positive future for the organization? How is the sense of future communicated? Is the picture of the future sufficient to provide you and others with a motivational thrust? State the picture as you see it. What is the image? ——————————————————————

    ——————————————————————————————————

    Is it well communicated? ————————————————————————————

    Does it motivate you? How? ————————————————————————

    ——————————————————————————————————

5. How effective do you believe your group or department is compared to what it could be? In effect is the organization productive and is your part of it in tune? Is the organization getting a good return on its investment in human resources? Why or why not? How effective is the organization as a whole? ——————————————————————

    ——————————————————————————————————

    How effective is your group or function? ———————————————————

    ——————————————————————————————————

    What is your evidence? ——————————————————————————

    ——————————————————————————————————

6. What major change do you believe would most enhance the effectiveness of people in your organization? Why? Is there support for such a change?
    Change that is needed ——————————————————————————

    ——————————————————————————————————

    Why do you feel it is needed? ——————————————————————

    ——————————————————————————————————

    Is there support in the organization for this improvement? ——————————————

    ——————————————————————————————————

Ideas for Action: Improving Climate Environment

1. A good H/R environment is one that respects people as individuals. People feel their differences are understood, that someone cares about their needs, and that they are used for their unique capabilities. It is as if everyone expects them to act as adults and supports them when they do.

    something
    to try

    a. Modify your practices to increase the sense of employee participation and ability to participate in decision making and other important organization activities.   ( )
    b. Assist the individual employee in taking charge of his or her growth and development.   ( )
    c. Open new and effective channels of communication about organizational improvement, for adjudication of grievances, for improvement in understanding of goals and direction.   ( )
    d. Change your style so as to enhance your employees' opportunity to act as adults and to demonstrate your respect for them as individuals.   ( )
    e. Change policies or practices that expect the employee to be dependent to ones which require independence of action.   ( )

2. A good H/R environment is a type four (humans are enhanceable) environment.
    a. Increase the freedom employees have to ask for changes in work which will improve their match with the organization, their opportunities to change roles as they pass through the passages of life, their opportunities to learn.   ( )
    b. Enhance educational and training availability and improve its relationship to work and employee needs.   ( )
    c. Set up measures and or analyses of the organization's H/R environment which will make management more conscious of its quality and the need for improvement.   ( )
    d. Search for and change policies or programs that are inconsistent with expecting the individual to take responsibility for personal development.   ( )
    e. If your organization has someone or some group activity working to improve the H/R environment devote some time to getting acquainted with their activity. If not, work to set up such an activity.   ( )

3. A good human resource environment is evidenced by good morale and a desire on the part of those outside to join the organization.
    a. What is the morale in my group? What is the morale in the organization? Is it declining or improving? Establish a program or programs to work at ways of improving morale.   ( )
    b. What is the outside image of our organization as a place to work? Are we transmitting an accurate picture? Work to improve the image.   ( )

    c.   What is the relative value of our H/R environment when compared with work environments in other organizations? Can we learn from things others are doing? Establish a program to improve the quality of the H/R climate.   (   )

4.   The individual manager represents the organization to the employee. No matter how positive or negative the overall H/R environment is, the immediate manager may modify it as the interpreter and transmitter for the specific employee.

    a.   Make changes to improve my communication of an honest and clear image of the goals and intent of the organization to my employees.   (   )

    b.   Take actions to improve the work climate for my employees by being more responsive to their needs and by providing improved opportunities for using their capabilities..   (   )

    c.   Work to improve the quality of my feedback to my employees on their performance by letting them know where they stand.   (   )

    d.   Improve the quality of my coaching and support of my employees.   (   )

    e.   Increase the opportunities for my employees to participate in decision making.   (   )

CHAPTER
3

Work Values

Work Motivations

Work Quality

Work Values, Motivation, and Quality

Why do people work? Why do you work? The most normal response is to earn money. Yet actually we work for many reasons. Over time, with different needs and values and as we move from phase to phase in life, these reasons change in priority. We work, therefore, to fulfill various needs or expectations. We expect to be paid. We expect to gain some sense of contribution and accomplishment. We expect recognition and reward. We expect work associates we like to be with. We expect if we do well we will get increased responsibility. Our expectations are numerous and varied. Our evaluation of whether we have good work and a good place to work relates directly to how well our expectations are met. Generally when we are meeting our needs, getting the rewards we need and want, we work more effectively. All the manager has to do, therefore, is to set up the conditions where each one of us feels we are meeting our needs and goals, where our expectations are reasonably met, and we will be motivated to work and will consider that the quality of work is good! This is not easy because of the variety of employee needs, the various needs of the organization, and the needs of the manager. Often these needs conflict, and many are beyond what can be done within the budget, the time, the physical conditions, the technology, the laws of the land, and on and on. The manager's role requirement is to do the best he or she can within the constraints and in response to the multitude of needs and expectations of the people and the organization. In developing your most effective style and your personal thrust as a manager you should understand work values, motivations, and quality.

Work Values

From my perspective the best kind of work is work through which I can gain self-actualization. This is work that you might describe as a calling. What do I mean by that? First, that the interest in and motivation and skill for the work seems to develop as much from a source inside as outside the person. It is as if the individual is both drawn toward the work because of the values he or she ascribes to it and pushed toward it by some inner plan or pattern.

Second, it means to the individual that the work is important and meaningful. That is, with his or her scale of values the person believes that a contribution to society will result from doing the work. Certainly those attracted to ministerial activities and health services would understand and generally reflect this feeling. However, one could apply the same outlook to laying bricks, plowing a field, or searching for new chemical compounds. The value is not absolute; it is represented in the expected outcomes to which the individual ascribes a value, a measure of importance. One person might ascribe a high value to an activity that someone else values much lower. In one case the work would be meaningful. In the case of the other person it would not.

Third, I consider work of high value if it utilizes the person's skill. A sense of being needed comes from a person's belief that he or she brings something unique to the activity. The fact that the individual does it is good because some unique understanding, creativity, skill, energy, or knowledge is brought to the process. The individual is able to imprint the accomplishment with his or her insignia, or mark. The accomplishment is owned by the individual.

Fourth, for me, work of high value is work which the doer enjoys, work where there can be a sense of fun, of play, as well as of satisfaction. Such work makes life more enjoyable, the individual a better person, and relations with other people are often better because of this. Such work makes it desirable to get up and go. Such work provides the doer with psychic needs of accomplishment, reward for achievement, and a sense of movement toward something. It also gives the individual a way of creating a balanced outlook toward life since he or she is better able to face negative incidents when work is going well.

Fifth, I do not separate work from life. They are intertwined. People were born to work. Yet for some people work is not life. For these people work is what they do to get the money to live life, which is something separate from work. I would be less than honest if I didn't say I believe my outlook is the better one. I am acknowledging my values. It is important that I as a manager identify the fact that this is my value judgment. This value judgment may or may not be shared by those who work with and for me.

This brief review of my values should tell us something about work values. The value is not only in the work itself; more importantly, it is in an attitude, an outlook which we bring to the work. These attitudes come not only from our experience, our learning, our families, and our history but also from who we are. That is, they result from an amalgam of inner and outer worlds. Work values are personal and individual. Although general cultural beliefs about work ethics undoubtedly influence the individual, each individual has a personal outlook. Thus, in telling you about my values I'm under no delusion that you will necessarily share them. For us as managers it is important to understand our work values, the outlook we bring to work, and very important that we attempt to listen for and understand the work values of those who work for us. If we assume our work values are universal, we start with at least one strike against us in searching for effectiveness in H/R management. It is as if nothing else we do will make sense. We will not come across as authentic. We will start with a communications gap or, worse, a blockage that portends failure.

One of the best descriptive systems for values associated with work I have discovered was developed by Clare Graves. It was later the basis for an American Management Association survey of managers. This survey of about five thousand AMA members was published in 1975 by AMA as a survey report entitled *Managerial Values For Working*, by V.S. Flowers, C.L. Hughes, M. S. Myers, and S. S. Myers. This is not the only way of looking at values but is rather a way that can be used to demonstrate how a manager and an employee having different values may conflict.

The system identifies seven different sets of values. Only six are useful in the world of work, and of these we will use just a couple to make our point. *Tribalistic* is the first. An employee holding to these values generally believes that being part of a tribe (team) that is well run by a strong leader is the good work situation. Such an employee is willing to do routine work if treated fairly, accepted by the group, and recognized as a team member by the boss. Such a person wants and expects specific direction. Being a good team member is of prime importance to this person.

If this person works for a manager who either shares or respects these values and manages this person in that context, things probably go well. If, on the other hand, the manager's values hold that people should want to grow through work, to gain a sense of self and major satisfactions from work, there is a potential conflict. If the manager cannot understand that the employee holds different values or if he or she fails to manage in the employee's context, there will undoubtedly be conflict. Respect and communication are built on shared values and experiences.

Another value set identified by Graves is labeled *conformist*. This person views security, well-defined rules, and loyalty as central. The employee expects reward for loyalty. Everything the employee does reflects the belief that being like the group in dress, behavior, and action will pay off.

    If this employee comes up against a manager who has a *manipulative* value set there is potential trouble. The manipulator's values stress freedom to wheel and deal and to be paid off for results. In this scheme there is no payoff for conforming; rather there is payoff for individual initiative. If the manager senses this difference and acts to bridge the gap, there may be success. Failing to do so augurs for conflict and an employee who feels he or she has been treated unfairly.

    At the end of this chapter there is a brief work values checkup. The intent behind the set of questions is to help you to understand your work values and to equip you with the types of questions which will help you identify the work values held by others.

Work Motivations

Work values are the stuff of which work motivations are made. But values tend to apply to more situations and are deeper, more tightly held, and harder to dislodge. By comparison one's motivations can often be tied to a

specific task. That is, if I put a load of shirts in the washing machine, I am probably doing so because I need clean shirts. The immediate and specific need and motivation is to have a clean shirt to wear. However, the basis of this specific motivation is my value that a clean shirt is more comfortable or that a clean shirt is a constituent of success.

The following brief review of the various theories of motivation is not presented to sell you, the manager, on a motivational theory but to aid you in becoming cognizant of the theories and to provide you with a base for developing your own operating strategy. Remember that a theory is only of value as a way of bringing order and understanding out of complexity. It is of value as long as we don't have a better one and as long as it works for us. Each of the following motivational concepts has something of value. Motivation is a set of learned responses. We cannot motivate someone else, but we can establish conditions where it is probable they will motivate themselves because of their values, their needs, their expectations, and outlook.

Broadly, motivations fall into two categories. Physiological motivations come from a change in the chemical balance of the individual. Except in extreme cases, such as a group literally starving, managers don't need to deal with or do anything relative to these motivations. It is with the second category, learned or social motivations, that the manager must deal. Such motivations are almost infinite in number and include the following needs:

- · to acquire things
- · to conserve things
- · to have order
- · to build and construct
- · to be better, to improve
- · to achieve and accomplish
- · to show off, to exhibit
- · to be recognized
- · to have privacy
- · to defend self
- · to influence or dominate
- · to be autonomous, self-regulating, self-managing
- · to be affiliated, to belong, to have friends
- · to play
- · to understand and to be understood

Motivations, needs, and the expectations which they establish form the basis for the psychological work contract. If an individual agrees to work for you, it is fundamentally because he or she feels that in doing so some needs will be met. The basis for the psychological work contract is communication about needs and capabilities and an interpretation or perception of fulfillment and utilization. The psychological work contract, most often undocumented and unwritten, can be the source of a successful match of person to job. Improperly established, it can be the basis for employee grievances and failure.

Many philosophers, psychologists, scientists, researchers, and managers have added to our understanding of social or learned motivations, the basis in psychological work contracts. Here are some of the significant contributions associated with the names of the contributors.

SIGMUND FREUD   established the thesis that many motivations are subconscious, that is, unexpressed and often unidentified. Generally this suggests that the individual is conscious of, identifies with, and acknowledges only the tip of the iceberg of motivations. This means the motivation you ascribe to someone's behavior generally rests on something far deeper.

ALFRED ADLER   called our attention to the power motive, the need to influence others, to get others to do our bidding. This motivation is evident in the young child who tries to control the parent by crying. Sometimes this behavior continues into adult life. This motivation is strongly evident in some people and seemingly unidentifiable in others.

ROBERT WHITE   added to Adler's identification of power. He identified the need to understand and manipulate our environment, the need to have power over things as opposed to people. This is seen in our desire to make things happen and extends to our desire for mastery, for personal competence.

STANLEY SCHACHTER   identified and clarified the affiliation motive, the need to relate to and be with other people. This can range from the need to belong, to identify with a work group, to the very personal need for someone to share experiences with, and to the need for support from others. It includes our desire to be of assistance to others, to find people to converse with, and to have others to exchange ideas and thoughts with.

ABRAHAM MASLOW   was a humanist with a deep caring for people. Starting with a physiological need like food, he saw needs proceeding up a ladder of importance through shelter, security, self-esteem, and self-actualization. His belief was that until the individual satisfies the lower-order need the higher-order need does not motivate. He proposed that when the lower-order is satisfied it is of considerably less importance in motivating. He pointed out that needs have no absolute value.

FRED HERZBERG'S contribution is often called the two-factor theory. He theorized that wants or needs can change, when satisfied, from motivators to hygiene factors. A motivating factor spurs us on. A hygiene factor is negative when absent, but doesn't make us work harder when present. The oft-questioned motivating affect of money falls in the category of hygiene.

B. F. SKINNER, a behaviorist, sees human activity as based on stimulus-response theory. Simply stated, he proposes that we work to achieve satisfying and pleasurable rewards. Rewards represent positive reinforcement. When we can make the connection between what we do and what happens, and if we like what happens, we will do more. Behavior modification, an approach of current management interest, builds on the concept of positive reinforcement. The important lesson is that the reward must make sense to the recipient and be related in his or her mind to what was done.

DAVID MCCLELLAND pointed out that the need to achieve becomes an achievement habit. The need for accomplishment and the satisfactions which come with it are conditioned, or learned, in our culture through assessment of personal experience. Bernard Haldane suggests use of this principle as a way of developing a good career; develop the habit of success.

DOUGLAS MCGREGOR heightened our understanding of management style, based on a belief about human beings, and its affect on motivational climate. His theory X, that people are basically lazy and must be motivated with carrot and stick, is contrasted with his recommended theory Y, which is based on the understanding that people are motivated by psychic needs, and want achievement and responsibility. Those who debate the pros and cons of the two theories often miss the main point. It is not which is right in an absolute sense, for they both can be right in particular circumstances, but that the manager's style establishes an environment and thus influences motivation.

LYMAN PORTER, EDWARD LAWLER, AND VICTOR VROOM added what is generally termed expectancy theory. Our sense of rightness, of satisfaction, of reward relates to what we expect; events do not have absolute values. A person can be motivated to do boring work if that is what he or she expects. But that same boring work is nonmotivating if what they expect is exciting work.

The subject of motivation is complex; there is no one theory that will do the job for us. As managers we must realize that, in a specific situation even with our attempts to identify the whole iceberg of values and needs, much of what motivates people will remain a mystery. Nevertheless we should not throw up our hands in despair. The best advice seems to be to try to set up environments where values and motivations will be an open topic for discussion. In addition the manager should try to establish an environment where each person is free within some limits to discover and use his or her motivations. It should also be an environment where individual differences are respected. We as managers create and affect the climate for motivation, and our style should vary from individual to individual and situation to situation. But these variations should fall within a broad strategy of overall direction and goals.

Work Quality

Quality work is work I feel good about. For you quality work is work you feel good about. Quality work is therefore personally defined. For me quality work is work that fits my work values. For me quality work is work where I can respond to my values and needs in my way, and not in the way someone else feels I ought to be motivated. This makes quality work sound selfish, and its definition seems to flow from some narcissistic theme. Personal definition is part of it, for as individuals we are responsible for managing our lives, our careers, our stress level, and our health. All these things in some way relate to quality of work.

Yet definition of quality of work has universal characteristics. These are characteristics to which each individual may assign different values, but characteristics most of us will agree are necessary. In another sense work researchers have also found that these characteristics transcend the individual. Because most work takes place in the context of an organization and this involves group activities, group specifications of quality and group needs are as important in defining quality as are individual needs. But the search for quality goes even further since the activities of the organization affect the quality of life for the community, the society, and the nation. Thus, quality work takes on values in the broader social sense. As an example, most would agree that work which contributes to the betterment of the human race is of better quality than work which damages the environment or contributes to depletion of human life. These broader community- and nation-based philosophical and value judgments are becoming increasingly important. However, for the purposes of this book we will not debate them. We will concentrate on discussing quality in the area where we as managers can have a direct impact, that is, improving quality within the mission and goals of the organization.

From the foregoing discussion of values and motivations it should be evident that quality of work has to do with the fit of the person to the work. If my work matches me, my needs, goals, and capabilities, then the probability is that I will judge it to be quality work. The fact that it matches means that the probability is high that I will be motivated and that I will gain outputs of value to me. The fact that it matches also means that there is high probability that I will be an effective employee, and thus the organization will gain the outputs that it desires. Both the individual and the organization gain from a good person/job fit.

What is there to match between person and job, and what is the role of the manager in making this match? At the most basic level we are trying to match the skills and knowledge of the individual with the organization's needs for skills and knowledge. Thus a good match on these characteristics is one where when the work needs analytical ability the individual brings analytical ability, where when the work needs powerful muscles the individual brings powerful muscles, and where when the work needs sales ability the individual brings sales ability. Another example might be where the individual brings a need rather than a capability. If the individual needs to have compatible and stimulating co-workers and the organization is made up of such people, as the individual views them, then a good match is possible. The individual brings both needs and capabilities. Matching is not a one-time act. Matching is an iterative adjustment process. Neither the organization nor the individual stays constant, and probably neither party can achieve all of what they want out of the match except for short periods.

The manager can be likened to a catalytic agent assisting in the match. The manager is the one who describes and interprets the needs of the organization in terms of tasks and assignments. Good communication is essential to making a good person/job fit. Thus the depth of understanding of the organization's goals and the skill with which the manager interprets them in terms that have meaning to the employee directly affects the quality and character of the match. The creativity of the manager lies in understanding both the organization and the individual well enough to find or create meaningful ways for them to come together. Many times in my management career I have seen an employee staring at a need (work) and not recognizing it. Such an employee often says there is nothing to do; management intervention is necessary first to make the need visible to the employee and then to show how the need can be broken into tasks. By contrast, the creative, interested, and committed employee is also a participant in this matching process. And, in the cases I remember, most often the failure to identify and take on work really represented lack of experience or motivation on the part of the employee.

Matching is further complicated because neither the organization nor the individual is seen as they really are. Matching occurs between subjective impressions. Each of us sees the organization and its needs and capabilities through glasses colored by our biases and experiences. Thus if I feel that I've been victimized by organizations, that they've gotten their pound of flesh, then I will see the organization's needs and goals with a negative bias. In this case I will feel that the subjective organization with which I'm trying to make a meaningful match should be viewed with suspicion, never taken at face value, and assumed to be asking for too much from its employees. Work experiences create work expectancies for the employee.

On the other side, the organization (represented by the manager's eyes) views the employee subjectively and is also biased by experience. If as a manager you are dealing with the employee represented above, you will probably view the employee as never truly offering full measure. Managerial experiences create the manager's expectancies. This matching of the subjective organization with the subjective person is shown in Figure 1. First let us get acquainted with the diagram. It shows an individual interfacing (coming together with) work as a subjective match. Mediators are people, actions, policies, and personal needs that can affect the match. Of these, task characteristics is the first and includes whether the work is complex or simple, repetitive or varied, of short duration or long, and so on. The values and norms are both the organization's and the individual's. For example, an organization may put a high value on profit, and this will affect the match. Norms are unwritten rules, and a norm of interpersonal competition will affect the quality of the match. Strength of needs represents how hard either the organization or the individual will fight to attain their desired ends. The outlook is the expectancy and the positive or negative view brought by the employee. Managerial style represents how we try to influence the match.

Responses are the first-order effects of the attempted match. Adjustment of expectations is shown feeding back to the matching process since it can make it easier or harder. If you have stepped up to sawing a felled tree into fire logs with expectations of the energy required based on past experience, you may revise expectancies based on performance. If the wood is wet and the saw dull, you will probably downgrade your expectations for output. If the process of doing the work is less successful than you expected, this disappointment can cause anxiety. In the extreme you may worry about being fired. In this case you will undoubtedly have a stress reaction. Anything from a tense back or a headache to a heart attack is possible. On the positive side, if the match is good the satisfaction that flows from this can spur productivity. Emotional behavior, such as sharp

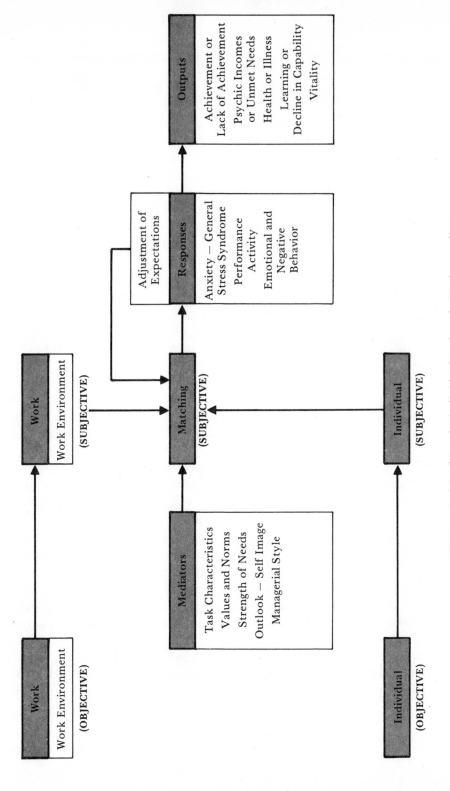

Figure 1 *Matching the individual and work: Understanding motivation and work quality*

words with the boss, is another type of negative response flowing from poor fit.

Outputs are second-order effects. This means they represent the ultimate effect from trying to work. These are paired in positive and negative pairs. Achievement suggests the ultimate effect is success in quantity, quality, or whatever measure is important. If we gain psychic incomes like satisfaction, a feeling of self-worth, recognition from peers and manager, these are positive. If we fail to achieve them, and expected them, this leaves us with our original needs unfulfilled. If the fit is a good one, we should gain in capability, knowledge, and vitality.

In trying to understand work quality we must look at the mediators, responses, and outputs in Figure 1. You and I as managers are mediators. By our style, through our implementation of our values, and with our skill at communications and managing people, we can positively or negatively affect this match. Undoubtedly we do both. What's more, it is probable we are not really sure which impact we are having even though we are trying to be a positive influence. Being sure of the response can only come about through assessing feedback. Feedback may be a verbal response from the employee, work output or its lack, or many of the other things indicated in Figure 1. But the feedback is often delayed, and thus it becomes very difficult to associate the action we took with what happened.

The characteristics of the task will create quality when they use the individual's capabilities. If we are dealing with a strong motivator (need) on the part of the individual, then this augurs well for quality feelings about the match. Just think of your own reaction when you know the organization is really depending on you. Incidentally, this need could be too strong and thus overwhelm the individual. It must be within the tolerance range of the individual. And even that tolerance range is a variable!

Responses represent the individual's assessment reaction to the quality of the match. If you as my manager helped me to change the desirability of accomplishing an unattractive task by pointing out how it could lead to something better, this could result in a feeling of quality. Stress reactions can be positive or negative. If the individual uses them to motivate for the work and works them off in the process, this would be positive, or eustress.* In such a case the reaction to the work would probably be positive. Outputs, the end result of this attempted match, also affect judgments about quality. Achievement, gaining something of value, is positive as are psychic incomes like a sense of personal worth. The sum

---

*The term eustress was created by Hans Selye because stress became a word with only negative connotations, and positive stress is the stuff of achievement, of life, of adventure. Eustress is positive.

total of reactions and outputs must be judged as positive for work to be judged as quality work.

In matching, the manager can do little to change what the individual brings. However, the manager can work at achieving accuracy of perceptions, modifying the values in the work environment, and toward good fit by understanding skills, knowledge, interests, and goals. Quality work exists when this process of matching achieves positive results and especially when it leads to learning, growth, satisfaction, and increased vitality.

SUMMARY

To work at good work, work that meets needs and uses capabilities, for a good organization, one with a supportive and open work climate and meaningful goals, is to have quality work. Quality work occurs when there is a good match between the individual and the organization. A good match is one which benefits both the organization and the individual. Working to achieve this match is a prime job of the manager. Others representing the organization and the individual employee should not passively stand by and wait for the manager to do it. However, the manager is in the key position. On the one side he or she interprets the organization. On the other side, he or she helps the individual to present self to the organization. The manager is the marriage broker. Job/person matching takes place best when both the parties, organization and individual, are clear about their values and their motivations. Only open and honest communication can lead to good matches. Yet such communications are not easy since our identified and acknowledged values and motivations are often only the tip of an iceberg. Much of what is to be matched is subjective and often subconscious.

Motivations for work come from our values and our needs. There is no one theory of motivation that we should universally use. Rather, each of the theories of motivation add a bit to our understanding. For the manager to establish the environment and the conditions where the employee can use his or her motivations to stimulate attention, interest, and commitment to the work there must be understanding and openness. In good job/person fits, both the individual and the organization benefit, creating the conditions for people to be motivated. Motivation is not something the manager does to the employee. Motivation is something the employee does to himself or herself under the right conditions.

Work Values Checkup

1. My main reason for working is to (number in order of priority, 1 most important, 2 next, etc.):

    ____ earn money   ____ fill the time   ____ gain power
    ____ provide a purpose   ____ provide a sense of   ____ achieve status
         for my life   influence/power
    ____ help others   ____ find myself   ____ support my hobbies
                                                                     and interests
    ____ achieve a unique   ____ create a sense   ____ use my skills and
         contribution   of belonging   knowledge
    ____ other _____   ____ other _____   ____ other _____

2. I feel most useful and gain the greatest sense of accomplishment when I (number in order of priority, 1 most important, 2 next, etc.):

    ____ inspire others   ____ provide direction to   ____ add to the total of
                                               others   knowledge
    ____ work alone
    ____ am a member of a   ____ teach others   ____ provide a useful
         team   product
    ____ create a concept   ____ help others to   ____ provide a needed
                                               achieve   service
    ____ other _____   ____ other _____   ____ other _____

3. Success for me can be defined as (number in order of priority, 1 most important, 2 next, etc.):

    ____ being the top manager   ____ being able to buy/   ____ gaining a higher level
         of a large organization   build the dream house   of knowledge, skill, and
                                                                     education
    ____ being the immediate   ____ living where I want   ____ writing a book/
         manager of a small   in the style I want   inventing something
         group of high talent
         people
    ____ being an individual   ____ being able to travel   ____ being consulted and
         contributor of note   where and when I want   looked to as the expert
    ____ other _____   ____ other _____   ____ other _____

4. It is important to me to gain the following from my work (number in order of priority, 1 most important, 2 next, etc.):

    ____ a sense of play   ____ an opportunity to   ____ my name on the door
         and fun   gain more self-   and carpet on the floor
                                        direction

    ____ utilization of   ____ the money to set   ____ greater numbers to
         my skills   up my own business   supervise
    ____ some new knowledge   ____ the chance to be   ____ a job I am proud of
         or experience   promoted   ____ more free time
    ____ concrete measurable   ____ more money as a
         achievement   sense of increased
                                        personal worth

    ____ other _____   ____ other _____   ____ other _____
    _____   _____   _____

5. Think about a task at work or at play which is fresh enough in memory that you can review it. Pick a task about which you feel very positive. Try to analyze what happened and list the aspects of that task which were motivating to you.

    _____   _____   _____
    _____   _____   _____
    _____   _____   _____
    _____   _____   _____
    _____   _____   _____

6. Pick the statement which best reflects your belief about people at work.   (   )

    ____ a. Employees are best suited for formated and carefully defined work and need to
             be told what to do.
    ____ b. Employees generally want good pay and loose supervision but respect a tough
             manager.
    ____ c. Employees are generally interested in security and fair treatment and don't
             want responsibility but will put out if they feel they will get rewarded.
    ____ d. Employees generally want freedom to direct their own work, variety of work,
             and feel responsible for their own success.
    ____ e. Employees are most interested in belonging to a good work group with friendly
             people sharing a common goal.
    ____ f. Employees need to achieve at the highest level of their capability and are
             therefore interested in challenging work.

7. Pick the statement that best represents your feeling about a quality work environment.

( )

   a. The most important aspect of a quality work environment is to have challenging work in which I am interested and which utilizes my skills.
   b. The most important aspect of a quality work environment is to be free to make decisions about what to do and how to do it.
   c. The most important aspect of a quality work environment is to gain recognition for accomplishment and a sense of personal worth through accomplishment.
   d. The most important aspect of a quality work environment is to have associates I want to be with and who are stimulating.
   e. The most important aspect of a quality work environment is to have the facilities and tools necessary to do a good job.

8. What do you know about the work values and motivations of those whom you supervise? Do you believe their outlook is the same as yours? Pick the most representative statement and then check it out through discussion with some of those who work for you.

( )

   a. To work here we must all share the same values.
   b. Generally those who work for me share the same values and put similar priorities on aspects of work equally as I do.
   c. Those who have worked with me over a considerable period share the same work values and priorities as I do but the newer ones do not.
   d. There is a broad variety of work values in the group, and only about a third share my values and views.
   e. There is only a chance relationship between values held by me and those of others in the organization.

9. Are there evidences of negative outcomes of work in your area? Here are some examples. Do any of them seem serious in your area?

( )

	serious	don't know	not serious
a. There are minor evidences of stress outcomes which may be due to poor job-to-person fit such as absenteeism, short tempers, interpersonal friction.	( )	( )	( )
b. There are evidences of serious stress-related outcomes such as ulcers, psychosomatic disorders, heart attacks.	( )	( )	( )
c. There are evidences that people are turning off to work in this organization such as low motivation, low commitment, increasing turnover.	( )	( )	( )
d. There are significant evidences that people feel a lack of achievement through increasing complaints about lack of promotion and personal growth.	( )	( )	( )
e. There is evidence of increasing turnover among new employees with indications our environment and work is not what they expected.	( )	( )	( )

Ideas For Action: Things The Manager Can Do To Aid In Creating Quality Work

		something to try
1.	Help the employee to feel good and make it easier to like himself or herself.	( )
2.	Provide job and tasks with risks which fit the individual's tolerance for probability of success much of the time.	( )
3.	Provide task variety and a job which will be perceived as changing and enduring.	( )
4.	Provide each employee with the opportunity to gain a sense of accomplishment as well as a feeling of gain in psychic income.	( )
5.	Make work fun and allow the freedom to create some playlike aspects within the job.	( )
6.	Try to create a system for fairly sharing repetitive, boring, painful, frustrating work that has to be done.	( )
7.	Provide each employee with the opportunity to gain a sense of meaning, a sense of being needed, and a social purpose which contributes to the well-being of humankind.	( )
8.	Act in a way which creates the feeling that what you do affects what you are paid (that is, good performance leads to good pay).	( )
9.	Assign tasks in a way which creates a sense of wholeness, where the pieces tasks, and parts (duties) fit together into something which feels like one job.	( )
10.	Make assignments which require the knowledge and skills which the employee brings and, is interested in developing.	( )
11.	Work with the employee to provide job assignments which have a sense of closure and not just tasks which go on interminably.	( )
12.	Provide each individual with a sense of decision-making freedom and responsibility—the opportunity to choose when and how to do what.	( )
13.	Assign stretching work, work which causes each one in his or her own way to reach beyond former accomplishments, which is challenging and causes the individual to compete with his or her own past achievements.	( )
14.	Try to create jobs which provide each person with a sense of purpose, a calling, a career which draws the individual to it.	( )
15.	Provide each person with a part of a total responsibility. This means assignments where the individual's goals fit within the overall goals and mission of the organization in an understandable and communicable way.	( )
16.	Provide feedback which creates a sense of impact so that the individual feels he or she makes a difference.	( )
17.	Create techniques for establishing accountability so that each person is measured fairly with shared agreement on the timing and character of the measurement.	( )
18.	Work to provide each person with a sense of freedom, of not being trapped, a situation where the individual is able to leave but stays out of free choice.	( )

19. Create an environment where the individual has freedom to change interests, to move to another function in response both to personal need changes and changing needs of the organization.

20. Make sure jobs require learning in order to stay with them.   ( )

21. Work to provide each person with a sense of belonging, of being part of a team to which he or she contributes and which will provide support in return.   ( )

22. Provide an environment which supports openness and freedom of communication, one where people don't feel they have to be defensive and protective, where people don't try to draw limiting boxes around positions and function.   ( )

23. Provide each person with the opportunity to be seen as an individual and to develop his or her uniqueness and special identity.   ( )

24. Provide the freedom to stand up for individual beliefs, feelings, and judgments, an environment where people are expected to do so and respected when they do.   ( )

25. Provide occasional opportunities for each individual to get away, to look back, to reflect on the job and work and to set new goals.   ( )

CHAPTER
4

Learning

The Challenge

Growth, Learning, and
Individual Development

Growth can be viewed as physical, as hierarchical in the sense of position and responsibility, as an increase in skills and knowledge, as social in our ability to live with and work with others, and as personal in the sense of enhanced self-understanding. Historically management attention has centered on hierarchical and social growth, and increased skills and knowledge. Although this is still so, many managers are beginning to understand that understanding self is a necessary base for all other growth. One question facing us as managers is: What is the function of the organization and thus the manager in personal growth and individual development? Learning, in the sense we will discuss it, is similar to growth and included in it. Growth takes place only when our personal learning can be integrated into our behavior. Learning in the abstract is not growth. As William James said, "The greatest thing, then, in all education is to make the nervous system our ally instead of our enemy." Integration of learning with self is growth.

In the perspective of this chapter, individual development, true personal growth, should take place in the organization and through work as well as in other aspects of life. The role of the manager, as a manager of people, is to reduce the threshold at which learning takes place, to make learning easier and more natural. While the outlook is that the manager is a teacher, an exemplar and a mentor, we are not suggesting stuffing knowledge into someone else but rather making self-motivated learning possible. This may require somewhat more time than just achieving job results. The role of the manager is to turn work assignments, where possible, into activities that accelerate learning. By doing this the manager supports one of the longer range goals of the organization. This goal is to cause the partnership of person and organization to become increasingly effective in the pursuit of organizationally meaningful and valuable goals. Achievement of this goal should increase organizational profit and thus provide a payout for the individual, the organization, and society. The role of the manager is one of catalyst, for useful combinations of people and organizations, as a designer of situations and environment. By setting work context such that it not only encourages and rewards performance but also rewards individual development and utilizes new learning, the manager is aiding achievement of both short- and long-range organizational goals. It is the conflict between short-range goals and long-range goals that makes this area difficult.

Learning

We learn through doing, using our skills and capabilities, which results in feedback that suggests how we modify future actions to improve our success. These actions/learnings may be muscular as in learning to ski, to skate, or to play tennis. They may be control of our expectations, our outlook or our thoughts. This is the kind of learning which takes place when we discover that by choosing a positive outlook we can create better outcomes than when we choose a negative outlook. As I write this chapter I am caught in a situation where I must be present to help others who have a free choice to come for that help or not. If my outlook is negative, and they don't come, this is wasted time. This is time I need to invest in other pursuits. Yet I have chosen to use the time, to write. I am taking advantage of the situation. All that really changed was my outlook. I chose to turn a negative into a positive. I recognized I had control and did not have to feel I was being controlled. Now, however, when someone comes I must shift my perspective again. Having made the first adjustment, I might now view their coming as a negative, an invasion of my time. Or I can choose the perspective that it was good I stayed and I am now able to serve, to help. By becoming conscious of my choices and my control I can increase my learning, my personal development. This kind of learning is both personal and social.

We generally learn as adults because of a conscious choice to learn. Through some process of creating value priorities, we make learning an outcome that is important to us. In the pragmatic sense we probably choose to learn because we believe our future state will be better as the result of the learning. We also learn because the process of learning is itself sometimes fun and satisfying. This is the sort of learning which occurs when we are intrigued by a book in an area of interest, so intrigued that we can't put the book down. This is the sort of learning we generally associate with hobbies and recreation. While this learning may also have future value, there is a current (today) value of pleasant occupation of time and energy.

Sometimes we learn because we are part of and with a group which is learning. This can be viewed as a learning situation or context. Enrollment in a class establishes this situation. You and I as managers may create this situation. In this context the individual is responding to a prior learned behavior, that of going along with the group perhaps for the sense of belonging, or the social support, or the feeling of being part of a larger activity or purpose. We also learn best when we are ready to learn. Perhaps you have had the experience of being presented with new data, a situation where learning is possible, and letting it slip by the first time and only the second time being able to catch on. This readiness is internal; it may be outlook, it may be need, or it may be simply that the signal gets through. Before we blocked it, didn't see it, or didn't hear it. We learn when we respect, trust, admire, or are turned on by the teacher. There is an interaction between teacher and learner which might be described as a sort of chemistry or energy field that attracts us and opens us. Understanding employee needs, readiness, and the chemistry of our relationships are all important if we as managers are to enhance learning. This concept of attention, of being open, of readiness, can be addressed in another way. It can be looked at as willingness to become emotionally involved. We learn best when we care in the emotional sense. We also block learning by emotional attachment to the old or prior way. Emotional openness is different from the conscious intellectual choice to learn. This is a choice to learn that is at the feeling level. Although we normally consider that we have volitional control over the intellectual or rational choice to learn, we generally assume that the emotional choice, the decision to really be involved, is somehow unconscious and not controlled by choice. This is probably partially true, but getting emotionally involved can also be a choice. It involves letting down some of the protective barriers we put up to maintain our stability, our sense of who we are, what we know, and what we can do. These barriers are erected to reduce the risks of change to a tolerable level. Real learning involves risk, for to learn is to change and changing means letting go of some old concepts as well as taking in new thoughts, ideas, concepts, and beliefs. This aspect of growth can be thought of as an internal process of giving yourself permission to change, to break boundaries and limits you previously erected to keep your world under control. Because of the rapidity of change in today's society, many people have intensified and strengthened their barriers to change and individual development. They are scared. Reducing the anxiety and increasing the comfort with change is the function of a good teacher-manager.

This discussion of learning started by presenting the need to receive feedback and assess it for learning to take place. Feedback enters the human system through one of our senses. For each of us there is a tuning,

a preferential bias for use of the several senses. Thus some of us learn better by doing as in the case of learning through tactile and muscular involvement. Others learn better through their eyes and their ears. The best learning situation involves the individual in the use of several sensory systems. Thus in many new educational designs we are learning to combine visual and auditory signals. In the design of learning systems or situations in the work organization, however, we are not usually talking of the classroom setup where we have a projector for visuals and a lecturer for auditory signals. So the manager must become conscious of the desirability of involving several feedback channels and what this requires in the design of the learning situation.

Biofeedback, the process of amplifying an internal body signal of which we are not usually conscious, so that we become conscious of it and can accept it as feedback, has taught us more about the need for feedback for learning. The lesson is that sometimes we must translate, convert, or amplify the feedback to make it useful in the learning process. This fact learned from body function control is also so in the organizational sense. Think of the situation where you as the manager see the results of an employee's work, see them in a way and from a perspective not available to the employee. Perhaps you receive field trouble reports on a product that can be related to a process in your department. It is then your role as manager to be part of the feedback loop. Whether the feedback is useful and contributes to the employee's learning is directly related to your ability to translate, amplify, attenuate, and focus the signal to create a needed change in behavior.

The Challenge

The challenge for the manager is to make work situations where the most normal, expected, desired, and measured output is some service or product and assure that the additional product, of learning and personal development, also takes place. Learning is a psychic need or income for the employee. Learning is an aspect of quality work. Learning contributes to the individual's sense of growth and achievement. But learning also contributes to improved performance and usually output of greater quality and quantity. Learning increases the power, the vitality of the organization, its profit, however measured, and its chances for survival. So learning is beneficial both to the individual and the organization. However, the organization under stress, perhaps failure in the marketplace or tough financial times, usually finds it difficult to take the longer view, the one of requiring employee development.

Even in the best of organizational conditions where the need for employee development is recognized, as managers we all know of work assignments and jobs where no learning is required. In fact many employees are already overeducated, overprepared, underutilized, and unchallenged. What can the manager do here? Certainly more learning in this situation would seem to lead to further underutilization, frustrations, and dissatisfaction. One attack is to eliminate such jobs by turning them over to machines. If the organization has the capital, sees the change as economically desirable, and recognizes the need to change work quality, this may be viable. In fact, managements have done, are doing, and will do a lot of this type of job redesign. However, if, as it often does, it means less jobs in the short term, is this socially desirable? In fact, how do we know whether the individuals involved, even if they could stay on new jobs that demand more and require learning, really want to do so? Shouldn't it be possible for the individual to choose to take a job which underutilizes, underchallenges, and does not require learning? The answer is most certainly yes, yet one wonders whether if exposed to the positive experiences of personal development the individual who now chooses not to become emotionally involved and committed would still choose that job.

In these days of changing social values it is important to present another alternative. This alternative is to deliberately take jobs away from machines and give them to people in order to restore to people some of the work values (satisfactions) of a simpler, earlier time. The thesis is that the reason people are underutilized is that we have pushed the use of machines too far too fast. This is the thesis behind E.F. Shumacher's *Small Is Beautiful* published in 1975 by Harper and Row and Ernest Callenbach's *Ecotopia* published in 1975 by Banyan Tree Books. This is the thesis behind some of the experiments with industrial democracy and improved quality of work life. My personal position is that many of these improvements in job satisfaction, job challenge, personal utilization, and quality of work life can be made without the more drastic suggestions of going back to a simple life. Discussion of person/job fit and matching, introduced in the last chapter, as well as managing change will reveal some of these ideas.

What can you and I as managers do to increase learning at work? A partial answer seems to lie in the following statements, each of which in its own way is not only an answer but also a challenge:

· Create task division so there is a range of jobs which require different levels of commitment, involvement, growth, and learning.
· When change in process and work organization is necessary, gain the participation of employees in deciding how to change the jobs

and what is to be the requirement for learning and other psychic needs.

· Create an environment, to the extent possible within organizational requirements, which offers more freedom for individual experimentation, choice, and mobility. Rotation of assignments is an example of this type of adaptation.

· Work as a citizen and manager to create new ways to make the broader organizational and society-based decisions about numbers and kinds of jobs in the context of the implications these choices have on use of energy, pollution of the environment, and quality of life and work.

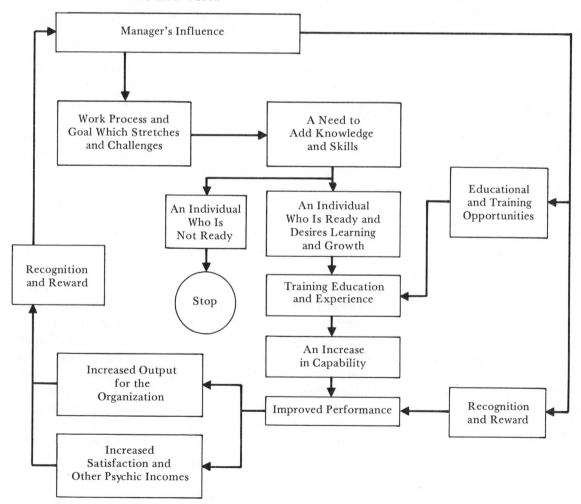

Figure 2. Learning at Work

Some of the things which the manager can do to create a learning cycle are graphically demonstrated in Figure 2. The four specific areas of managerial impact are:

· in the *design of the job* to create the need for learning
· in the *support of learning* through training and opportunities for experience
· in the *recognition of performance* based on new learning
· in the *enhancement of satisfaction* by creating additional rewards that flow from the improved psychic income

Learning takes place through work when it is needed or required for success and achievement at work, or to achieve some future goal. This pictorial representation starts with work which requires learning. The manager can influence this need through design of assignments. If the individual wants to learn and is ready, an increase in capability can occur. The manager influences the process by providing the opportunity for learning and the new information or experience. The manager can reinforce this positive gain by recognizing improved output. Additional reinforcement may occur when the manager works to enhance the satisfactions. One technique might be to provide opportunities, which meet employee personal goals, that come about because of the learning, increased sense of worth, and other positive outcomes.

SUMMARY

We know that individual development, growth, and change are necessary components of a life of quality and vitality. We suspect that the organizational world, the world of work, has not been well designed to respond to this need. In fact, we have many examples of work which is nonstimulating, nonchallenging, nongrowth requiring. We also have many examples of people who say they are satisfied with this work. Yet we suspect that many individuals and most organizations as well as society as a whole would benefit from our being able to build more learning, more human renewal and growth, into work. The result of such a change would be both personal and organizational profits, not just profits in the economic sense. These gains would evolve from a better fit between people and work.

By reviewing and discussing why humans learn, this chapter has provided some clues about how to make improvements in the world of work. Sometimes these improvements lie in redesign of the work or shifting some work to machines. Sometimes these improvements lie in sharpening the manager's skills in creating meaningful feedback. Sometimes these improvements lie in the individual's gaining increased personal understanding of which senses contribute most to learning or making those personal changes in outlook which are necessary precursors to learning. These are but a few of the actions that may be taken once we decide that learning in work is a desirable goal.

The managerial challenge is thus one of how and what to do. It is also one of achieving the proper balance between short-term goals of profit and longer term goals of improved employee capability. The challenge is also in a larger sense a societal problem. We must learn to weigh alternatives as dissimilar as apples and oranges (meeting a schedule or helping a person to grow) and make rational choices for a better world both of work and of life in general.

Learning and Personal Development Checkup

1. What value is placed on individual learning and growth by the organization in which you manage? Pick the most appropriate statement   ( )

    a. A great deal. Both through policy and action the organization supports learning and growth as a desired output of work.
    b. Some. The organization supports education but does little to integrate learning with work.
    c. So-so. Sometimes yes, sometimes no; there is no clear signal about support for learning.
    d. Not much. There is no evident support of personal growth or investment in human resource improvement.
    e. None. We hire people for what they bring and throw them out when we no longer need them or they become obsolete.

2. What is the need or requirement for those you supervise to continue learning to perform their jobs? Pick the most appropriate statement.

    a. A great deal. In order to survive they must learn.
    b. Some. There is moderate continuing need for learning.
    c. So-so. Tremendous variability.   ( )
    d. Not much. There is little chance to use new learning.
    e. None. They are overqualified now.

3. In assigning tasks, in creating jobs, what do you do as manager? Pick the most appropriate answer.   ( )

    a. I seriously and successfully consider building in a need for learning.
    b. I consider learning as a need but find it very difficult to build into the job.
    c. I try to supplement the job with training and learning experiences.
    d. I never really think about learning as a need unless brought up by employee.
    e. I never consider learning and personal development as part of a job design.

4. If through the job or other means, a member of your group grows in skill and capability, what do you do? Pick the most appropriate answer.   ( )

    a. I work aggressively to seek a better job for the person in or out of my group.
    b. I fill out the papers and take actions, though not very aggressively, to improve the person's job challenge and job capability needs.
    c. I try to encourage the employee to take personal actions to get a better job.
    d. I tell the individual that learning and growth is fine but improvement of job depends on openings which neither of us control.
    e. I try to hold on to the individual in the same job because that is the only way you can get my job done.

5. Are there evidences of frustration with or blocking of personal development and growth which come to you as complaints? Here are some examples. Are they serious or not?

		serious	don't know	not serious
a.	Career frustrations with people complaining about lack of opportunity and a failure to gain through hard work.	( )	( )	( )
b.	Resignations because people have not achieved the growth in position, responsibility and pay they expected.	( )	( )	( )
c.	Evidences that people feel overtrained, overeducated, and underutilized which come out of attitude surveys or individual counseling interviews.	( )	( )	( )
d.	General non-use of a policy of tuition refund and other support of education.	( )	( )	( )
e.	People drop out of or avoid company education programs, demonstrating a general low priority on learning and growth.	( )	( )	( )

6. Which of the following statements best represents your belief about how employees feel the organization supports individual development?   ( )

a. There are lots of opportunities for individual growth and advancement and management is both open to and supportive of personal growth.

b. There are some opportunities for individual growth, and management is supportive when individual development is not in conflict with short-term business needs.

c. There are minimal opportunities for individual development, and they are entirely dependent on chance.

d. Managers appear to own employees and are allowed to hoard human resources and block personal development.

e. This organization will hire from the outside rather than provide opportunity for employee growth.

Ideas for Action: Learning and Individual Development

		Something to try
1.	Search aggressively for work assignments which stretch people and demand learning and growth.	( )
2.	Consider rotation of tasks and assignments in the group to provide learning, broadening, and variety. Consider rotation of some employees out of your group.	( )
3.	Have a personal development counseling session with each employee to search together for ways to improve personal development.	( )
4.	Forcefully present to upper management the needs for new assignments of people in your group who have stopped growing or are blocked.	( )
5.	Consider reorganization, shifting of function boundaries, taking on new functions, and other changes to increase growth opportunity in your group.	( )
6.	Search for opportunities inside your organization and outside it. Consider in addition trips, visits, and experiences which will accelerate learning and development.	( )
7.	Search for and keep a list of available courses and programs. Use them aggressively by actively encouraging enrollment of your employees.	( )
8.	Create a department or group discussion session where you and your group have an open two-way talk about schemes for improving learning and personal development.	( )
9.	Consider a group problem-solving, team-building session where the group learns about how it learns and improves as a group and its ability to take charge and influence what happens.	( )
10.	Consider changes in your own learning and personal development behavior which will transmit a positive message about your belief because you do it. Become an exemplar.	( )
11.	Visit the education group serving your area or if there is none a nearby educational institution and see what's available, or better yet influence the creation of an applicable course.	( )
12.	Create an ad hoc learning program in your group where members take responsibility for studying a new area and then teaching it to the group as a whole.	( )

CHAPTER
5

The Story

Aspects of the Individual That Impact People Management

How To Find Out Who You Are

Who Are You?

Who you are, who you believe you are, who you want to be, and who others think you are—all affect your ability to manage people. Yet I believe this is probably the first human resource management book of recent vintage with this chapter heading. Why is this so? Why have we ignored or removed the person from the role of manager? I believe the reason is that we have been searching very hard to understand what managers do, working diligently to find teachable principles and techniques, even trying to make management a science with decision theory and mathematical models. We have left the realm of the person to the psychologist. Yet, to manage people you must communicate with people. You must come in contact with people. You must have many and varied relationships with people. This interpersonal behavior, required of the manager, underlines the importance of knowing and managing who you are in these transactions. Who you are makes a difference.

Despite the title, this chapter will not present a set of personality characteristics that define a good manager. The nature of our discussion will not be prescriptive but rather will demonstrate the need for personal assessment and insight as a basis for stepping into the arena to manage other individuals. An anecdotal story will open the topic and make the point.

The Story

Manager Ruth was bright and eager. She had graduated with high honors from the university, been fought over by several companies who wanted to hire her, and risen quickly, in about three and a half years, from her starting position as a young engineer to her first job managing other people. She was a high-energy person, always in early and working late. She liked to organize and control things, was a self-starter, quick and doggedly persistent. In fact, it might be said, she tried too hard, didn't know when or how to let up, was seen as aggressive and overeager by others, and demonstrated type A behavior with its increase in probability of a heart attack. One might also observe she had apparently taken on all of the supposedly male characteristics believed to lead to personal success in the organization.

She had a small group engaged in an important task. They had tight deadlines, limited budget, and a real technical challenge. In fact the probability of success was not very high. Ruth viewed this as a personal test and was, as was characteristic of her image and style, pushing everyone, including herself, very hard.

One day she called one of her employees, an engineer, into her office because she felt things weren't going well. Let us assume that her intent was to be helpful. She said, "Your part of the project seems to be going slowly. Are you having some difficulty I can help you with?"

The engineer responded, "The computer room is awfully slow in getting my data back; sometimes I have to wait several days."

Ruth said, "I notice you are not putting in any overtime. If I were you I'd work longer hours when I was behind. That's the way you demonstrate hard work. And I notice too that you're sending stuff to the computer room that you could do with a little extra effort. I just don't think you're working hard enough."

I needn't carry the story further. Ruth's style and outlook were built on her beliefs and values. While trying to be helpful she was imposing her beliefs, her goals, her outlook on the other person. Incidentally, from the start of the conversation it also looks as though she was going to tell, not listen. That is an aspect of style. For the moment, however, the point is not to criticize Ruth but to understand that who you and I are, who we want to be, our values, our beliefs, our goals, all impact how you and I manage. I am not out to change either Ruth or you, although you may choose to do that. Rather I am trying to increase our mutual understanding of the process of managing people. The impact of personal strategy and style are discussed in chapter sixteen. And now to the impact of our several selves on our ability to manage.

Aspects of the Individual that Impact People Management

There is literally no aspect of self which does not impact our ability to manage. Our style of thinking, our goals, and our aspirations affect it. For example, if your goal is a more responsible position with more people, there is no way you can hide that goal; it will color everything you do. As you and I review some of these aspects or characteristics of self, it would be useful to keep in mind the following:

1. I am not trying to change the characteristics of the person, your characteristics; rather I am pushing for understanding them.
2. I am not, in most cases, evaluating the usefulness of the characteristics. That is, many of them are not in themselves bad or good.
3. I am trying to identify the characteristics to help you as a manager become aware of how they may affect your management.
4. These characteristics of self are not the exact equivalent of a list of personality traits, or behavior modes, or any pure list since the list includes such aspects as goals, values, interests, and energy level.
5. The list is not all inclusive; rather it is representative.

The following list is best thought of as characteristics, or parts of us as individuals. It is an attempt to provide a window through which you may view both your several selves and the things which tend to shape those selves. Thus, for example, values lead to goals, and our goals will tend to influence our behavior. Our behavior is seen by others as us. If I am pursuing a goal aggressively you will tend to see me as aggressive. Yet in another context I may not be aggressive. I also may not view myself as aggressive. Dominance, by contrast with values, can be viewed directly as an aspect of personality. If in interchange with other people you view me as trying to dominate and control, then that is an aspect of the self you see as me. Opening our thinking and our personal sensitivity to these aspects is best done by reviewing some examples.

Values.   The values, concepts, goals, and beliefs that are important to the manager affect the manager's outlook, and this colors his or her relationships with other people. If, for example, not damaging the ecological balance is important to the manager, this value could cause the manager to insist on using both sides of every sheet of paper. Such a rule would seem strange, maybe even improper, if we did not understand the underlying value held by the manager who imposed the rule. If viewed purely as an aspect of personality we might call the manager a penny pincher. This would not be as helpful as understanding the underlying values.

Goals.   Where the manager wants to go with his or her life affects relationships with others. If, for example, it is important to the manager to use the job to support another interest like skiing, this can affect scheduling of activities and attitudes about weekend work in the ski season. Or the manager's goal may be to make a scientific contribution, or to gain some organizational position or some income level; in other words, the goal can be of major or minor importance in the total life of the individual. Yet in each case it can affect how that manager deals with other people in the work situation. One problem is that human goals, like values, are often unexpressed, and so we guess. Often we guess wrong and this contributes to organizational malfunction.

Interests.   Subject interests directly related to work as well as hobby and avocational interests affect what we read, what we feature in our conversation, and thus how we relate to others. For example, in my own relations with others the lack of an interest in major professional sports like baseball has limited my openings in conversations, sometimes even my acceptance by others. I could change that if it was viewed by me as important. But forcing the change without true interest would not be authentic and would probably not work well. I chose not to change my interests. But, knowing that and occasionally getting it out in the table, telling others, has helped in my ability to relate to others and to manage people.

Energy level.   High energy level is evidenced in both speed and duration of sustained activity. Being around a person of high energy level can make one of low energy level uncomfortable, perhaps resentful, and sometimes just tired. It is important, as a manager, in making assignments, in judging performance, and in communicating, to understand your own energy level and how it may color your outlook. It is also important to be sensitive to the energy levels of those whom you supervise.

Dominance.   As very young babies we learn to control our mothers by crying and wetting our pants. From this experience and many others, including how we get our sense of security, some of us develop a strong need to control others. A person with a high dominance need, will often overpower others, will generally not listen openly, will often by force of personality and even by just getting more words in, attempt to control others. The manager should assess his or her need to dominate since this directly affects interpersonal and managerial style. A high dominance person would generally find creating a participative work environment very difficult. This doesn't mean he or she should not try but rather should understand the difficulties that must be overcome.

Cultural background.   In the United States, because we think of ourselves as a nation of essentially one class, built by those who sought frontiers and freedoms, until recently we have not been sensitive to the affects of ethnic, class, and cultural backgrounds. However, the belief systems imbedded in an ethnic or class culture can have a major effect on managerial style and approach. For example, the manager in England is generally from an upper-class background, and this colors his or her outlook. The manager with a Germanic background will generally put high value on hard work and control.

Initiative.   This factor refers to the individual's ability and need to start things, to sense a need and take action. The manager's level of initiative will affect his or her response pattern to the needs, problems, and challenges of the organization. The manager's initiative will affect what he or she expects of others.

Flexibility.   Some of us are highly pattern oriented. Once we have learned how to do it our sense of personal safety comes from repeating that pattern. Thus our level of flexibility, our relatively high need for the predictability of the known, will affect our expectations of others. If we have a high need for predictability and are inflexible, change imposed by the organization or the employee will seem threatening. If by contrast we like risk taking and experiment, we will probably have little patience with a manager or a person we supervise who has a strong need for the known and a fear of change.

Thinking style.   Recent brain research has heightened our understanding of the difference in the thinking modes of the right and left hemispheres. The right hemisphere is generally better at imagination, artistic thoughts, visualization, and thinking about the whole, or the forest. The left is generally better at rational, sequential, number-oriented thinking and analyzing the individual tree. How you assign duties to these brain hemispheres and how they work together is your individual mindprint. It is as unique as your fingerprint. If the manager's mindprint is unique and the employee's is unique, it follows that communication and understanding require shared perceptions or shared thinking approaches. One way of describing and classifying these was developed by Isabel Briggs Meyers. She builds into her test, called the Type Indicator, a breakdown into whether we are taking in information (sensing), finding facts (left hemisphere), or working on intuition, which means developing relationships beyond what is brought in through the senses (right hemisphere). Second, she believes our style is influenced by whether we pair this approach with thinking, impersonal analysis of cause and effect, or feeling, based on caring. Her test provides a way to get in touch with this aspect.

Extroversion/Introversion.   Extroversion and introversion refer to our general orientation; extroversion emphasizes the outside world and others, and introversion characterizes people who are most comfortable working alone and inside themselves. This type of orientation colors our relationships with others and affects our expectations of others. If they view the world as we do, they seem to have the right perspective and are relatively easy to communicate with. If they view the world from the opposite perspective, we may have difficulty communicating with them.

Figure 3 is designed to demonstrate graphically how individual characteristics can affect manager-employee relationships. Just one function, communication, is used. The illustration, using only three aspects of self, portrays these aspects as filters affecting communication. Actually they are more than filters, for sometimes they amplify as well as block or distort. If, as in the Figure, we assume that the communication started out as coherent and clear, only part of it gets through the filter of our selves. Furthermore some that gets through is changed in direction and character. Who we are definitely affects our ability to communicate.

Figure 3 demonstrates that a consistent message (parallel lines) starting from inside the manager must first escape the filters of goals, personality, and interests. These were chosen merely as examples. Some part of the message gets stopped. Some parts may get through, as illustrated by the one straight line. Some parts of the message get through but get distorted (wavy line) or redirected as they go out. On the receiving end the process of filtering and distortion is repeated. Response by the employee goes through a similar but reversed path. From the figure it seems a miracle that any clear message ever gets through.

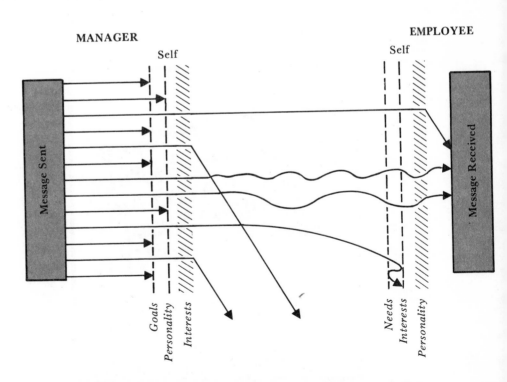

Figure 3. *How individual characteristics affect communication*   **65**

How to Find Out Who You Are

Finding out who you are requires analysis of feedback from actions and self-assessment. Your assessment may be supplemented by some tests and input from others. One of the challenges is that the very process of measuring changes the context and thus may alter the individual image which is projected and viewed. This can be demonstrated in the physical sense by thinking how you dress when working on your car or in the backyard as compared to how you dress for a party or work. Now think about how that would change if I told you a photographer from the local newspaper was due to photograph (measure) you at work in your back-yard. In the behavioral sense there are two parallels we've all experienced. The first is looking in the mirror. Note how you stand up straighter, smile, and become more attractive when viewing yourself in the mirror. The measurement process, looking in the mirror, affected you. As a second example, think back at how your behavior changed in school when being tested in a subject versus just chatting with friends about the subject. In the business world, a modern approach, called the assessment center, where each individual's behavior is viewed and reported in structured exercises may well be an equivalent. In matters of measuring who we are and how we behave we must be cautious about how the process of measuring may affect the behavior.

If measurement changes the person's behavior, how can we ever be sure of who we are? The answer seems to be to collect data many times in different situations. When the same or similar answer shows up repeatedly, we can accept that it has some validity. With this caution, you may wish to try some of the questions at the end of the chapter. In a nonthreatening way, because only you see the answers, we have provided some questions to start you on self-discovery and self-assessment. Suggestions about where to find workbooks, tests and other ways to enhance your self-assessment have also been included.

SUMMARY

There is no known way to separate the role and duties of managership from the person. Therefore, who the manager is, in all aspects of life, personality, character, goals, and interests, to name a few, shapes the approach to management. No one style, no one set of characteristics, is the right one. This is true despite the many attempts in history to name characteristics of the successful manager. Rather it is important for the manager to understand that these aspects, traits, and characteristics of self are part of the picture. It is also important for the manager to be open, to communicate about values and some of these underlying determinants of action, style, and content in order to improve communications with others. And it is important, using self as the example, to realize that everyone you as a manager manage also has these several selves all affecting his or her relation to work and to you. Last, it is important to the manager to recognize that if any of these aspects are interfering with success in managing people he or she has both the responsibility and the power to change them.

Self Checkup*

1.   Pick the statements which most nearly reflect your personality as a quick way of determining whether you generally tend toward being an introvert or an extrovert.

     a.   I often choose a quiet place for concentration, and enjoy being alone.   (   )
     b.   I tend to be quick and often dislike complicated and specifically defined business procedures.   (   )
     c.   I often have trouble remembering names and faces.   (   )
     d.   I generally communicate well and keep employees informed.   (   )
     e.   I am interested in the idea or concept behind a task, job, or action.   (   )
     f.   I generally like to have people around, am usually with a group.   (   )
     (a/c/e tend to reflect introversion; b/d/f tend to reflect extroversion.)

2.   Some people tend to rely more on their feelings as a basis for action and others on rational, logical assessment of facts and information. Check those statements which most nearly reflect your usual approach.

     a.   I find it very hard to tell people unpleasant things (for example, a negative performance appraisal).   (   )
     b.   I like to analyze and organize data.   (   )
     c.   I work to create harmony and dislike political struggle or disagreements.   (   )
     d.   I seem unemotional and uninterested in feelings. Often enjoy disagreement.
     e.   I tend to make decisions based on likes, dislikes, and wishes.   (   )
     f.   I find little difficulty in disciplining employees, making organizational changes and even dismissing people. (   )
     (a/c/e tend to reflect feeling reaction; b/d/f tend to reflect rational, data-oriented behavior.)

3.   Pick the words that seem most descriptive of your managerial style.

     a.   ask   (   )   f.   question   (   )   (a/d/e/f/j tend toward parti-
     b.   confident   (   )   g.   argue   (   )   cipatory style; b/c/g/h/i
     c.   tell   (   )   h.   measure   (   )   tend toward authoritarian
     d.   suggest   (   )   i.   achieve   (   )   style.)
     e.   listen   (   )   j.   accept   (   )

---

*Think of these questions as a rough guide since there are no validation studies or proof they reflect what they say they do. Accuracy of reflection is also highly dependent on your outlook toward the question.

4. Check the statements which most nearly reflect what another person would observe who watched you as a manager:

    a. Is most often observed making decisions. Will give an answer to any question and is action oriented. ( )
    b. Spends the majority of working hours with those who work under him/her. ( )
    c. Spends the majority of working hours with upper management. ( )
    d. Is often observed helping an employee to understand what is required. ( )
    e. Is most often in his or her office. ( )
    f. Is regularly seen in exchange with one or more employees and is viewed as accessible. ( )
    g. Spends a lot of time on budgets, reports, and measures. ( )
    h. Generally is observed with a dour expression and is seldom seen smiling. ( )

5. Which statement best reflects your outlook? ( )

    a. I believe that knowledge and skill combined with hard work are the most important ingredients of success.
    b. I believe knowledge and skill and hard work are important in success but feel how you apply them is important too.
    c. I'm not sure whether knowledge, skill, and hard work or how you relate and your outlook is more important in success.
    d. I believe how you relate and your attitude and your outlook are more important but that skill, knowledge, and hard work count too.
    e. I believe that how you relate to others and your attitude are much more important in success than what you know or how hard you work.

Ideas for Action: Possibilities for Assessing Who You Are

Something
to try

1. *Unguided Self-Assessment.* Just taking some time to think about your values, your goals, what you like and dislike, your successes and failures, is a valuable way of finding out who you are. The success of approach is highly biased by who you are and by your habits of self-assessment. Alone on a beach or in the mountains is often a good time for reflection.   (   )

2. *Experimental Self-Assessment.* This is a further refinement of the first sugges-tion, but in addition you keep some kind of a record of experiences to assure that your data is more factual and that experiences needing analysis are remembered. With this technique it is possible to sample changes and record the results. This is a more proactive, exploratory process than number one.   (   )

3. *Use of Workbooks.* There are many guided self-assessment books available. Generally these are books of questions, experiments and exercises which will help you sharpen your perception of yourself. They provide a sort of active mirror. Several are listed below.   (   )

4. *Use of Tests.* There are many tests designed to help you learn about yourself in sharper definition. These range from Rorschach ink blots, which is very open and right hemisphere oriented, to measurements of your personality and style, to identi-fication of your thinking patterns, to comparison of your interests with interest related responses of people in various fields of endeavor. In general they need interpretation by one trained in the use of that test. Several are listed below.   (   )

5. *Professional Service.* Career counselors, family-oriented social service coun-selors, counseling psychologists, psychoanalysts, counseling philosophers, and psychiatrists all in their own way are geared to help you find who you are and in most cases aid you in change. Often a nearby college or university is a source for this type of assistance. This level is suggested only for those who are having real difficulty in getting in touch with their needs and capabilities. For the purposes of making yourself a better people manager, engaging in the first four suggestions is probably more in line with your needs.

SUGGESTED SOURCES OF ACTION POSSIBILITIES FOR
SELF-ASSESSMENT

Books

R. N. Bolles, *The Three Boxes of Life* (Ten Speed Press, 1978).

F. Flach, *Choices: Coping Creatively with Personal Change* (J. D. Lippincott Co., 1977).

S. J. Harris, *The Authentic Person* (Argus, 1972).

S. M. Jourard, *Healthy Personality* (Macmillan, 1974).

D. B. Miller, *Personal Vitality* (Addison-Wesley, 1977).

C. R. Rogers, *On Becoming a Person* (Houghton Mifflin Sentry, 1961).

R. Samples and R. Wohlford, *Opening* (Addison-Wesley, 1975).

N. W. Weiler, *Reality and Career Planning: A Guide for Personal Growth* (Addison-Wesley, 1977).

Workbooks

D. B. Miller, *Personal Vitality Workbook* (Addison-Wesley, 1977).

G. A. Ford and G. L. Lippitt, *Planning Your Future* (University Associates, 1972).

J. H. Zenger, D. E. Miller, J. Florance, and P. Harlow *How to Work for a Living and Like It* (Addison-Wesley, 1977).

J. W. Loughary and T. M. Ripley, *Second Chance* (United Learning Corp., 1975).

T. V. Bonoma and D. P. Slevin, *Executive Survival Manual* (CBI Publishing, 1978).

Self-administered Tests (Require professional interpretation)

Strong-Campbell Interest Inventory, Stanford University Press.

Meyers-Briggs Type Indicator, Consulting Psychologists Press.

Birkman Method, Life Style Grid, Birkman and Associates, Inc.

Style Awareness, Personnel Predictions and Research, Inc.

PART II

The Manager's Human Resource Functions

This part is designed to help you understand the human resource management functions for which you as a manager have basic responsibility. These are the classical core functions in managing people.

CHAPTER
6

Deciding On The Need

Sorting Applications

The Interview

Other Review Processes and Techniques

Positive Correlations

The Hiring Decision

Selection and Hiring

One of the most important decisions a manager makes is whether or not to hire a person. Most often the decision is based on data supplied on an application, a resumé, in an interview, or all of these. The decision represents a risk and a potential for success for the organization, the manager, and the applicant. Like most managerial decisions it must be made with what seems like incomplete data. The quality of the choice is dependent on the ability of the manager/interviewer both to communicate the specifics of the need and to evaluate the applicant. The quality of the decision depends, therefore, on the interview abilities of both manager and applicant. It is generally more dependent on subjective evaluations and feel than on factual data. However, we like to believe we make the decision on facts. One of the reasons for organizations to search for tests and to create probationary hiring categories has been to substitute facts for subjective feel. This need to rely on subjective feel is a prime source of anxiety and stress for the manager.

Some organizations, especially large ones, have tried to supplement and sometimes even replace the manager in this selection process. They do this by using personnel professionals to make the hiring decisions. If people are hired by personnel professionals, they are generally brought into a pool or training program. This moves the line manager's decision inside the organization and limits it to a prescreened group. It limits the manager's range of freedom to consider the broad field of applicants. The hope is that it raises the general quality of hiring practices since the professional interviewer is thought to be more objective and to take the longer view. Managers are seen as taking a hiring perspective which reflects the opening rather than the individual's career.

Even in organizations that do not establish central groups of recruits the personnel professionals try to assist the manager primarily to assure meeting the organization's broader objectives. Who has the primary and who has the secondary responsibility in choice varies with the culture and policies of the organization. Where the manager has the clear responsibility, the personnel professionals' role is one of helping to avoid big mistakes and assuring compliance with various governmental antidiscrimination rules and equal opportunity goals. The threat of discrimination charges has clouded the hiring and selection process and considerably increased the stress created in the process. This threat has made many people and organizations defensive in their hiring and selection strategy.

Because of the divergence among organizations in how the function is managed, we must deal with concepts and principles, guides and suggestions. It is up to you as a manager to translate this information, to become clear about the hiring processes, goals, and policies in your organization. It is up to you to know clearly where the responsibility lies. You as a manager have much to gain by being vitally involved in the hiring decision because your ability to accomplish tasks and to achieve goals is dependent on the people you have. When you are excluded from the choice you are seldom freed from responsibility for results.

For the purposes of our discussion we are assuming that the organization rather than the manager does whatever is necessary to locate applicants. This process, normally called recruiting, has become very sophisticated in the gathering of potential applicants from the university campus, and in the case of scientific specialties and certain executives and managers. It is less sophisticated for unskilled and semiskilled people hired on a local market. Attaining minority hiring goals has heightened the competition. Sometimes organizations use professionals, affectionately called headhunters, in locating those with particular skills, experience, and education. In the case of the entry-level and semiskilled openings, recruiting may entail no more than putting an advertisement in the paper. Sometimes it is based on recommendations from those you already employ, or just dealing with walk-ins, people who come to your door asking for work. If you are running your own small enterprise, you must find the recruits. You must find a way to have a group of applicants from which to select.

Deciding on The Need

The need for new employees comes about in two main ways. They may occur because of an increase in the organization's activities that causes a requirement for more people or new people with special attributes. They may occur because of the loss of an employee either through action on your part or action initiated by the employee. In both cases you have an opportunity. In the sense of your group your opportunity is to add a person who will add to the group capability and one who will allow you to enrich or change assignments within the group. Many managers overlook this opportunity and seek instead an exact substitute for the person who was lost. Or they see the opportunity as a specific need for a specific talent which needs to be added. While sometimes correct, it is wrong to assume that filling a slot or a hole is the correct approach. Rather, as a manager you should ask yourself what set of attributes and skills would enrich the group and the long run strength of the organization? Who should the manager look for if part of the goal is to improve work quality, interest, challenge, and development opportunities of others in the group? Who should the manager look for if career hiring, hiring for the long haul, is the emphasis? Are there perhaps several different types of openings you could fill rather than just one? Does the nature of the opening change when viewed from the career perspective? Further, one should ask whether you even have the opportunity to hire. Is there someone else already in the organization who should be rotated into your group? The real opening is then somewhere else in the organization.

After you have reviewed these questions and assured yourself that you are the one who should be hiring and have set up broad specifications, there are still some steps to take before starting to review applicants. The first is to get in touch with the conflict between the immediate and the long-run need. As a manager your shortest route to restored or expanded capability in your group is to hire the person who can quickly be productive, the experienced person. Yet in the long run, because of a different experience base, such a person may not have the flexibility, or the adaptability to remain vital in the organization. You must judge the right balance of response to short and long-term needs.

You must also decide what level of competence, skill, and education you need. Generally speaking, we as managers tend to hire the highest level of preparation we can attract. This probably results from our feeling that we are measured by performance, and reserve power (underutilization) helps us to gain results when we are given a new task without the relevant human resources. This incidentally is almost universally the case. Organizations normally ask for increased performance without allocating increased human resources. If we can really challenge the overqualified person, that may be fine. But overall, people like James O'Toole, a futurist and one who studies work and learning, feels we are underutilizing most people, about 80 percent of the professionals in the United States. If this is really so, we have all hired overqualified people. Together we are wasting tremendous amounts of human capability. You must make a decision on the level of competence you need before looking at applicants. Figure 4 is intended to put the overall process in perspective.

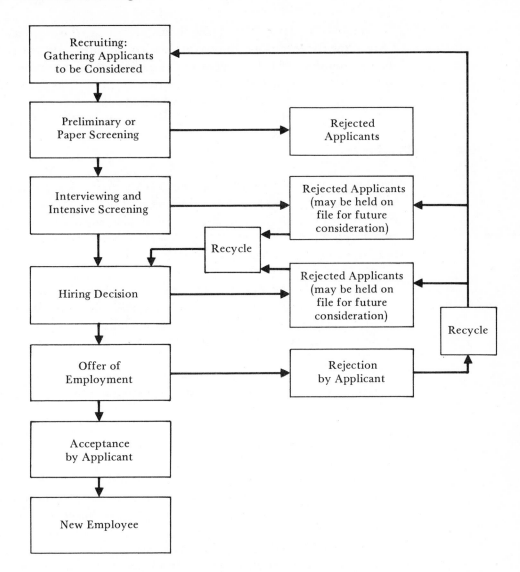

Figure 4.   *The selection and hiring process*

The selection and hiring process is critical to organizational success. Only by attracting and selecting qualified employees can the organization succeed. The process starts with gathering applicants to be considered. To give some feeling of the magnitude of the process, most major organizations that recruit on college campuses for professionals see from twenty to twenty-five students in preliminary campus interviews (the gathering process for this group) to hire one person. Preliminary screening is a review of

79

information on paper. The desire is usually to cut the number to at least one quarter for the more intensive, time-consuming, and costly process of interviewing and further screening. The hiring decision requires choosing from those who make it through the interview process as ones to be considered.

Sorting Applications

Whether you have just a few applicants or many, you need to do some initial screening using the data which is on the application. This will narrow the field so that you can spend the requisite time for a more thorough review with a few. Basically the application (sometimes supplemented by a résumé) gives you information about:

· work experience, and often a record of accomplishments
· education, and some feeling of the quality of educational achievement (class standing or grade point average)
· communications ability (how well the individual has presented himself or herself in writing)
· skills and knowledge not necessarily reflected in either the education or the work experience (often seen in hobby or extracurricular activities)

From this information it is necessary to determine:

· *The relevance of the work experience.* Does the work relate to the kind of work you would expect the person to do, now or in the future?
· *The quality of the work history.* Did the person demonstrate an increase in learning, skills and capability by a job sequence of increasing responsibility, and does the sequence of jobs move in a planned direction? Does the work experience seem to represent a theme?
· *The quality and applicability of the education.* Education in an area of knowledge which can potentially be used, now or later, on the job is better than education in areas which cannot be used. However, successful educational achievement in any form can demonstrate an ability to learn. This is a skill that is necessary for adaptation and job growth, for a career.
· *The capability at communication.* Although limited in the scope of its test, the application provides an opportunity for the individual to present himself or herself. Those who do a better job are better at communication, a skill required on most jobs.

- *Motivation and drive.* Continued improvement in jobs and in education demonstrates a commitment, as does working while going to school. This demonstrated drive may be used to differentiate an applicant from another without this evidence. Significant extracurricular, community, or hobby activity may also demonstrate energy and drive.
- *Potential for growth.* Sometimes reported extracurricular activity, the educational sequence, or the job sequence can reveal evidence of growth and personal development. Past evidence of personal development is no guarantee of future growth, but it increases the probability of that type of behavior. In selecting on an initial screening, demonstrated growth can make the difference in whether you further pursue the candidate.

Whatever you and the people in personnel do, the review process should be orderly, and your criteria, even though subjective, should be documented. Being able to demonstrate equality of review and consistency in the process is important in today's world of confrontations, disputes, and litigation.

The Interview

From these screened and sorted applications you should have identified a group whose qualifications you would like to explore further. The general purpose of the interview is to learn things about the applicant that were not on the application form and to tell the applicant something about the work and work climate. During the interview you and the job are being sized up by a sincere and capable applicant just as you are sizing up the applicant. Some of the major characteristics of a good interview are:

- The applicant is comfortable and not under unnecessary stress.
- The applicant has your total attention.
- You act as a catalyst for the applicant to talk about himself or herself, to cover such factors as goals, inner desires, interests, and experiences. The applicant should do the greater part of the talking although you must do enough to communicate a picture of the organization, job, and future.
- There is a plan, not rigid, but there are a set of questions you want to cover and some things you plan to say about the work.
- There is a real meeting between two people, and no matter what the outcome the applicant should go away feeling that a fair and reasonably complete exchange, without overselling, took place. You

can often measure the authenticity by looking for a correspondence between the nonverbal cues and the verbal statements.

· There is understanding of the psychological, the social, and the legal contract governing employment. The applicant must understand your expectations, and you must understand the applicant's expectations.

· There is understanding that there are some subjects you can't talk about such as age, religion, proprietary technical information relative to the former or current employer or the job under consideration.

· There is appropriate discussion of the family and outside work impacts, ranging from relocation to continuing education, overtime, and any social expectations, to company norms, rules, and policies.

· There is an understanding relative to the quality and applicability of the applicant's experience and education and a real discussion of both applicant and job strengths and weaknesses.

· There is closure; that is, each person knows what to expect as the next step if any.

· There is prompt documentation of the facts learned and the judgment made about the hirability of the applicant and the rationale for it.

A good interview feels right. There is normally a subjective and intuitive reaction that there has been a good, open, and complete exchange. Each person, manager and applicant, feels that concerns were shared and specific questions were answered. There is a feeling of freshness and authenticity, and although there is usually no on-the-spot commitment, each person should walk away with a feeling of knowing where they stand. Future events and actions should verify the accuracy of these feelings and attest to the quality of the interview.

Other Review Processes and Techniques

For some positions, particularly where there is a specific measurable skill involved, interviewing is often supplemented by testing. A typing test measuring words per minute and accuracy is a legitimate way of establishing a factual measure of typing skill. Tests must be shown to have a valid, measurable relationship to the actual work. Tests must be shown to be free of bias on race, religion, sex, and age. For these reasons tests oscillate in their acceptability and move in and out of favor. The decision to use tests must be made carefully and, in today's world, with competent professional advice. Failure to do this opens the possibility of future confrontation or litigation over applicability and discrimination. Some tests relate not to job skills but to intelligence, interests, personality, and interpersonal style. It is hard to validate and to eliminate aspects of unfair discrimination from these, and a professional should always be involved. Social legislation and changing values have considerably reduced the value of tests.

Team or sequential interviewing, or both, by several individuals with different perspectives is another way of enhancing the quality of interview screening. Agreement among several skilled interviewers who are related to the job by field, subject, or responsibility and at least one personnel professional reduces the risk of making a hiring error. However, there are applicants who do not interview well. There is not always a one-to-one relationship between a good impression in an interview and good performance on the job. Some hiring errors are inevitable.

Reference checking is another way to supplement the interview. In earlier times many organizations used professional credit and other investigative organizations to do some of this information gathering. Today, because of privacy sensitivities and the questionable tactics of some of these organizations, fewer organizations use them. However, even though you know the reference names presented are those the applicant believes will give positive references, it is a good practice to check some of them. Usually a phone conversation is better than a letter because you can follow the unplanned leads created in the conversation and gain some information from tone of voice and what is unsaid. Not only should references be checked but to catch any misrepresentation on education, some data work, history, and so on should be checked for accuracy. Checking former employers should of course wait for permission from the applicant.

Sometimes a problem-solving or stress interview is used. This can vary from asking the fresh Ph.D. to describe his or her dissertation research to a group, to asking a model maker to make a part, an engineer how he or she would approach a problem, and a computer operator to actually operate a computer. If such supplements can be worked in and it doesn't overwhelm the interview by eliminating the opportunity to cover other aspects, actual performance simulation can be of real value. However, the stress interview may really be a two-edged sword. The interviewee may consider such a tactic unfair. But such supplements can help to determine if the interview quality differs from the capability to perform in the work situation.

Sometimes an interview is supplemented by a social event. This can vary from lunch with potential co-workers to dinner with spouses. Not only does it provide inputs in a more relaxed social setting, but it also provides an opportunity for the more subtle sell when you are in tough competition for the person. Many times in my experience this technique has been the one that made the difference. Either it provided input to a new side of the person or it helped me to answer applicant questions and reservations not covered in the formal interview.

One shouldn't underestimate the value of personal attention as an important part of this process. Demonstrating that you believe the applicant is important can immeasurably improve the quality of the communication and information exchange. Just imagine how different your reaction would be if you were promptly greeted in the lobby, offered coffee, and a warm informal rapport was established. Compare this to cooling your heels in a lobby for two hours waiting for the person to be free to interview you and when you finally go into his office having his attention interrupted by a phone call. A decision as important as the hiring decision should be given your full attention.

A personal experience may serve to reinforce this point. At one time when I was searching for a new position I traveled over a thousand miles for an interview. The trip was paid for by the prospective employer who had my application and a resumé. On arrival at eight in the morning I waited for an hour before anything happened. I was then interviewed by a personnel representative and told the executive who had invited me was tied up but would see me later. I made myself comfortable in the lobby. At lunchtime three members of the potential organization took me to lunch, and we talked informally. At about half-past four I finally got to the executive's office. I had spent most of the day in the lobby. He was occupied with several problems, and there were several people in his office. After fifteen minutes of interrupted conversation, I was rushed by company car to the airport. They checked my references by phone (often a half to full hour long-distance call) and made me an offer of a good position at several thousand dollars more than the one I took. On receipt of my rejection the executive spent over an hour on a long-distance call questioning why I'd turned down his offer and arguing I'd made the wrong decision. Do you think I did?

Positive Correlations

Extensive studies in many organizations have attempted to find correlations between facts and information gained from the applicant and future success. These are soft studies. That is, there are so many individual variables it is hard to be sure of any broad principles. The principles and results also vary with the culture of the organization. However, here are some things which seem to correlate positively with a successful work experience:

- *Academic record.* A good record does not guarantee good work performance. But those who succeed in the organization most often are those who had a good though not superlative academic record. For example, it is not just grade-point average but the trend which is important. Did the student have trouble early in college and end on a high level? Or was the trend the reverse, with a down slide and lower marks in the career-related subjects? The first trend is preferable.
- *Extracurricular activities.* Those who engage in something other than study while in school seem to do better at work. Activities that predict success can range from part-time work, athletics, or drama, to newspaper publishing or hobby-related activities such as photography or skiing. Holding a leadership position in one of these activities has good positive correlation with work success.
- *Tangible evidence of work accomplishment.* The person who can demonstrate that, in whatever jobs they have had, they accomplished something is demonstrating a good predictor of future organizational and career success. Where creative skills are involved there is usually a portfolio, a tangible demonstration of accomplishment.
- *Interpersonal skills.* Any activity, work related or not, which demonstrates ability to relate to others, such as teaching or leading, has a high correlation with work success. Having been a scout leader is an example. Both leadership and qualities of being a good team member may be involved in this capability.
- *Business awareness and understanding.* This is most often demonstrated through the interview. It is a sort of business sense, a feeling of what works in the practical world that correlates with later organizational and career success. By contrast the person who does not have it often suffers from an inability to translate knowledge and skill into useful organizational accomplishment.
- *Evidence of interest in the organization.* Especially among professional, managerial, and executive applicants evidence the applicant has sought information about the organization is a positive indication of strength of interest. If the applicant has gone beyond just looking up the organization in a directory and dug into annual reports/or asked people who work in the organization or knowledgeable experts about it, this augurs well for future success. It means that the

organization passed the applicant's screening and that the applicant has established positive expectations.

· *Attitude and expectations.* Work attitudes and expectations are changing in our culture. However, although you may not discover the "Protestant work ethic" you can often discern through interview whether the individual is in touch with (can understand and communicate) his or her expectations. You must be the judge as to whether these expectations are achievable in your work environment. Work attitudes and expectations which are viewed as positive in your organization's culture will usually correlate with organizational and career success.

· *Goal definition.* An individual who has goals and objectives he or she can communicate to you is usually a better employee than one who has not defined goals and cannot tell you about them. This does not mean the goal must be detailed to the last dotting of the i, but a sense of direction of theme and purpose should be evident.

· *Energy level.* More high energy people are successful in organizations than low energy people. They also, however, are often those people who show up with growth frustrations (complaints about not moving fast enough) and high stress reactions (anything from ulcers to heart attacks). Energy level which is a good match with job requirements and organization culture is a good predictor of success.

· *Interviewer rating.* Despite the variability of interviewers and managers there is most often a positive correlation between the rating manager/interviewers give and the applicant's eventual performance. Any manager may be wrong in the specific case but in the overall, positive interviewer ratings do correlate with job success.

The Hiring Decision

The result of the interview process should be a narrowing of the field of applicants. It is now necessary to make the decision, to take the risk, to pick the applicant who is best qualified overall. There is no scale that alone measures applicant quality. There is no single characteristic which determines success. In fact, the matching of person and job, of individual and organization, is a multifaceted, iterative, and continuous process. You as the manager can create the work environment, pick the assignments, and influence the match with your positive outlook and expectations. However, you are a long way from controlling all the factors. Your participation in the hiring decision augurs well for the success of the person you select.

His or her success is a validation of your judgment, so to some extent you work to make it come to pass.

In making the decision you are weighing the evidences you have which indicate the person can be successful in the short term (on the immediate assignment) and have potential for the long term (career growth). Remember you are responsible for determining what balance is appropriate. In making this decision you are in some sense measuring the strength of desire the applicant has to be hired for your opening. This aspect is controlled by the applicant. You are also judging whether the addition of this person meets the goals of the organization for skill needs, for career potential, and for equal opportunity. This goal is under the control of the organization, the management. You are making a judgment about the strengths and weaknesses of each applicant and, on some kind of scale of your own devising, ranking the applicants in overall quality. However subjective, and it is good not to be afraid of that fact, you should be able to document the rationale for your choice. This provides both a good learning base for you as you review this decision against actual performance and documentation to support your decision if its fairness and objectivity is ever challenged.

A checklist of some elements to consider in making your hiring decision follows.

· *Defensiveness.* It is relatively easy to demonstrate that you picked the most qualified if you choose the person with the most relevant experience. This may not, however, always be the best person, the person with growth and adaptability potential. You need to find your comfort level and that of organization management on this issue. Don't assume the need for a defensive position without checking it out. This is one of the prime dangers in our litigious times.
· *Risk aggressiveness.* Taking the long shot in hiring may pay off, yet sticking with some of the factors which seem to correlate with success is also important. Your tendency to take a given level of risk in hiring probably relates less to the characteristics of the applicant than to your own sense of security and personal success.
· *Personal bias and group balance.* Bias is not used here in the negative sense of unfair discrimination; rather it is used to suggest that you should be conscious of how your own values and beliefs (who you are) affect the hiring decision. The probability is that someone with values and ideas similar to your own will be rated higher by you. Yet a strong group is not usually one in which every person is alike. Think about the need for some counterpoint, some differences, in a good, balanced, and strong work group.

- *Overqualification.* This is a negative word, an unmentionable in the hiring process. To admit hiring an overqualified person is some kind of a sin. To refuse to hire a person because they are overqualified is also some kind of a sin. You must be comfortable that the applicant's level of qualification makes it possible for the person to be challenged by the work. You must be comfortable that you are not rejecting someone because, probably subconsciously, you see this person as a threat to your position because of the strength of their qualifications and potential for development.
- *Collaboration.* In most organizations there is someone else involved in the decision, either your superior or a personnel professional. Be clear about who is advising and who is deciding. If you are making the decision, listen to the advice but don't hide behind it. Use advice of others as a sort of general insurance against failure. No insurance provides complete protection against risk. Don't use the advice of your manager or a human resource professional as a way to escape your responsibility for the choice.

SUMMARY

The hiring decision and the screening process which precedes it represent two of the most important activities and two of the most important decisions a manager can make. Your success and the organization's success depend on the quality of the decision. It is also important for the individual applicant to feel that you fairly and properly represented the organization with all its pluses and minuses, for that person's future is dependent on this decision.

The screening process consists first of an evaluation based on paper input. Usually this paper is the organization's application form and often it is supplemented by a resumé. The paper evaluation is necessary to reduce the number of applicants on whom you concentrate your energy and time. The interview is the process in which you check the data previously reviewed and fill in the blanks. The interview is a process of letting the individual tell about himself or herself. It should also include some questioning on your part and some description of the work. Remember that in the interviewing process you are also being interviewed. Your responses, your nonverbal cues, your reflected feelings help the applicant decide whether he or she wants to work in your organization, in this environment. Applicants are becoming more sophisticated. More and more the applicant is becoming selective about the quality of the work and the work environment, and you should not distort them just to make a sale, to hire a person. The hiring decision is based on the overall evaluation of applicant strengths and weaknesses. Key factors range from the applicant's capabilities to the motivation he or she has to use those capabilities. It is important to be fair in your judgments and it is important to pick the best-qualified person for the organization.

A Selection and Hiring Check-up

1. Do you outline or plan your interview?
   (   ) yes   (   ) partially   (   ) occasionally   (   ) not normally   (   ) no

2. Do you feel comfortable and capable in the applicant interviewing role?
   (   ) yes   (   ) somewhat   (   ) so-so   (   ) somewhat uncomfortable   (   ) no

3. Do you believe that the people you have interviewed as applicants feel you thought they were important and devoted your full attention to them?
   (   ) yes   (   ) many did   (   ) occasionally   (   ) seldom   (   ) no

4. Have you indentified the factors which you feel are most important in determining the qualifications of an applicant?
   (   ) yes   (   ) to a major extent   (   ) to some extent   (   ) poorly   (   ) no

5. Have you ever openly discussed the applicant interview process with other managers or personnel professionals to try to learn more about the process?
   (   ) yes   (   ) informally   (   ) I guess so   (   ) haven't thought of it as important   (   ) no

6. Are you proud of the people you have hired and their success in the organization?
   (   ) yes   (   ) significant numbers   (   ) some   (   ) a few   (   ) none

7. What percentage of the time in an applicant interview are you generally listening as opposed to talking?
   (   ) 80   (   ) 60   (   ) 50   (   ) 40   (   ) 20

8. Do your opinions about applicants coincide with those of other managers or personnel professionals who interview the same people?
   (   ) almost always   (   ) moderately well   (   ) occasionally   (   ) not well
   (   ) don't know

9. Do you generally gain for your group (win against internal and external competition) those applicants you want to hire?
   (   ) yes, generally   (   ) sometimes   (   ) once in a while   (   ) I don't feel that strongly   (   ) I don't usually compete

10. Have you had experiences with people you have hired which suggest, through problems which have occurred or through employee feedback, that there was incomplete communication in the employment interview or mistaken expectations?
    (   ) yes, definitely   (   ) quite a few   (   ) an occasional one   (   ) not that I am aware of   (   ) no, none

11. Have you done anything, enrolled in training, discussed the process, or read about interviewing as a definite effort to improve your applicant screening capability before reading this chapter?
    (   ) yes, quite a bit   (   ) some   (   ) nothing formal   (   ) no, nothing   (   ) I don't remember

12. Select the statement which best reflects your outlook about applicant screening.   (   )
    a. I believe it is one of the most significant and important roles of the manager.
    b. I feel that it is generally important but believe I can get useful work out of most people.
    c. I am careful about selecting people to key positions but not particularly careful in selecting the others.
    d. I rely on personnel to get the people I need and I manage the people assigned to me as best I can.
    e. I've never really thought about it before.

Ideas for Action: Selection and Hiring

		Something to try
1.	Discuss this chapter with fellow managers and/or personnel professionals.	( )
2.	Enroll in a training program on interviewing techniques in general or applicant interviewing as a specific process.	( )
3.	Read further about the process. Suggested references are L. R. Sayles, and G. Strauss, *Managing Human Resources* (Prentice-Hall, 1977), chapter five, "Interviewing: The fine art of listening." R. F. Irish, *If Things Don't Improve Soon I May Ask You to Fire Me* (Anchor Press/Doubleday, 1976), chapter seven, "How to read a person."	( )
4.	Work with my management and personnel to better define roles, responsibilities, hiring policies, and human resource goals.	( )
5.	Keep a log of what I do and how I perform in an interview to improve my understanding of the process.	( )
6.	Specifically set aside some exclusive time to devote to applicant screening and thus learn by doing. One way is to offer my services to personnel even if I have no immediate openings in my group.	( )
7.	Start working out a plan for my interviews including the objectives of the interview and key questions I intend to ask.	( )
8.	Conduct some role-playing interviews with friends who will allow the interview to be recorded so that I may listen to my tone and manner in an interview.	( )
9.	Interview some of my employees about their hiring interviews. Find out how they reacted and how they now feel about the quality of the interview with respect to finding out about them and their gaining information about the organization.	( )
10.	Review the original applications and recruiter interview comments about employees now in my group. Determine if there were clues which relate to the performance levels and attitudes you now observe.	( )

CHAPTER
7

Who Is Responsible?

What Is It We Are Matching?

The Problems and Causes of a Mismatch

Improving The Match

Matching People and Work

Effectiveness and achievement are dependent on the quality of the match between the individual and the organization. Individuals bring needs, like the need to utilize personal capabilities, the need to learn, and the need to grow. Organizations can provide the opportunities to fulfill these needs. Work thus becomes rewarding. Individuals also bring capabilities to work. Capabilities include knowledge and skills they wish to use. By providing an opportunity to use these capabilities the organization makes it possible to gain a sense of worth. Matching, gaining congruence between the individual and the organization, is not easy. Both the individual and the organization are changing and usually not in regular or predictable ways. Matching is also subjective because perceptions and expectations are involved. Matching people and work is a prime challenge for the manager.

Organizations also bring needs and capabilities to the work situation. Needs for the organization vary from goals of profit, leadership capabilities, and productive service, to utilization of ideas and facilities. Capabilities for the organization range from the technical process, which represents the mission, to the ability to pay for work, and to provide tools, equipment, and money to purchase materials. Like the individual, these needs and capabilities change over time. The person responsible for representing the organization and negotiating the match with the individual employee is the manager. That is why achieving the person/job fit is a primary human resource function for the manager. The quality of the match affects output and performance (organizational goals) as well as the assessment of work quality, morale, and satisfactions by the individual. Not only is matching very important on an ongoing basis; it is very important in the start of a work relationship between an individual and an organization. There is evidence that the quality of the first match sets the pattern for what is to come throughout one's career. If the individual employee starts the first job with a match that leads to personal success, this sets a pattern for future jobs. A good match leads to continuing success in the organization. A poor match leads to more poor matches and a lack of success. This is not an ironclad rule but a probability. An example will make the point.

I once had the sad duty of conducting the exit interview with an employee of thirteen years. This employee had been on projects for thirteen years that were not successful. I'm not sure to this day what was cause and what was effect. What I do know was that this employee realized there was little chance he would ever be on a successful project. He was labeled by past experiences. The probability of his getting assigned to a project with a high probability of success was small. He joined another organization and has had a very successful career.

Who is Responsible?

Classically it was the manager's total responsibility to choose the assignment and pick the person who best fit that assignment. The generally accepted management view was that the employee was passive and dependent in this process. Curiously, however, if the employee didn't fit it was somehow seen as the employee's fault. Today we see a shift in responsibility for matching to include the employee. The ratio of sharing is dependent on organizational climate, type of industry or organizational mission, the nature of the specific work, the level of education or preparation necessary to work in that area, the manager's style, and the employee's job outlook. Thus, there are today situations approximating the classical view where the responsibility is all on the manager's shoulders and situations where the responsibility is almost toally on the employee's shoulders. As a manager you should find yourself somewhere on this continuum. Being able to assess where you are, where your organization expects you to be, and which direction you are moving in is important in learning to manage people better.

Generally the trend in management today is toward increased sharing of the responsibility for matching job needs with the employee. This is reflected in the interview where the applicant is interviewing you in some cases as intensely as you are interviewing the applicant. In such a case the applicant's view is one of personal responsibility for the quality of job fit. To gain increased employee participation and responsibility for job/person fit we must set up conditions that support this personal responsibility and expectations that matching will be a shared activity. In the simplest sense this means you must ask the employee to communicate with you about job outlook, expectations, needs, and capabilities. In this complex world it really means making statements, creating policies, taking actions, and using words which continually demonstrate your expectation and your reinforcement of the process.

The responsibilities of the manager and the employee are shown in the following listing:

Employee Responsibilities	*Managerial Responsibilities*
to choose to take some responsibility for the match with the work and for establishing the quality of the work	to set expectations for and give clear signals about the balance of manager and employee responsibilities in job/person fit
to actively assess self, goals, needs, capabilities, transitions in value, and career direction shifts	to describe and communicate organization and subgroup goals, needs, and capabilities
to actively assess organization needs for opportunities to apply self	to encourage and listen to employee statements of goals, needs, capabilities
to actively present self to manager, communicating about goals, needs, and capabilities	to offer suggestions for modifications (job redesign) to improve person/work match
to negotiate openly for change (improvement) in work design and to manage personal change to improve match	to provide support for improvement in person/work match such as better equipment, support availability, coaching, training, task rotation, variety
	to work at the iterative changes necessary for a match and not to assume it is a one-time process

For the employee to fulfill his or her responsibilities there must be managerial and organizational statements and activity that make it both desirable and expected. For the manager to fulfill his or her responsibilities there must be policies, a supportive climate, and higher management expectations which encourage it. Both manager and employee need training in the process, which is neither taught in school nor handed us at birth.

What Is It We Are Matching?

We have used terms like goals, needs, and capabilities to describe what it is we are trying to match. We have said we are matching the person to the work. Despite all of the studies of work and people there is no standard or universal way of delineating what it is we are dealing with. First, individual differences are so great that they cloud our understanding and impede the creation of generalizable principles. Second, there are many different work contexts. Work situations vary with the technology, the specific organization's pursuits, and the culture, or organizational climate. Here we are using culture in a double sense: first, to describe the organization's culture, and second, to indicate the specific country's culture, which is also a variable. Thus, it is difficult to talk about the match even from experiences in two cultures with as many shared heritages as the English and American cultures. Third, the very process of asking about and describing the aspects to be matched can change the matching process and conditions. Just asking a person about goals, for example, may modify individual goals. This serves to emphasize the next challenge. We are dealing with variables, not fixed characteristics. Just thinking about the changes you notice in the work and work environment when you return from vacation will emphasize the changes in the organization and work. Thinking about how your values may or have changed with the birth of a child or the reading of a book or the impact of a new law may heighten your sensitivity to personal changes.

One aspect to be matched is goals. Ideally a good match of goals exists when the person can say, in the process of doing what the organization wants, "I am doing what I want to do and I am working toward one or more of my goals." If the individual wants to learn a skill and the job requires learning that skill and provides the opportunity to learn, this would represent a goal match.

The broad category of needs represents other aspects to be matched. Needs may or may not relate to personally defined goals. Fulfilling the need to learn provides a type of psychic income from work and meets the person's goals. However, the need to belong, the need for recognition, and the need for a sense of accomplishment are needs which do not represent a particular goal. Personal needs are recognized and defined by some individuals in some cases and not recognized, not consciously admitted, in other cases. For example, the need for income and the associated recognition which comes from it is often discussed and acknowledged. By contrast, the need to belong is seldom discussed, addressed, or admitted with respect to work or the work group. Many needs represent an income desire, income in the broad and psychological sense as opposed to the monetary. On the other hand, some needs are physical such as a space in which to work, tools to work with, and materials. Some needs may be ones which would be better satisfied by some other aspect of the individual's life, but because they are not, the individual brings them to work. Not only does each individual have a broad spectrum of unique needs, but the relative importance of these needs is different and changing with time. Personal priorities of needs differ. Here is a partial list of the range of the needs a person may bring to the work situation.

to use skills	to do something	to use knowledge
to accomplish tasks	meaningful	to write
to find self	to leave an imprint	to analyze
to enhance self-worth	to have power	to fill time
to belong	to gain status	to support others
to communicate with	to earn money	to be recognized
others	to be busy	to earn reward and
to learn	to make decisions	recognition
to gain a sense of	to contribute	to gain esteem
growth	to be loved	
to achieve goals		

Capabilities represent another group of things to be matched between the individual and work. If the individual brings a particular skill it is usually accompanied by the personal need or desire that it be used. If the organization needs that skill, then placing that person where it can be used is important to the organization. Such a placement represents a person/job fit. However, since we all have multiple skills, all our skills will generally not be used or needed at the same time. Also the individual's level of skill may not match the organization's need. For example, a secretary might type at thirty words per minute but the job might require fifty words per minute. As in most cases of matching some adjustment is necessary. The most normal adjustments are learning and skill improvement by the individual or supplementing the person with equipment that helps to bridge the gap. A further complication in the matching of people and work is the fact that needs are not always matched to capabilities. Needs may be matched to needs, capabilities to capabilities, and needs to capabilities. This is shown in the following diagram:

Employee	*Organization*
need for recognition ⟶ ⟵	capability to recognize with position, status, and pay
need to utilize skills and knowledge ⟶ ⟵	need for particular skills to manage organization activities
capability to work alone ⟶ ⟵ (self-management)	capability of providing work where individual can work alone

The Problems and Causes of a Mismatch

A mismatch (poor job/person fit) represents underemployment and underutilization and thus lost opportunity and lost human energy. A mismatch has the potential for creating stress in the individual and thus stress-related illness. A mismatch has the potential for causing a deterioration in the organization's capability to pursue its goals. A mismatch has the potential for spawning other mismatches. A mismatch invariably ends up as a problem for the manager and may lead to either voluntary or involuntary turnover. A temporary mismatch may set up the forces for resolution and improvement. A long-standing mismatch is negative and usually starts a longer negative cyle of negative job incidents.

Mismatches occur for many reasons. They may, for example, come about because the manager does not really understand the work. If as managers we do not really understand what skills, knowledge, and tools are required, we may put the wrong person on the job. Mismatches may occur because of poor communication between the employee and the manager. If as an employee I fail to tell you, my manager, about my goals, needs, and capabilities and you fail to elicit this information, then the match is made blindly. A most frequent type of mismatch results from a failure to reach goal agreement between manager and employee. Both feel they have communicated, both think they know what is expected, but a real meeting of the minds has not taken place.

Mismatches may occur because of change. In a rapidly moving organization the need, the task, and the assignment change often from the beginning to completion. Thus the person who starts out on the job and is a good match to the work may, because of change in the work, be the wrong person later in the cycle. Mismatches may occur because of a change in the person's goals and needs over time. For example, the person who relocated geographically from one company location to another to take a job that represents a good fit and loses, through divorce, wife and family in the process is a different person with different needs from the one who accepted the position. While this example seems dramatic, it portrays one of the types of changes in the person of which we are often not aware. One case like this led to performance degradation, alcoholism, and financial problems. Such a person is really a different person from the one who accepted the position.

A cause of mismatch is the programmed or formulated aspect of a job. A programmed job is one in which the technology or the process limits the degree of freedom for the individual. The classic example is the paced assembly line such as in automobile manufacture where the individual's duties are limited, timed, and proscribed in great detail. This causes mismatch because every individual needs some degree of freedom, some sense of control over the job. At the other extreme, jobs we normally think of as professional and demanding of individual initiative and decision making may also be seen as programmed. An example might be the work of an engineer whose degree of freedom is limited by extensive design standards or even proscribed computer programs. This latter case may be even more damaging because the professional approaches the job with higher expectations of freedom to control his or her work than the unskilled worker who expects some limits to freedom. Both, however, are key examples of negative aspects in our current world of work.

Mismatches may occur because of outlook and expectations. It is possible for a good match of skills and interests, what looks like the perfect match, to be wrong. This is perhaps the hardest part of this challenge. Whether or not there is a good job/person fit depends on attitude, outlook, and expectations. For example, suppose an employee brings to the work place an expectation that six months on this job should result in a promotion and an increase in salary. By contrast you and I as the managers believe it normally takes about a year and a half. (The commonly accepted idea of a normal time for promotion among managers is a sort of managerial myth.) As soon as it becomes apparent to this employee that his or her expectations are not going to be met, the fit may be disturbed by compensating actions by the employee. These may range from simply not working as diligently to diversion of energies and interests, to group disturbing actions, or even to sabotage. Thus matching is not real in the objective sense but only in the subjective sense. Matching is in the minds of the manager and of the employee.

Person/job fit is affected by the employee's future outlook. If we believe that changes will occur which will improve it, we will generally see today's fit as better than if we see the situation deteriorating. A simple example of this is the promise of rearrangement and refurbishment of space or a projected move to a new facility. I have seen groups put up with crowded and poor working conditions when they expect improvement. The same group with the same conditions not projected to improve will make the poor work conditions into an almost insurmountable problem. This same concept can be used to test the employee's feelings about future changes, such as organizational shifts or geographical moves. In this case we might use the question as part of an attitude survey (a periodically administered set of questions about opinions used to sample employee morale).

Improving The Match

It should be clear that anything which is done to improve person/work fit must be a joint manager-employee enterprise. The manager can and should set the climate for improvement. However, actions intended to improve work taken by the manager and not the result of joint interest and effort with the employee can be made to fail by the employee. Employee attitude, outlook, and expectations strongly affect the results of change.

Probably the prime danger in setting out to improve matching is that we as managers will assume something which is not true. We might, for example, assume that we know what the employee wants and needs. This would be the case if we were to apply our values and decide everyone wants challenge because we want challenge. This is the case when we decide that a particular routine which we see as boring is boring for everyone.

But many people on dull, routine jobs provide the input to smooth or adjust the fit by daydreaming, creating music in the mind, rationalizing that it could be worse, and other creative, imaginative techniques. If the

101

employee wants the job to fit it can often be made to fit. This is not to say that adjusting to a bad fit is right in the long run, but it may well avoid stress-related problems and help us to last to the next opportunity to modify the relationship. Open exchange, open discussion, and true participation are the cornerstones of person/work fit improvement.

Improvements may be categorized in the following ways:

Changing what needs to be done.   This is the case when we choose a useful goal (meaningful to organization and individual) over one of less value. This is the case when we can actually eliminate a process or an activity. This is the case when the organization can give up a specific goal and substitute another.

Changing how something is done.   This is the case when we change the sequence of activities, change work boundaries, redesign the workplace, and add new tools or equipment.

Changing who does things.   This is the case when we share activities in different ways between members of a group. This might include rotation of assignments or increase of the individual's depth of activities as in the case of adding setup of a machine to the duties of running the machine.

Changing the span of the activity.   There is extensive study which supports the concept of wholeness of a job as an improvement in quality. Including more parts of a cycle or process in the activities of one person can improve the sense of wholeness. An example might be making an individual responsible for assembly of a total device previously assembled in stages on an assembly line.

Changing the skills and knowledge of the individual.   When we provide education and training so that the individual brings enhanced capabilities to the job, we change the probabilities governing the person/job fit.

Changing the expectations.   Through open discussion, training, and participation in goal setting and in job redesign we have the opportunity to bring expectations and reality into better alignment. Often negative expectations may be turned into positive expectations when frank and full communications and discussion of goals replaces inadequate communication.

The responsibility of the manager is to set up work conditions that fit the environment, the organizational culture, and the mission, and also to encourage working at improvement in the person/job fit. For some groups this may require group meetings and participative job redesign. For other groups establishing the right environment may mean setting up educational activities. For others creating support may simply be the manager's opening up to suggestions. For other individuals creating the supportive environment may mean extensive one-on-one (manager-employee) career-related discussions. The purpose of this discussion was not to prescribe what you should do to improve the job, but to state clearly that job change for improved job/person fit can and should be an active thrust of the manager. Yet while recommending this outlook, we must add the caveat that all jobs can't be improved and every employee does not want to improve his or her fit. Some employees simply don't see the job as that important or something in which they wish to invest that much energy.

SUMMARY

The person/job fit is important. It is important to the organization because it directly affects output quality and quantity. Good fit usually means the organization moves toward its objectives. It is important to the organization also because good fit directly contributes to positive morale and thus the ease with which a group can be organized to pursue the organization's goals. The fit is generally important to the individual because a better fit means both more psychic income (satisfaction) and better performance which should affect real dollar income. Person/job fit is most important to those individuals who see work as important in their lives.

Person/work matching is a mutual or shared responsibility between employee and manager. A good match requires good communication about goals, needs, and capabilities. A good match requires managing change and adjustment. People change their values, goals, and interests. Work changes as the result of technological and business changes.

Person/work matching is difficult because it is subjective and thus affected not only by real measurable things such as skills available and required but also by mind set, by outlook, and by expectations. When the employee's and the manager's expectations and the reality of work conditions are out of alignment, the match is poor. This is true even if goals and capabilities are well matched between the organization and the individual.

Person/Job Matching Checkup

1. Can you list the organizational *needs,* including their strength (priority) which you represent for the company in matching work to the people you supervise? (Try it and then respond to the question.) Pick the most appropriate statement.   (   )

    a. I feel I can list almost all.
    b. I feel I can list many.
    c. I feel I can list some.
    d. I feel I can list but a few.
    e. I've not really identified them.

2. How do you communicate these needs to your employees? What is the quality of the communication from your perspective? Pick the most applicable statement.   (   )

    a. I have frequent, two-way, participative discussions about the nature of organizational needs and goals for our function. I work actively to translate these for the individual so they have meaning. My employees understand the needs and goals very well and have helped to shape them, so they own them, and accept them.
    b. I have group and individual discussions as needed and there is very open communication about organizational needs, goals, and tasks. Most of my employees have a clear understanding of and agreement with these goals.
    c. I have the required discussions necessary to establish performance plans and interpret organizational goals and needs to help with defining and outlining tasks for individuals.
    d. There is evidence of need for improvement in my communication of organizational needs and goals. I am discovering difficulties in acceptance of appraisals and missed objectives which relate to a lack of understanding of needs and goals.
    e. There is considerable evidence in my group of misunderstandings about needs and goals despite my attempts at communication.

3. How would you characterize the openness and quality of your attempts to match people and jobs? Pick the most appropriate statement.   (   )

    a. The definition of the job is a mutual process openly carried on between the employee and me. We consider reassignment of work, adding facilities, and investing in training as usable ways of improving person/job fit.
    b. There is considerable flexibility and adjustment, shifting of tasks, redefinition of work based on open communication.
    c. There is open discussion, some adjustment of tasks, support for training, and ability to alter support and facilities.
    d. I define the job and listen to the employees' needs and capabilities, and then make the choice of best fit.

e.   I define the job, and it is generally up to the person to adjust to it and meet our goals.

4.   Are the capabilities you provide (facilities, support, training) on behalf of the company of high quality and diversified, or poor and relatively inflexible? Pick the appropriate statement.   ( )

a.   They are good, flexible and able to be improved as needed.
b.   They are reasonably good and moderately adjustable.
c.   Some are good, others bad, and I can adjust the support if I fight hard.
d.   Support is barely adequate for the process and does little to enhance the capability of the people.
e.   Support is insufficient, poor, and I seem unable to improve it.

5.   How do your employees see the person/job matching process as you manage it? Pick the most appropriate statement.   ( )

a.   It is open, adult, constructive, supportive, and responsive to employee needs and employee individuality.
b.   It is mostly open and supportive and responsive to individual employee needs.
c.   It is generally good but somewhat limited in flexibility. Employees feel they must bear most of the adjustment burden.
d.   There is almost no possibility of employee modification of the requirements.
e.   It is closed, arbitrary, and parental. Employees are expected to adjust to fit organizational needs or leave.

6.   How do you believe your employees feel about the following statements? Pick the most appropriate answer.

a.   Their utilization of their skills and capabilities on their job is: ( ) very good ( ) good ( ) so-so ( ) poor ( ) very poor
b.   Their ability to talk with you and modify tasks and measures. ( ) very good ( ) good ( ) so-so ( ) poor ( ) very poor
c.   Their understanding of organizational goals and department or group goals and needs is: ( ) very good ( ) good ( ) so-so ( ) poor ( ) very poor
d.   Your understanding of their goals and needs is: ( ) very good ( ) good ( ) so-so ( ) poor ( ) very poor
e.   Their ability to be challenged and have the freedom to develop and change is: ( ) very good ( ) good ( ) so-so ( ) poor

7.   Have you checked up on the perceptions you documented in (6) by having an open discussion with your group? ( ) yes ( ) sort of ( ) no

8.   Pick the statement which best describes the frequency of your actions on this subject.   ( )

a.   Conversations and adjustments of work requirements with employees are so numerous and frequent I am not keeping score.

b.   Within last few days I have had a large number of conversations about person/job fit and job requirements with employees.

c.   Within the last month I have had a few conversations with employees about work fit and job requirements.

d.   Within the last six months I have had a few conversations with employees about work fit and job requirements.

e.   I can't remember a specific open, two-way discussion with an employee about needs and capabilities and matching them with our work.

9.   Select the statement which best reflects your assessment of evidences of poor fit between persons in your organization and jobs. (Try to take a dispassionate view, not blaming yourself.)

a.   I am unaware of stress-related symptoms in my employees, have recently assessed fit, and find a high level of satisfaction with work quality.

b.   I am aware of some negative morale in my group, feelings of work quality being poor, and some evidences of job-related stress disorders.

c.   I find my flexibility to modify work severely limited and therefore am aware of negative reactions to work quality, poor morale, and several cases of job-related stress disorders.

d.   There has been turnover, and I am having difficulty in replacing people. I relate this to poor matching, job stress, and the perception of poor work quality in my area.

e.   There has been considerable evidence of job-related stress, poor morale, high turnover, and I relate this to poor job matching.

10.   How would you categorize your feeling about your ability to deal with the issues of people/job fit? This is a reflection of your assessment of the environment in which you work.   (   )

a.   I feel the environment is highly supportive and encourages me to work creatively at matching people and work.

b.   I feel the environment is supportive of creative matching only when the business weather is good, but I have considerable freedom and control.

c.   I feel the environment is neutral, and therefore I am quite free to work at creative matching of work and people.

d.   I feel quite limited and constrained in matching people and work both by the process and by the environment.

e.   I work in an environment where matching people's needs and work is neither encouraged nor supported, and I feel I have little control and small freedom in working in this area.

Ideas for Action: Improving the Person/Job Match

		Something to try
1.	Select and hire people with the right skills and interests and/or make changes in hiring and selection to improve the probability of good job/person fit.	( )
2.	Create new ways of communicating more effectively about organizational needs and goals so as to build a better basis for matching.	( )
3.	Create new ways of listening and encouraging your employees to tell you about their needs, capabilities, and goals.	( )
4.	Change the climate, the expectations relative to the desirability of a good job/person match, and the need for joint responsibility and action to improve matching.	( )
5.	Establish or request new educational or training activities which will improve the matching processes.	( )
6.	Increase the opportunities for your employees to experiment with change and through experience improve their ability to tell you what they desire.	( )
7.	Consider asking the H/R training function to establish a program to help managers match people and work.	( )
8.	Analyze your own match to your job and through this process and discussions with your manager improve your fit to your work. Personal experience with the process should improve your ability to help others.	( )
9.	Take a course in a nearby university or in a company educational program which deals with job development and job and organization design.	( )
10.	Read more about organizational psychology and job development. Here are some suggestions.	

> T. F. Connellan, *How to Improve Human Performance* (Harper and Row, 1978).
> J. R. Hackman and J. L. Suttle, *Improving Life at Work: Behavioral Science Approaches to Organizational Change* (Goodyear, 1977).
> E. H. Schein, *Organizational Psychology* (Prentice-Hall, 1970).

CHAPTER
8

The Anatomy of A Leader

The Leader and The Group

Coaching as a Managerial Role

Leadership and Coaching

Leadership and coaching are both necessary managerial roles. In some senses they are contrasting roles. For example, to be a leader you need to be out in front, to be ahead in discovery and interpretation, to be ahead in trying new things, to be committed to change, and to be an exemplar. These elements of leadership tend to create in you a difference which may make it harder for others to relate to you, to understand you, and even to follow you. Because you are out in front you must believe in your values and goals, defend and fight for your beliefs and sense of direction. This push to lead may also, in some ways, increase the gulf between you and others. Leadership, along with some other functions like performance measurement and decisions about people's futures, tend to make the manager's role a lonely one. To withstand the rigors of being alone you also need ego strength. This too may increase the gulf between you and others.

Coaching, by contrast, requires empathy for others and the ability to be sensitive to their needs and struggles. Coaching requires that you be able to sense how it feels to be struggling as some of those you lead may be, to be a learner, to do these difficult new things, to change and to grow in capability. Coaching requires that you be caring and nurturing and a mentor for your employees and others. Coaching is probably the least understood managerial function. Because of this many managers are fearful of the coaching role. Through coaching others you get your reward, your sense of accomplishment, in the accomplishments of others. Often the initial rewards for the person chosen as a leader come through personal accomplishment. Yet the two types of rewards merge, since to be a leader you must have followers and to have followers you must communicate, teach, and coach.

Many of the human characteristics that are components of leadership and coaching are personal characteristics that are part of your basic personality. Other components are behaviors probably learned early in your life before you became a manager. It is for these reasons that many say managers are born, not made. Yet the premise of this chapter is that you and I can, from wherever we start, improve our leadership and coaching capabilities.

The Anatomy of A Leader

The leader I choose to follow is one I admire. This does not mean all aspects of the person are perfect or that I would choose to be like that person in all aspects, but rather that I respect the person and perhaps he or she has some outstanding aspects I would like to emulate. Thus one of the aspects of leadership is trust built on an authentic relationship. Another is probably some characteristics of personality, of behavior, and of accomplishment which I would like to develop in myself. The leader, then, must be good at what he or she does. For the manager this starts with being a good manager. Yet there is no one model of a good manager. Good managers are judged as good because they do what fits the environment, somehow sense what is necessary to do themselves and what is necessary for others to do. Good managers in any organization are those whose style, direction, and accomplishments attract people to want to be part of their group. Good managers set up a positive aura. Managers who are leaders are exemplars, generally people who set high standards for themselves, show how it can be done, and get their employees to rise to higher levels than they would without the manager's help.

Thus, another element of leadership and of good managership is that the individual brings out the best in those who work for him or her. Leadership is inspiring others to achieve, to grow, and to learn. One such manager for whom I worked, without ever saying I hadn't done as well as I could, caused me to compete with myself. Somehow in his presence, through the assignments and suggestions he gave, my motivations were enhanced. He didn't seem to force me or lay something on; it was as if he removed barriers, probably my own self-imposed barriers. Respect for the other person, as a whole person, with capabilities and a desire to use them, is what comes through as central to this aspect of leadership.

Most leaders I know are egocentric. That is, they believe in themselves; they have the courage of their convictions. To be a true leader I feel this is a necessary component. Yet in our culture we generally believe egocentricity is not a good aspect of personality. However, without a belief in self, life at a frontier (intellectual, business, or physical) is unbearable. You need the strength to fight for what you believe, to stand up against attack and odds that organizations are very capable of mustering against you. Yet if you develop too much ego strength (self-centeredness), it becomes easy for the organization to discount you and to all but eliminate your opportunity to be effective. Too much of this characteristic separates you from others and makes having followers difficult. Your strength alienates others by making them feel weak. Balanced egocentricity is what is desired. Balance is represented by enough belief in self to provide the strength to lead in the environment where you find yourself. Probably the components of balance are best described as a sense of humor, some evident humility, and some demonstrations that you are flexible, human in your reactions, and able to change and to adapt. One person I know describes this as the ability to lose a battle to win a war. Thus a part of achieving balance is the ability to take a larger or perhaps longer view.

Top management and organizations are also aware of this personal dilemma of leadership. From this perspective it is usually described as the need for individualism. Yet the desired individualism must be, within limits, acceptable in the organization environment. Thomas Watson, Jr., made this need evident in IBM when he called for "wild ducks." Another top manager I knew described it as the ability to fight the organization above, but the sense to know when to stop fighting and do what it has been decided should be done as if it was your personal decision. The fighting represents the personal strength. The carrying it out as if it was yours represents the support of the organization.

Many leaders pursue their area of expertise in the sense of a calling. Their career and their job are not something they have been arbitrarily pushed into. Their work and their careers drew them as a powerful magnet. There was something about their inner program and this type of activity that was sympathetic and compatible. For some managers the managerial role of leadership does attract and feel right. For others leading always remains strange. Creating a personal feeling that the leadership role in management is a calling is probably not something over which we have active control. Not having this one aspect of the anatomy of a leader does not disqualify one for leadership. Having it, however, makes up for some other aspects of the anatomy of leadership that may be missing or weak.

Closely related, but hard to separate from the sense of the calling by things we see the person do or say, is belief. Good leaders believe in what they are doing. Good managers believe in what they are doing. This belief seems to go beyond the objective data at times. That is, the decision the leader makes seems to be in spite of the data and in response to some overall theme. This belief provides a sense of central purpose, of direction, and makes seemingly unrelated actions understandable. Belief in the necessity for management, in the rightness of the role, and in the creative aspects of leadership is probably as important as one's belief in the organization or one's personal field or area of specialty. These beliefs are seldom identified as beliefs and not often communicated. Yet those in management should take time to identify and assess their beliefs.

Other parts of the anatomy of a leader can be grouped or described as a sort of communications sensitivity. One aspect of this communications capability, being in touch with where the followers are, keeps the leader from outdistancing those managed. Another aspect of this communications capability keeps the leader in touch with the context, the organization's goals, direction, and climate. This has the feature of increasing the credibility and the usefulness of the leader to the followers in the role of an interpreter of the organization. A third aspect of communications capability has to do with timing. When one is pushing at a frontier, trying to create movement and action or introducing change, there is a time to push hard and a time to relax. Part of timing is sensing that the followers are ready to accept movement; and the organization, change. Often the single most evident aspect of good leadership or management is this sense of timing. The good leader just seems to do what is necessary at the right time.

Although we could go on discussing many aspects of the anatomy of leadership, only one more aspect of leadership, energy, will be discussed. Being a leadership manager takes energy. High energy people have a greater probability of being leaders in dynamic and fast-paced organizations. Energy seems to be the single most important factor which can be identified in the majority of leaders.

Another way to look at leadership is to look at the roles leaders in management play. The anatomy previously described can be likened to the structure of the manager. Roles, by contrast, describe what the manager-leader does.

Many leadership roles are interpersonal. That is, they are viewed as activities between the manager and other people. One role is as figurehead, both symbolic and legal. In this role the manager's relationship with others is generally outside the organization. One role is motivational, or at least lowering the threshold at which the individual is self-motivating. In this role the manager is dealing with the employee-follower or with other managers. And another interpersonal role is as communicator and liaison. Here the manager seems to receive and sometimes search out messages, translate or interpret them, and communicate the message to employees or other managers. Leadership roles are informational and include monitoring the work flow and process, disseminating information about problems or accomplishment, and being the representative or spokesperson for the organization. Leadership roles also include decision making about using resources, settling disputes, and placing emphasis. The anatomy, or characteristics, of the person affect how the individual interprets and plays all these roles.

Unlike human anatomy where we can say that every bone or organ seems to occur in each human, leadership anatomy is not consistent. Rather than consider this discussion and listing as complete or definitive, therefore, it should be considered as representative. The characteristics which make up leadership capability must fit the individual, the business context, and the culture of the specific organization. In assessing which of these factors and others define a good leader in your organization, you must be in touch with the organization climate and observe the characteristics of those considered leaders.

The Leader and The Group

Not only must the leader fit the context and needs of the organization, he or she must be flexible in style and technique in response to the needs of the group. The primary role with respect to the group in the context of human resource management is to enhance and clarify the employees' psychological expectations which result in the motivation to do what the organization needs. These activities include:

· Recognizing the stimulating employee needs for outcomes (work results) which the manager can in some sense control.
· Opening the opportunities for individual employee payoff and the route to payoff (personal satisfaction and growth) through coaching and direction.
· Assisting the employee in clarifying and communicating personal expectations and goals.
· Reducing or eliminating frustrating barriers to work performance and personal achievement.
· Increasing the personal payout, sense of satisfaction or value of outcomes, as perceived by the employee, for performance that results in organizational goal achievement.

· Setting the climate of the work environment to achieve a good balance between individual needs and group needs, and understanding and using the collective needs for further stimulation of performance, assistance in determining direction, and recognition and rewards for group accomplishment.

From this list it can be seen that in managing the group the leader must strike a balance between response to the individual's needs and response to the group's needs. Sometimes personal motivation results from individual tailoring and interaction with the manager. Sometimes it results from response to the group's norms, mores, and needs. Sometimes the most effective motivation is at the group level. Sometimes motivating requires bruising, creating a challenge for the group, something for them to bump against. A manager managing a mature, self-sufficient, self-directing professional group will, for example, need to provide less actual direction of the tasks than one managing dependent, lower skilled, non-self-directing people. The style of leadership appropriate for the first group is not appropriate for the second. However, as the learning and self-management capability of the second group increases, the manager will need to back off in detailed direction of the work.

To further our understanding of the manager and the group, it is important to understand some characteristics of groups. First, groups are groups because the individuals are drawn together and bound to each other in some way. The source of this cohesion may be in a common background or set of experiences. In this sense college graduates hired by an organization off the same campus in the same year might see themselves as a group. A group may be created by a common activity or purpose. Thus, in organizations departments with a specific function are often defined as a group. A group may be defined by close contact. Thus the passengers in a car may be defined as a group, and those working in close contact, relating to the same process, may be defined as a group. These same people might also be defined as a group because of common skills or common status. A group is sometimes created when people come together to exert power they cannot exert alone, such as in a caucus or a union. Sometimes a group is defined by communication needs and a shared vocabulary.

The strength of the group is created by the bonds just discussed and some social characteristics. One social characteristic is the amount and kind of support the group gives its members. Support might be in the form of job help, assistance in knowing what to do. Support might be in passing along the norms (unwritten rules) of behavior. An example would be in telling the new group member how much work is enough work. Another aspect of support may come off the job in providing friendship and activities. These things can vary from poker groups and bowling teams to car pools and aid in personal work projects at home. Support may come in the form of protection. This may involve taking the employees' side in a difference with the manager or even providing physical protection from rival groups.

Groups also have leaders. These are people around whom the group rallies. The leaders vary with the topic or the perceived group threat. The manager must identify these informal leaders and involve them as a supplementary communication route to the group.

This understanding of groups suggests that we as managers must look at the personality of the group to determine what different managerial styles are required. For example, managers must learn to sense the group's need for person-to-person care and emotional support. Some people and groups need a lot of managerial attention. For them frequent attention is part of the feedback which assures them that they belong, that they are noticed, that they are important. Other groups and individuals are much more self-sufficient and demonstrate less need for attention. If you give a group with low attention need the level of attention required by one with high attention need they may well feel that you are bugging them, that your constant attention shows a lack of faith in their ability, and that you don't trust them.

Managing the group is a balancing act. On the one hand, the manager has a set of characteristics which form his or her style. Whatever is done must fit with this style. The manager must also recognize the social characteristics of the group and adjust style to fit group needs and the perceptions on which the group is based. All of this must be done within the environment and goals of the organization. As if this is not complicated enough, a manager must also balance the operational view of the group's need for structure (detailed direction) and its need for participation (the opportunity to be self-directing).

A review of the literature on motivation, on how to get people or groups to do what you believe is necessary, is really a review of leadership patterns, or style. When Frederick Herzberg is talking about hygiene factors he is talking generally about the factors important to those individuals or groups needing high structure. When Abraham Maslow is talking about self-actualization he is talking about self-managing, self-sufficient people who need low task structure and direction. They supply their own structure and control. They don't need a manager who does. When Rensis Lickert is suggesting that we use System 4, a participative management style, he is talking about a management system which works best with those needing low task structure and direction. He is also talking of a style that is relatively high in required interpersonal relationships. When Douglas McGregor is describing theory Y he is talking about those who need low structure; theory X, those who need high structure.* The point is that none of these styles or systems are specifically right or wrong. Any system or style can be right when it fits the context and the group. It must, however, also be a style that the manager can use and still be authentic. Figure 5 presents the continuum in visual form and summarizes what we have just discussed.

Coaching as a Managerial Role

A coach is a helper. A coach is someone who brings out the best in you. A coach explains the ropes. A coach provides feedback which helps you learn. A coach often provides positive stress (eustress). A coach may relieve negative stress or anxiety. A coach makes personal change and individual

---

*For a description of Herzberg's, Maslow's, and McGregor's theories see chapter three.

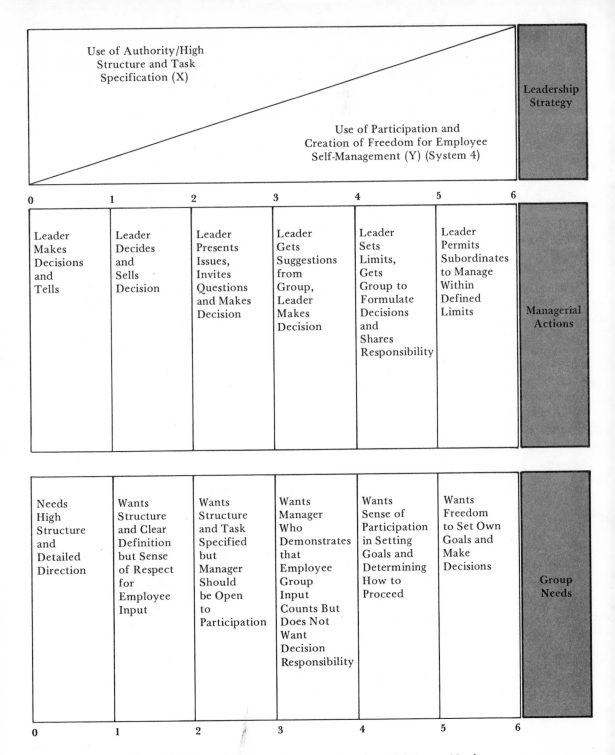

0	1	2	3	4	5	6

Use of Authority/High Structure and Task Specification (X)

Use of Participation and Creation of Freedom for Employee Self-Management (Y) (System 4)

Leadership Strategy

0	1	2	3	4	5	6
Leader Makes Decisions and Tells	Leader Decides and Sells Decision	Leader Presents Issues, Invites Questions and Makes Decision	Leader Gets Suggestions from Group, Leader Makes Decision	Leader Sets Limits, Gets Group to Formulate Decisions and Shares Responsibility	Leader Permits Subordinates to Manage Within Defined Limits	

Managerial Actions

0	1	2	3	4	5	6
Needs High Structure and Detailed Direction	Wants Structure and Clear Definition but Sense of Respect for Employee Input	Wants Structure and Task Specified but Manager Should be Open to Participation	Wants Manager Who Demonstrates that Employee Group Input Counts But Does Not Want Decision Responsibility	Wants Sense of Participation in Setting Goals and Determining How to Proceed	Wants Freedom to Set Own Goals and Make Decisions	

Group Needs

Figure 5. *Matching Managerial Action With Group Needs*

117

development less threatening for you. A coach cares about you. A coach provides you with another perspective — a helpful way of looking at events and activities. A coach impacts your life. A coach is often an exemplar, a model. Coaching is an art — an art including many positive relationships between people. Personal development is often accelerated by a caring coach who appears at the right time and elicits a response in the individual. Coaching and teaching others is important in work and in play. Coaching is a very necessary part of managing people. But coaching is misunderstood and a role which raises anxiety in the manager.

Coaching is defined as doing whatever is necessary to aid the individual in self-achievement. Coaching is not telling as much as it is creating the situation where the individual discovers. It is showing, but stopping short of doing it or being so explicit that the individual becomes dependent on your skill. It is providing support and encouragement, but not so much that the individual fails to learn to stand on his or her own feet. It is providing performance feedback for the individual so he or she can do the necessary self-assessment and make personal choices. It is not deciding for the individual. The manager who feels coaching is telling, being the expert, is the manager who fears the coaching role.

The manager's coaching role has first to do with the pursuit of the tasks and activities of the job. In this role the goal is to accelerate individual and group learning and the development of skills and knowledge necessary to do the job. This aspect of coaching can be considered production or output oriented and tends to have a short range and immediate focus. The nature of this coaching is specific to the job and the culture of the organization. Good coaching of this type has the following elements:

- understanding the employees' motivations
- explaining the nature of the task and the measures of completion and quality
- watching performance and providing feedback which accentuates useful and positive evidences of successful performance in order to improve performance
- being available for job counsel and advice but not so available as to eliminate learning and the development of self-management skills
- providing access to appropriate references and training experiences
- providing recognition for growth and accomplishment

In thinking about how to assist managers in their coaching roles one searches first for good examples, since there are no absolutes. One experience comes to mind which was the way one of my managers assisted me in adjusting to a new job and a new city. First, he was not the manager who had hired me, so first we had to get acquainted. At this stage he made certain I knew that he knew I had special expertise and experience that he respected and needed. Second, he made it clear that he would help me to get to know the organization. He took me to meet key people. In early assignments he asked me to come back and tell him how I thought they should be approached. As we reviewed my plans, he suggested contacts and ways to get the organization to respond. At an early opportunity he took me along on a trip to another location. This provided me some one-on-one time without the pressures of daily operations. On this trip he found out about me and he transmitted some of the lessons from his experience. The main feeling which he trasnmitted was that I had his support. He later demonstrated that as I made presentations and pro- posals. When I became interested in operations research, cross disciplinary and mathematical analysis, and found a two-week educational program at Case Western Reserve University, he supported my enrollment and found the funds. When I came back he expected me to tell others about OR, and I conducted some informal seminars. He attended and, by so doing, en- dorsed the activity.

Both he and his wife enjoyed entertaining in an informal manner. We were soon introduced to people in the community through the me- dium of their parties. Many may feel this was beyond what was expected and many might feel uncomfortable with such entertaining. The message is that he and his wife did something that fit their style and it helped. When a promotion and a change came along, he provided plenty of op- portunity to talk it through and helped me to identify the pros and cons.

Longer-range coaching has a goal of improving career manage- ment, the total lifelong iterative development of the individual. Here again the emphasis should be placed on being supportive but not so supportive as to become a crutch. There are, for example, people who would like to be able to put the responsibility for making career choices on the manager. They thus can blame someone else if it does not work out. A good career coach is not one who makes career choices but rather one who establishes conditions which aid the individual in making career choices. This means, for example, aiding the individual in becoming sensitive to value and need changes. It means providing the feedback which inspires the individual to spend the energy necessary for the tough job of self-assessment. It also includes providing information about opportunities, not in the sense of jobs but in the sense of organization needs and challenges.

The role of the manager in career counseling is covered more fully in chapter fifteen. However, in discussing coaching there are some important additional points to make here. Careers are now multiple, thus people need support in managing transitions from one career to another. The coach has some specific things to do here. First the manager-coach needs to make as clear as possible what the individual should do and what opportunities are available to prepare for the next step. As I have investigated complaints of employees, the failure of the manger to spell out what the individual can do to improve the potential for promotion, individual growth, and a change of career is a recurring theme. Certainly this is partly a failure of communication. No manager can, or should, try to lay out a specific sequence of activities. There are too many variables, and readiness for change is not the same in two people. However, exploring and helping the individual to think through possibilities are coaching functions.

The manager-coach should also provide a window to opportunities. This may mean describing specific opportunities, but more often it means describing types or classes of opportunity. Basically the process is one of interpreting organizational direction and its meaning for career planning. An example might be to translate a technical trend into what it may mean in job trends.

The manager-coach should provide support for assessment of specific opportunities when they come up. In this role the coach should assure that the individual thinks through the alternatives, the satisfactions to be gained or those that may be lost, and the risks of change and nonchange. The manager cannot offer assurance against failure, but the manger can describe the support, the fail-safe aspects of the organization. In this sense the manager reduces the apparent risk or understood risk without changing the actual risks.

What can be learned from our review of coaching? Are there some guidelines or principles of good coaching? Here are some to try:

1. The coach provides information and transmits experience both in the sense of how to accomplish things in the organization and in the sense of how to get ahead in the organization.
2. The coach provides information and experience in accord with the needs of the individual. That is, the coach senses what is needed and when it is needed by viewing the situation from the perspective of the person to be coached.
3. The manager-coach helps the employee to prepare for promotion, personal change and growth, and transition to new jobs and new careers.
4. The coach is not an expert and should not take the responsibility for choices off the employee's shoulder. The coach highlights and

makes more evident signals (feedback) which the individual might not identify. The manager then creates an environment for objective review by the employee.

5. The manager-coach is supportive of the employee and does those things which reduce the apparent risk to the employee of choices and change.

6. The manager-coach interprets the organization's goals and the norms of the organization for the guidance of the individual.

7. The manager-coach does those things that fit the style of the manager and the organization's environment.

SUMMARY

The successful manager who is a leader and a coach causes others to rise above themselves and to achieve more. Leadership and coaching techniques are not so much telling and directing as creating the conditions for others to become self-directing. Leadership requires being out in front, setting standards and goals, but always being sensitive to the followers. A good leader does not outdistance the followers by so much that they are not inspired to follow. A good leader is in communication both with the long-range goal and with those people he or she leads. A good leader provides a bridge and inspires people to cross it.

The manager who is successful in coaching is the person who is able to sense the individual's need for attention and support and then to respond to those needs. Yet in the response the coach is restrained lest he or she become a crutch. The coach provides feedback that helps the individual to become more sensitive to what is being done right, what works. The good coach is a mentor and an exemplar. Much of the value of coaching is not in what is said but in what is done.

121

Leadership/Coaching Checkup

1. Do your employees understand and accept the direction you have set so completely that they pursue it vigorously even in your absence?

   yes, definitely (   )   reasonably well (   )   they would try but are confused (   )   probably not (   )   no, I must be there (   )

2. Select the statement which is most descriptive of your leadership style and technique.   (   )

   a. I am very successful at stimulating others to achieve more and have frequent feedback which confirms this.

   b. I can cite examples of people who have followed my leadership and achieved higher levels of accomplishment as a result.

   c. I am not very sensitive to my impact on others and do not know whether they accomplish more or less because of me.

   d. I am aware of the fact that I have failed to provide inspiration and leadership for some and am working to improve my leadership.

   e. I am aware of a real lack of ability to inspire others and don't know what to do about it.

3. Pick the most appropriate descriptive phrase. I am able to   (   )

   a. regularly and successfully vary my style to fit the needs of specific individuals and the group.

   b. sense the need and vary my style as required in most situations.

   c. sense the need and vary my leadership and coaching style to stimulate a few.

   d. create the right leadership relationship with an occasional person and not inspire the majority.

   e. achieve only one style and approach and hope that it will be right for some.

4. If you came upon a large group of people intent on committing mass suicide, marching into a river for example, which of the following actions do you feel you could successfully use to save some?   (   )

   a. I would get out in front of the crowd and say, "Follow me—this way to the river!" and actually lead the group away from the river.

   b. I would walk along beside the group, convince a few to change their minds, and ask them to become agents to help change others' minds.

   c. I would walk along beside the group and try to convince a few individuals to change their minds.

   d. I would stand in front of the group, yelling "Stop!" and lecturing them on the folly of their action.

   e. I would not feel capable of doing anything and I would turn the other way.

5. Think of your role as an examplar, being a model for others, and pick the most
    appropriate statement.   (   )

    a. There are many of my followers spreading my style and approaches
        throughout the organization and others. I have many "graduates" of my school.
    b. I can see my influence in the actions, style, behavior, speech mode, and outlook
        of many members of the organization.
    c. I can identify one or two people who have adopted some aspects of my style
        and behavior.
    d. I have some evidence that people are modeling their behavior after mine in my
        presence, but it does not seem to last after they leave.
    e. I have no evidence that anyone is modeling themselves after me.

6. Pick the statement which best describes your outlook on your role as a coach.   (   )

    a. I actively search for the right coaching mode with my employees and with
        others in the organization. I see coaching as one of my key roles as manager.
    b. I take a positive, active stance on counseling and coaching and set definite
        times for one-on-one sessions with my employees, thus formally establishing
        expectations that I will be their coach.
    c. I see that I have a role as a coach, and through highlighting accomplishment
        and providing some advice, I try to set the climate where employees will look to
        me for help.
    d. I believe that coaching is important and have been responsive to requests by
        employees for talking/listening time with me. I, however, generally wait for them
        to make the first move.
    e. I see my managerial role mostly in terms of managing the work and do not see
        myself as a coach. I feel people should generally stand on their own feet.

7. Think about your coaching activities and identify the frequency and pattern most
    nearly representing your style.   (   )

    a. Coaching is so much of my activity and so continuous I can't tell when I am not
        coaching when in the presence of members of my group.
    b. I can identify a half-dozen coaching events in the last day or so.
    c. I can identify a half-dozen coaching events in the last week.
    d. I can identify a half-dozen coaching events in the last month.
    e. It is hard for me to identify any coaching activity in the last month.

8.   Check the appropriate responses.

		generally	sometimes	almost never
a.	It is difficult for me not to tell the employee what to do.	( )	( )	( )
b.	I find it tough to help the employees feel comfortable and open with me.	( )	( )	( )
c.	I find it easy to provide useful feedback to the employee.	( )	( )	( )
d.	Listening, letting the employee find the answer, is easy for me.	( )	( )	( )
e.	Sensing the employee's individual needs (motivation) is easy for me.	( )	( )	( )
f.	Setting tasks jointly and defining performance measures is hard for me.	( )	( )	( )
g.	Providing employees with recognition for accomplishment is easy.	( )	( )	( )
h.	I have little difficulty in identifying the need and creating the appropriate training experiences.	( )	( )	( )
i.	I find it difficult to make the time for counseling.	( )	( )	( )
j.	I have personally used someone as a coach to me.	( )	( )	( )
k.	I can sense the need for leadership, the vacuum which requires me to step out ahead.	( )	( )	( )
l.	I find there are so many staff aides and people second-guessing me that it is difficult to take responsibility.	( )	( )	( )

Ideas for Action: Improving Leadership and Coaching

Something
to try

1. Get together with fellow managers to discuss leadership styles and roles so that we can share ideas for improvement.   ( )

2. Take a formal college course in leadership or coaching.   ( )

3. Engage your group in an open discussion with you about leadership and coaching to elicit their expectations of you and suggestions for improvement.   ( )

4. Become more attentive to how you spend your time and to your managerial roles by keeping a small notebook and recording what you tried and how it worked.   ( )

5. After a coaching session with an employee elicit that employee's feelings about how it went and how you could be more helpful.   ( )

6. Engage in some volunteer (public or professional) activity where your leadership capability is stretched and sharpened because of the absence of pay and work relationships on which to rely.   ( )

7. Set up a gamelike situation at lunchtime or during some leisure activity where you deliberately try to win over a group to a point of view not generally held by these people.   ( )

8. Take an assessment test dealing with your style and thus get to know your style better. (For examples, Meyers-Briggs, Personnel Predictions, Birkman.)   ( )

9. Take time at the end of a meeting of a group of people to analyze who led the group in what aspects and why that person was successful or unsuccessful. In other words, start looking at the leadership process around you.   ( )

10. Read about leadership, especially biographies of leaders in fields related to yours or of significant interest to you.   ( )

CHAPTER
9

The Performance Plan

The Appraisal

The Appraisal (Performance) Interview

The Total Process

Cautions and Caveats in Appraisals

Performance Planning
and Appraisal

I want to be measured because that means what I do is important. Knowing how I am doing is necessary for me to progress. Yet measurement is in some sense control by my manager, and I resent it. Therefore, to feel that I am fairly measured I must feel that I had a say or at a minimum I clearly understood what I was expected to do. To gain this feeling, therefore, I want to work with my manager in laying out my assignments, tasks, and schedules and to know when I should finish them. Yet, I don't want performance specified in so much detail that I feel a lack of freedom to manage myself. I must also know what will be judged as acceptable completion and have some idea what I need to do to be judged as doing an outstanding job. If my job results in measurable output, as it would if I were assembling parts performance measurement, it is relatively easy. In this case I am expected to make a certain number of assemblies per day, and they must pass a quality check — they must work. Even in this case, however, I need to feel that, if my work is slowed because some of the parts don't fit or if my assemblies don't work because in some prior stage the parts weren't made right, this will not be held against me. Above all whatever performance measure is involved, I need to feel it is fair.

More and more, however, people are employed on tasks which do not result in easily measurable results. This means that the task of specifying what needs to be done and the task of establishing what will constitute satisfactory completion are both difficult. It puts a greater premium on the need to have good communication about the work and the measurements. It raises the priority for managerial understanding of performance planning and appraisal. The result of a good performance plan and a fair appraisal should first be that the employee knows where he or she stands. Second, it should be reasonably clear as to what the individual must do to improve and gain an increase in salary and a promotion in status. Performance measurement, normally called appraisal, should form the base upon which manager and employee can build job progress. Planning and appraisal, both processes requiring interaction with the employee, are necessary elements of managing output or productivity and individual development.

These processes are continuous if the employee and manager have good rapport. Why then is it necessary to have a formally scheduled and documented plan and appraisal? First, because having a formal process improves and assures communication. We all have selective hearing, hearing what we want to. This can occur even in a formal interview, but probabilities of getting through are increased, especially if the employee acknowledges the appraisal with a signature. Second, there are many of us who in the absence of a formal requirement will just not do it or will never achieve closure of a performance review. We will assume that the employee understands. Third, formality of process is necessary for the organization to assure that people are being treated in the same way. Finally, formality of process provides a record in case of misunderstandings or formal grievance reviews.

There are several types of appraisal. The management-by-objectives appraisal process is described here. This approach has been chosen because it is representative of the elements of most appraisal programs. Other appraisal approaches include:

· *Identification of traits, styles, and activities.* For example, the employee is dependable and finishes assignments on time, or irritates others, and is a disturbing influence in the group.
· *Identification of most applicable behavioral patterns.* For example, the employee is self-managing and needs little direction, does thorough research into procedures, or demonstrates great skill in the use of measurement instruments.
· *Ranking.* Simply take all members of a group and list them in the manager's order of perceived value to the group activity.
· *Measurement of quantity and quality of units produced.* Where a measurable physical output exists, those with higher numerical output are considered better performers.
· *Peer evaluation* A good example of the evaluation of one employee by another employee is the medical staff review in a hospital. The diagnosis, actions, and results that a specific doctor achieved or failed to achieve with a specific patient are evaluated by fellow doctors.
· *Self-appraisal.* As a continuing process, we assess how well we have done relative to our goals, our sense of capability, and our inner programs. Sometimes this can be and is formalized as part of the appraisal by the manager, who asks the employee to prepare for the appraisal interview and part of the appraisal is a comparison of self-evaluation with the managerial evaluation.

The Performance Plan

Matching the work goals to the employee's goals and the task needs to the employee's capabilities is the essence of the good performance plan. It is necessary for both the employee and the manager to know what performance is expected and how it will be measured. Successful performance is required both by the organization and by the individual. On-time quality accomplishment of tasks makes the organization viable. Meeting performance goals is necessary for the individual to earn pay increases, promotion, self-satisfaction, and career growth.

It seems axiomatic to say that the eventual evaluation of performance cannot be any better than the quality of the performance plan. The exception to this is where in the process of appraisal both manager and employee see that their failure results from incomplete early communication, and both parties then grow and change. In such a case the growth involved may well be more valuable than a good appraisal would have been. This example helps us focus on the dual goals in the process. The two goals of performance planning and appraisal are (1) managing the work in an orderly fashion so that productivity is a result, and (2) contributing to the employee's growth, change, and personal development.

A good performance plan results in a meeting of the minds between employee and manager. Only if this exchange is open and frank will the ultimate measurement of accomplishment be considered fair by the employee and perhaps others who review it. Unfortunately even with this almost miraculous communication, it is still possible for the employee to feel unfairly appraised. One reason for this is that the values and personality of the manager affect the measurement. It is equally true to say that the values and personality of the employee affect the performance. Standards of measurement also reflect the manager's interpretation of organizational rules. Achieving a meeting of the minds between employee and manager requires setting a framework in which the employee feels that he or she has been listened to and that although it is not an agreement between two people of equal power it approaches such an agreement.

To establish the plan an interview or often a series of discussions is required. Therefore, the planning interview is important. Good interview principles apply equally to the establishment of the plan and the performance evaluation upon completion of the tasks.

One of the challenges in setting up a good plan is that in most organizations job requirements are not static; they change over the performance period. Changes in tasks, schedules, and criteria for achieving completion are normal. It is therefore not uncommon for the manager and employee to arrive at the measurement time only to find the plan they set up is no longer valid. Ideally it should have been changed as things progressed, but in reality these changes are seldom documented. A good technique is, therefore, to review and modify the documentation of the plan as the measurement review approaches. As in setting the original performance requirements, both parties should provide input to this modification.

Another challenge to planning performance is that, at best, a plan usually hits only a few of the key items or parts of performance. Thus all elements are not documented. It must be clear to both parties at the outset that the plan is not and cannot be complete. For example, in review of many appraisals of managers by managers I have seldom found the requirement for planning performance and evaluating performance of employees spelled out as a detailed requirement. Yet a manager could fail by not performing these processes. For the employee a similar requirement is normally to be punctual and regular in attendance. Yet most performance plans take this as a given and do not spell it out. These examples identify that category of requirements, general in nature, which every person must complete just to hold the job. Performance plans, therefore, usually highlight unique aspects, not general ones.

A third challenge to the establishment of the performance plan is the meaning and interpretation of words. Even a word like *complete* can have different interpretations between manager and employee. The best technique for avoiding misinterpretation of words is to give examples. The manager should specify what he or she means by complete in concrete and specific job-related terms.

A fourth challenge in performance planning is the necessity for trust. Good and useful performance plans require that the two parties trust each other. Without trust neither the plan nor the evaluation is really possible; without trust both parties merely go through the motions. Such action lays the groundwork for future controversy. However, even with these difficulties, the great majority of job performance plans do not end in controversy. Despite the challenges, despite the problems of two people communicating accurately and openly, the process works out satisfactorily in most organizations most of the time.

Some cautions are in order. A performance plan, by its very existence, tends to limit degrees of freedom. The employee therefore sees it as an attempt by the manager to control. The greater the participation of the employee in setting the plan, the greater the employee's sense of freedom. Employees vary significantly in this need for freedom. Also we tend to specify measurable qualities in performance planning, and both employee and manager must be alert to the tone and process aspects which, although difficult to spell out, may literally make the difference between success and failure. Another tendency in performance planning is suboptimization. That is, in specifying what is required from a particular employee, the good and bad aspects must be made specific. Yet good individual performance, good group performance, and good organizational performance are in some senses mutually exclusive. Where possible individual performance criteria should be specified in respect to the group as well as the individual.

The Appraisal

To assure that all the elements are covered and to enhance comparison with your present appraisal form, we have included a conceptual model. In this model four key activities are recorded as part of the performance plan. There is a place to describe the expected activity in three or four words, a place for a more detailed description where specific expected behavior may be cited, and a space for indicating the relative importance of the activity in the overall work assignment for the person. All other parts of the model form pertain to the appraisal, the measurement of performance/ Performance appraisal is the process of making judgments about the work accomplishment with respect to the requirements of the job/Although the MBO (management-by-objectives) form has been used for illustration because it allows measurement against mutually agreed-upon statements, performance can and often is measured against standard statements. Examples might be as follows:

1. The employee has demonstrated understanding of the requirements of the job by completing tasks in the following manner: (   )

   a. always does more than expected and is accurate and timely
   b. often does more than is expected and is generally accurate and timely
   c. performs assignments as required and expected and is generally accurate and timely
   d. completes assignments only with significant managerial assistance and is inconsistent in quality and timeliness
   e. fails to complete assignments and is late/or inaccurate

2. The employee's ability to communicate with others, work as a member of a team, and be successful in interpersonal relations can be described as follows: (   )

   a. communicates clearly, is supportive of group goals, and others enjoy working with him or her, overall outstanding
   b. generally is understood, considered a good team member, but is somewhat inconsistent in quality of relations with others, but overall is considerably above average
   c. has some difficulty in communicating, works well as a member of the group most of the time, and despite some difficulty with others is satisfactory in this area
   d. has interpersonal relationship difficulties which require managerial assistance to correct but is still considered a desirable member of the group because some learning and improvement is taking place
   e. has considerable interpersonal difficulty, is a disruptive influence in the group, and does not seem to be making progress

3. The employee's capability to learn and grow to perform the job may be described as follows: (   )

   a. is a quick learner, progresses rapidly in increasing personal capability, and is helpful in assisting others to learn and to grow
   b. learns well and is improving at a reasonable pace, and occasionally is helpful in teaching others
   c. is learning and growing in capability at an acceptable average rate for the group

132

      d.   has difficulty learning but with considerable managerial assistance shows improvement

      e.   seems uncommitted and incapable of learning and growing in the context of this job

Whether using such standardized statements or whether measuring performance against specific requirements for a task or job, the process requires that the manager differentiate this individual's performance from standard expectations, or averages. Differentiation of performance quality, quantity, and timeliness should be with respect to what the individual can legitimately be expected to do. That is, it would be unfair and discriminatory to define a task that others would generally agree was beyond the individual's capability. In repetitive manaufacturing tasks, it is possible to have a reasonably valid measure because many people can be measured on the same task. In the case of knowledge workers this is much more difficult. It is usual in this case for acceptable performance to end up being what the manager feels he or she could do on the same task, modified for the experience and educational level of the individual employee. Seldom is the manager of a given employee in a position to have sufficient numbers doing exactly the same thing to come up with averages, standards, or totally defensible criteria. Our conceptual model provides the manager with space for recording the observed behavior and ranking the employee's performance on some scale (Figure 6). It is important on the MBO type of appraisal to make the statements similar to those in the examples. That is, the statements should describe the actual observable behavior. The statement, "completed the task on schedule with results beyond expectations," supplemented by an example, would be a good one. The statement, "did OK on the task," would be significantly poorer in describing accomplishment.

Most appraisal programs also provide for some general statements about the individual. Our model puts these in the form of general strengths and areas for improvement. Some performance appraisal systems and forms will provide a set of generalized areas on which all employees are to be rated. Examples might be work commitment, skills and knowledge, ability to learn, and communications ability.

Our conceptual model contains a place for an overall rating. Overall ratings are necessary shorthand for dealing with the management of salary increases based on performance, for assessing whether to consider an employee for a change in position, and other activities where some general qualitative statement is needed. Also the model has a place for recording the interview both from the perspective of the manager and the employee. Many systems do not directly provide form space for employee comment,

Name _____ Date of Plan ___/___/___ Date of Appraisal ___/___/___

Department _____

Job Title _____

Activity	Performance Plan: List Specific Job Requirements, Dates, Quality, etc.	Rank	Accomplishments: What Did the Employee Do Relative to the Plan?	Performance 1 2 3 4 5

Strengths: _____
_____
_____
_____

Areas for Improvement: _____
_____
_____
_____

Interview Summary: _____
_____
_____
_____

Employee Comment: _____
_____
_____

Overall Rating:
1. Outstanding
2. Consistently Exceeds Requirements
3. Exceeded Requirements at Times
4. Met Requirements of Plan
5. Failed to Meet Performance Plan

Employee Signature _____

Manager's Signature _____
___/___/___
Interview Date

Figure 6. Conceptual model for performance planning and appraisal

but even in that case the employee should have some way to contest, rebut, or agree. Written evidence that the interview took place and what happened strengthens the process and communication and provides a basis for later review.

The model also provides for the signatures of both parties. Having the employee sign assures that he or she saw the rating and that it was not recorded just for the record and without feedback to the employee. It is really the feedback to the employee for job performance improvement, individual development, and growth that is the prime function of performance evaluation. Use of the evaluation for salary purposes and consideration of promotions is really a secondary purpose. There are some states, and California is one, which require that the employee receive a copy of anything he signs. Since problem employees and litigious employees would probably collect old appraisals to prove their point, some corporations do not require signing in California. I believe the trend of legislation makes this a weak stance since employees are entitled to access to their files under privacy legislation, and the desirability of an open adult relationship between employee and organization makes such an act questionable. The best way is clearly to have an employee sign the form even though this means that the employee must be given a copy.

The Appraisal (Performance) Interview

The interview is what the appraisal process is all about. In an ideal world we would not require a form or a records system because managers and employees would be communicating effectively about job requirements, performance and improvement. The real gain from the interview should be learning by both employee and manager, growth in employee capability, and performance improvement. With this in mind here are some specifications for a good appraisal interview:

- *It should be planned.* The manager should decide what is to be covered, what he or she wants to occur as a result of the interview, and what it is necessary to say to have clear, open communication.
- *It should be open, frank, and positive.* A good interview is one where the two parties both talk and listen and where there is agreement on improvement. An appraisal that concentrates on negatives is usually one where communication is not open, the employee stops listening, and the outcome is a deterioration rather than an improvement in the employee-manager relationship.

· *It should contain no surprises.* Saving up incidents for the formal interview, which often comes but once a year, is dangerous and destructive. Rather, the interview should be a time for more complete and helpful discussion and an integration of many incidents already fed back.

· *It should be relatively comfortable.* It is normal for the employee to be under some tension and stress when being evaluated. Therefore the manager should do all he or she can to set the environment and tone so that the employee is not threatened by the event. Managerial attitude, nonverbal communication, timing, selection of topics, and physical setting are all important. (For example, it is recommended that the manager get out from behind the desk and create a setting conducive to communication.)

· *It should be natural.* Closely related to comfort is the need for both parties to be authentic. If, for example, the manager is passing on an evaluative comment from someone else, his or her belief or nonbelief will generally show through.

· *It should feature strong points and accomplishment.* There is much more to be gained in improvement by building on strengths than concentrating on failures. One seasoned career counselor, Bernard Haldane, suggests we would all gain from carrying a list of our accomplishments and successes for easy and frequent reference.

· *It should cast all changes and improvements in the context of the work.* A poor interview concentrates on traits and personality which are at best difficult to modify. A good one casts change in the context of job behavior.

· *It should end in an action plan.* A good interview is one where both manager and employee have something to do, and report back about, as a result of the discussion.

· *It should gain acceptance.* A good interview is one where there is agreement. This does not mean that the employee and the manager must like all aspects of the appraisal, but rather than they agree that it is a fair evaluation.

· *It should be documented.* Both what took place and the employee's reactions to the discussion should be recorded. All action commitments should also be recorded.

A good interview characterized by these specifications results in improved understanding between manager and employee. It should thus establish a basis for job performance improvement and growth in capability. The formal documentation should really be subservient to and supportive of these goals. Filling out a form required by the personnel system does not meet the requirements, even if it does get the system off your back. A good appraisal interview is one both parties feel was useful and constructive.

The Total Process

Figure 7 shows the total process in perspective. First, the manager chooses an assignment or assignments from the work available, based on his or her understanding of employee capabilities and interests. Next the manager explains the work to be done. A good interchange between employee and manager at this point will clarify the assignments and allow their modification to improve the job/person fit. The ultimate result of this discussion should be mutual understanding of what is to be done and how performance will be measured. The employee should, at this point, understand what constitutes satisfactory performance and what represents outstanding performance.

As the work is done the manager should provide coaching assistance and immediate feedback on critical problems. Critical problems should not be stored up for the appraisal interview. There should be no surprises in an appraisal. At the appropriate time the appraisal interview should provide the opportunity for mutual agreement on the evaluation of what has been done. If both parties agree, then the cycle starts anew with the additional information learned in the process as a basis for improving things the next time around.

If there is a failure to achieve a meeting of the minds, the employee faces a choice. Either the employee feels the issues are serious and escalates the problems for review, or the employee decides it is not important and goes along with the situation. Properly done, a review can clear the air and establish a new basis for communication and a better try the next time. Not well done, the differences remain and can cause a deterioration in the manager-employee relationship. This is often what happens when the employee chooses not to make an issue of the differences.

Cautions and Caveats in Appraisals

Discrimination has become a negative word. Yet for the purpose of employee counseling and determining pay, discrimination—distinguishing the difference between achievement of different quality or distinguishing between satisfactory and unsatisfactory performance — is the essence of

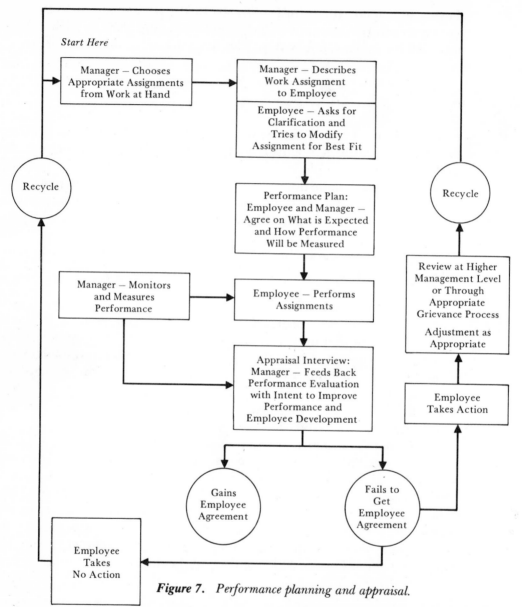

Start Here

| Manager — Chooses Appropriate Assignments from Work at Hand | Manager — Describes Work Assignment to Employee |

Employee — Asks for Clarification and Tries to Modify Assignment for Best Fit

Recycle

Performance Plan: Employee and Manager — Agree on What is Expected and How Performance Will be Measured

Recycle

Manager — Monitors and Measures Performance

Employee — Performs Assignments

Review at Higher Management Level or Through Appropriate Grievance Process

Adjustment as Appropriate

Appraisal Interview: Manager — Feeds Back Performance Evaluation with Intent to Improve Performance and Employee Development

Employee Takes Action

Gains Employee Agreement

Fails to Get Employee Agreement

Employee Takes No Action

Figure 7. *Performance planning and appraisal.*

This flow diagram shows the necessary steps and the alternate routes dependent on good, complete communication. It begins with the manager choosing what he or she feels are appropriate assignments; presenting these to the employee; the employee should then have the opportunity to question and to modify, where appropriate. Next both parties should achieve agreement on what is to be done and how it is to be measured. The manager monitors performance and feeds back observations and suggestions in the appraisal interview. If there is a meeting of the minds the cycle repeats; if not the employee either chooses to escalate the issues or not and after the review the cycle starts again. If the employee chooses not to escalate there is the possibility of deterioration in the quality of the process.

appraisal. Thus one of the overall cautions in the appraisal process is that assessment of performance is personal and must be kept private. It must also be a rating of the individual with respect to his or her own capability, not with respect to someone else's. It must be fair in the sense that the expectations of performance were reasonably within the realm of possibility for that individual, considering education and experience.

One of my responsibilities over the years has been the investigation and adjudication of differences between individuals and the organization. A prime source of grievances has been the performance appraisal. From these reviews I have sorted out a series of common problems. They are:

· *Failure to achieve closure.* In these cases the employee and the manager meet and talk but do not communicate well enough to arrive at a conclusion. The employee generally feels that the manager fails to tell him or her what is wrong. The manager feels he or she communicates but the employee doesn't listen. This failure can occur either at the time of establishing the work plan or at the time of appraising performance or at both times.

· *Assignment of a task with almost assured failure.* Most often in this case the employee is already failing to perform satisfactorily and the manager sets up a trial assignment that must end in success, demotion, or dismissal. The intent of the manager is good—a fresh chance with extremely clear limits. However, the measurement is unfair if a review of the employee's history indicates that at the outset the assignment was beyond the employee's capability.

· *Vague and undefined requirements.* In this type of case, usually with a professional employee like an engineer, the manager makes the assumption that a minimal description of what is needed is sufficient. Such an assumption might be all right, but the manager's second failure is not to get feedback, not to check to see what the professional believes is the assignment. The failure to get feedback and discover that the assignment is incompletely understood leaves both people at fault. Such an assignment is a weak basis for downgrading the assessment of performance of the professional. This is an area of many shades of gray!

· *Measurement against arbitrarily high or unfair standards.* Our most often used behavioral and attitudinal reference is ourselves. Thus, placed in the role of the manager, we are tempted to and sometimes use our own performance as the standard for rating others. An example might be the manager who devotes many extra hours to work and therefore expects all employees to do likewise. This may be very unfair.

139

In addition to these normal caveats or challenges, our current social legislation aimed at reducing discrimination and at improving the safety and quality of work has complicated the appraisal process. A specific area applying to appraisal is the growing pressure for validation of the process. Validity in this case means that the same performance should be appraised in the same way by two managers. Since there is no way of creating exactly the same conditions and since managers are human and make only semi-objective judgments, validity is an elusive goal. Ultimately this thrust for validity will probably force organizations to move away from management-by-objective appraisals that allow for individualized measurement criteria and toward some standardized measurement criteria. Like other attempts to create fairness through legislation, I expect this may well interfere with rather than improve our ability to match individuals and work. In the meantime what can organizations and managers do to move in the direction of improving job performance measurement fairness and validity? The following organization actions are suggested:

· Analyze jobs in a manner that sorts out, identifies and documents those activities that are really critical to satisfactory performance. This may require some combination of centralized study of jobs and training individual managers to be more adept at identifying the critical requirements for satisfactory performance. (Example: Satisfactory performance of this assignment will be measured by delivery of readable, accurate, usable specifications for parts manufacture to manufacturing by a specific date.)

· Standardize rating scales and to the extent possible anchor them in behavioral statements that can be used to differentiate and train managers in the use of these scales. (Example: Satisfactory performance will be demonstrated by answering all information calls (normally about ten per hour) politely and courteously and receiving no more than one complaint per month from a subscriber about your handling of an inquiry.)

· Standardize for all employees doing essentially the same type of thing the period and conditions under which observations are made and upon which ratings are based. This will be easier to do for highly structured jobs and very difficult for self-supervising professionals. (Example: Performance will be measured by a review of performance against schedule and specifications at the end of each month.)

· Employ professionals to conduct validity studies of the appraisal program and make modifications and improvements as possible.

(Example: Training sessions for managers where they all observe the same recorded performance, rate it, and compare ratings for consistency or studies of actual ratings by different managers of the same group of employees would qualify as an indication of interest to improve.)

For the individual manager the advice is: Be consistent. That is, whatever technique you use, use it with all the employees you appraise. For example, if in an investigation of a complaint I found that a manager had spelled out sixteen specific performance requirements for one employee and four for all others I would suspect discrimination. If I found some performance plans specifying time criteria for measurement and others not, I would ask further questions. The individual manager would also be well advised to have well thought out and documented statements of performance to support differences in performance ratings. In other words, if the form says "outstanding" because that is the organization's rating scheme, the manager should be able to describe the exact performance that he or she would rate as outstanding. Again, consistency is important. If to achieve the top rating you expect one employee to walk on water, then any employee who achieves that rating must be able to demonstrate that performance!

SUMMARY

Planning performance, that is, establishing a statement of what is required for satisfactory performance on a job, is necessary and desirable both for the individual and the organization. For the individual it provides a yardstick on which to determine progress and improvement and thus to test the fairness of pay and other rewards. For the organization it provides a basis for differentiating the employee reward for good and bad performance and for assuring complete communication about work requirements.

The best performance plan is one that is determined mutually between manager and employee. A meeting of the minds on requirements establishes a positive base for appraisal of performance. Appraisal should be primarily aimed at assisting the employee to grow and gain in capability. Whatever forms or techniques are used, they are secondary to the primary process of coaching improvement.

Appraising performance requires making judgments. The less structured the job the more subjective these judgments may be. The more subjective the judgment the greater the probability it can be attacked as unfair or discriminatory. Yet despite this challenge the great majority of appraisals are helpful. New social legislation and court decisions, however, are moving us toward some increased standardization of rating processes in order to assure validity. If action is to be based on the performance rating, especially negative action, then the organization and the manager must be able to demonstrate fairness.

Performance Planning and Appraisal Checkup

1. Which of the following is most descriptive of your outlook towards the performance plan and appraisal process?   (   )

    a. I enjoy doing it because the process provides an opportunity to work with the employee and aid in growth and personal development.

    b. I am quite successful with most employees and enjoy the process except when the employee has a performance problem.

    c. I have difficulty in establishing the appropriate open communication and am uncomfortable in evaluating others, but I'm working at it and trying.

    d. I do it as an administrative requirement, but I don't like to do it.

    e. I avoid appraisal and performance evaluation as much as possible and put the minimum effort into filling out the forms and talking with the employees about it. Many of my appraisals are overdue.

2. Pick the statement which you believe your employees would choose as descriptive of performance planning and appraisal.   (   )

    a. It is a useful growth-oriented process which is generally fair and provides for real communication between my manager and me. I feel I've been helped to improve and appropriately appraised.

    b. It is a useful process, and my manager has provided helpful suggestions for improvement and appraised me fairly. However, I feel that it is mostly for the record and not wholeheartedly supported.

    c. My manager sets the requirements and appraises me against them. On the whole he or she is fair but I don't gain much.

    d. My manager sets unclear job requirements, is inconsistent in the quality of appraisal, and provides me with little help.

    e. My manager sets unreasonable requirements, does not appraise all of us on an equal basis, I'm unsure of where I stand, and I get no real help from my manager.

3. How would you judge the quality of your performance appraisal interviews with your employees? Pick the most appropriate answer.   (   )

    a. They are open two-way sessions where I learn, and I am able to help the employee improve.

    b. They are mostly open and two-way but vary significantly with the personality of the employee.

    c. They are generally satisfactory, but where there is any requirement for change or need for improvement I am not too successful.

    d. They are short and primarily a session where I tell them what I've decided.

    e. I don't have them. There is no requirement to tell the employee how he or she is appraised.

143

4. How would you judge the acceptance of your appraisal ratings by your employees? Pick the most appropriate answer.   ( )

    a. My employees totally and completely accept my ratings. I've never been challenged.
    b. My employees accept my ratings as fair but there is some disagreement which we generally are able to work or talk out.
    c. There have been some challenges of my appraisals, but generally I hold my position through the power of the managerial role.
    d. There are many employees who wish they could challenge my appraisals and accept them only begrudgingly.
    e. I am frequently and formally challenged in my ratings, and I've had to change some.

5. The first thing you should do when sitting down to have a performance interview with an employee is: ( )

    a. to assure that you will have enough uninterrupted time
    b. to assess the mood of the employee by talking about something inconsequential
    c. to assure that the employee understands what the interview is about and what your interest is
    d. to hand the form to the employee and let him or her read it
    e. to ask the employee to tell you how he or she feels about performance
    f. several of the above might be appropriate

6. The most important thing to accomplish in a performance assessment interview is: ( )

    a. to make sure the person understands what he or she has done wrong
    b. to make sure the person understands what he or she has done right
    c. to make sure through asking for feedback that whatever is said is heard and understood
    d. to make sure that you listen to what the employee has to say
    e. to make sure that all aspects of performance are covered
    f. several of the above might be appropriate

7. To make sure that a performance interview is a positive learning and growth-oriented experience, it is most important to: ( )

    a. focus your comments on actual events where the type of behavior you feel is right was demonstrated by the employee
    b. focus on specific behavior or incidents where the employee did the wrong things or used the wrong technique
    c. ask the employee to tell you what he or she feels was done well and reinforce those incidents with your positive comments
    d. establish an action program for learning new skills and gaining new knowledge
    e. get the employee to essentially evaluate his or her performance, both strengths and weaknesses

Ideas for Action: Improving Your Performance Planning and Appraisal

something
to try

1. Have a department or group meeting and discuss the process openly, looking for suggestions for improvement and experimenting with some of the suggestions.   ( )

2. Take a course or workshop on appraisal and counseling either inside the organization if available or outside at a nearby college or from one of the organizations offering management development training.   ( )

3. Solicit open suggestions for improvement in the process of performance planning and appraisal from each employee at the end of the appraisal interview.   ( )

4. Establish the practice of planning your performance evaluation interviews and do the following:
Establish interview objectives.
   Write down a sequence of questions or topics.
   Pretest your attitude and pick positive times in your own cycle or mood.
   Arrange for uninterrupted privacy and physical conditions suitable to open exchange (i.e., don't sit behind your fortress desk!).

5. Critique your own interview after the fact. Ask yourself:
   What went well? Why?
   What could I do next time to cause it to go even better?
   What didn't work? Why?   ( )

6. Establish a time to sit down with your fellow managers and exchange experiences and ideas on the process of setting objectives and appraising performance.   ( )

7. Read or review some appraisals done by other people for ideas on content and style. Look at them to see what the words tell you and whether you feel it was a positive, helpful discussion.   ( )

8. Ask each of your employees to tell you what the several aspects of the job are which they feel are most important. Have them write a short description of these aspects, and if you agree use these as the aspects on which you will appraise for the next period. If you can, gain agreement on what will represent outstanding, satisfactory, or unsatisfactory performance.   ( )

9. Review each of your performance appraisals with your manager to gain suggestions, agreement, and to check to see if there are additional inputs you have missed.   ( )

10. Try one of my grandmother's technqiues. For each negative you feel it is necessary to include in the appraisal, try to find five positive things you can say. The ratio seems extreme, but try it!   ( )

145

CHAPTER
10

Recognition and Reward

Pay

General Pay Principles

Promotions

Recognition and Reward, Pay and Promotion

The fun part of management for many of us is recognizing and rewarding the employee who performs well and grows. Yet, many managers act as if the only recognition they can dispense is a pay increase or a promotion. One of the purposes of this chapter, therefore, will be to open up the concept of recognition and introduce the broad range of rewards. Recognition ranges from a smile to being assigned a high value task.

In our work culture hierarchical promotion is seen by most people as the main form of growth. So much value has been placed on pay and position that the concept of growth, as an increase in capability, as being able to do something tomorrow you can't do today, has been lost. Early job experience where pay increases and status changes are frequent set up expectations for a continuation of that form of recognition. Yet, promotion rates most often slow down with increased experience, and the positions at the top are few. This leads to an almost inevitable decline in morale and a reduction in positive feelings about recognition with increasing age and experience. The manager thus enters the arena of recognition, reward, pay, and promotion to deal with an often highly sensitized and perhaps somewhat unrealistic employee population. In fact, the manager is part of this culture. Yet, the good manager will be found fighting to change the system and expand the growth supporting uses of recognition, not just go along with the past.

Recognition and Reward

Recognition and reward are provided by us and by others. If you accomplish something that you feel has value, there is usually a personal reward in the accomplishment. This is the feeling of satisfaction you get when you

147

straighten up a messy desk, finish repainting a room, or complete any task you have set for yourself. Some of the key elements of this self-reward are:

· You choose the task and its completion has some *personal value* for you.
· *You are in control* of how and when it is done.
· You gain the satisfaction of completion and probably overcome some challenges and obstacles in the process.
· You learn and increase your capability in the process of doing the task.
· The end result has some aesthetic or creative value in your context and within your values.

Although this self-satisfaction, recognition, and reward are not usually sufficient, ideally they should be part of any recognition. In the work environment tasks that provide this personal, positive reward create a very strong base for acceptance of any other recognition. This is why we put so much emphasis in this book on the fitting of the person to the work. No external recognition, acknowledgment by someone else, even a manager, can totally substitute for personal, internal recognition. So as managers, even though it would seem we can only really control and use the recogni-

tion we supply, that is not true. We should start by trying to design tasks, jobs, and work so that the individual is able to achieve self-created recognition.

When we as managers think of recognition and reward, we most often think of what we can do to recognize the accomplishments of the employee. We have many ways, but as a group managers tend to narrow and specialize their thinking about recognition. Like the employee in the context of work, we generally limit our thinking about recognition to:

- praise or verbal recognition for task accomplishment
- increases in privileges or freedoms in the work environment
- increases in pay
- increases in status
- promotions to higher levels of responsibility
- monetary rewards, prizes, and trips

Actually the range of recognition techniques also includes the following:

- personal time, one-on-one time (manager-employee), and attention to the employees' needs and interests
- broadened exposure by allowing an employee to present a proposal to other groups or executives, or to visit other company locations or others in related businesses
- increased participation in establishing group goals, task assignments, and redesign of work processes
- opportunities for variety of tasks and special assignments within the work group, or temporary loan to another group
- exposure to a broader aspect of organizational operations and activities through a task force assignment or a temporary assignment to another part of the organization
- tasks and assignments that more nearly fit the goals and interests of the person
- free time to investigate personal interests or explore alternate approaches or create new answers
- work time for self-improvement either through special activities or educational programs
- time and support for professional or community activities

Undoubtedly both these lists could be expanded, but they should be sufficient to make the point. There are a myriad of changes or alternate activities which can be viewed as reward or recognition. Whether or not they are seen as recognition depends not so much on what we do as how the individual values and views what is done. Recognition is in the eye of the beholder.

This can best be seen by referring to the recognition model in Figure 8, which is based on expectancy theory. The diagram puts what we have been saying about recognition in pictorial form. Each of us approaches a task effort with an expectancy (Expectancy I) that a certain amount of effort will bring certain results. This expectancy is based on our prior experience, our abilities and interests and the context in which the task is placed. For example, if I am to cut up a tree felled in a recent storm, I approach this effort with expectancies of effort and performance based on my experience with a saw and my interest in the project. If I have to do this rather than something else I want to do, this sets the context and alters my outlook and expectations. For our purposes the context is the work environment. Expectations and outcomes will be influenced by our general feelings about work and the work environment. If we are generally positive this will tend to bias us toward positive results. If generally negative the reverse will be true.

So we start the task with expectation that a certain effort will bring certain results. Feedback as we do the task will modify our expectations. If we are sawing wood and the saw is dull, we will quickly adjust expectations. After we finish the task we gain our personal performance reward. This is the intrinsic or personal reward for task completion, the sense of satisfaction—perhaps even a nice tired feeling in our muscles. We approached the task with another expectancy (Expectancy II) that the completion would cause us to gain a certain sense of achievement. This may or may not occur. Our general feeling of personal achievement may or may not live up to our expected level of satisfaction. If it falls short we will tend to be disappointed. If it exceeds expectations we will be pleased. Our expectations are not absolutes; they are influenced by our attitudes and interests in the work process at a particular time.

As managers you and I are suppliers of the extrinsic reward. This also may or may not live up to the expectancy of the individual. Further its value depends on the value the individual assigns to what we do. Suppose you reward me with two tickets to a baseball game. If you do I'm disappointed because I don't like baseball. Someone else might be really pleased. In order for the manager to supply appropriate recognition, therefore, what the manager does must fit the context and, to the extent possible, meet the expectations of the employee.

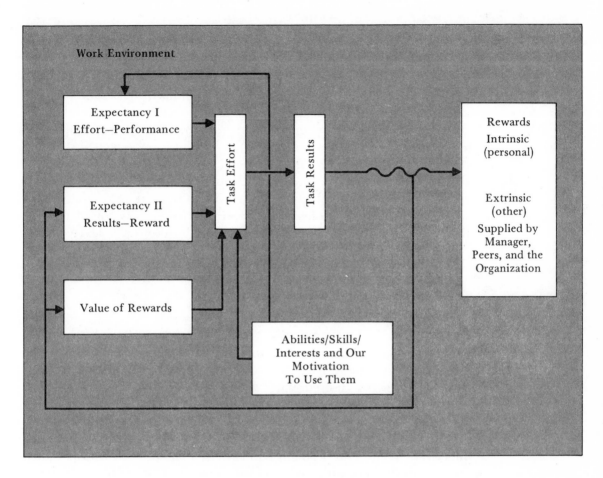

Figure 8. *Recognition model*

Everything else we say about recognition, reward, pay, and promotion can be understood in the context and principles we have just outlined. The purpose of managerial recognition of the employee, whatever the technique, is to create a positive feeling and associate it with accomplishment. Recognition for achievement is given in the hopes it will further encourage work toward the organization's goals. Good reward and recognition, therefore, must meet the following specifications:

> It must occur as quickly as possible so that it can be associated by the recipient with the accomplishment it is to recognize. (Example: Reward the completion of an assignment that was achieved today, today.)

- It should be in some proportion to the effort and difficulty of the task so that it meets some reasonable range of expectations. (Example: Don't reward punctuality with an increase in pay. The two acts are out of proportion.)
- It should be of value to the recipient and meet his or her criteria for a reasonable reward. (Example: If the employee wants increased freedom to direct his or her own activities, then this is an appropriate reward for job accomplishment.)
- It should be fair; that is, all people gaining the same achievement should be similarly recognized. (Example: Fairness is judged by recipients and others of similar status. If you reward one employee with an opportunity to leave early because the task is completed, then anyone who completes the task should be allowed to leave.)

Pay

The value of pay as a recognition is a subject of debate. Certainly what you are paid for your work contributes to your sense of personal worth, and this is part of recognition. Pay also provides you with the income to satisfy needs and purchase discretionary items. The debate centers around whether or not pay is a motivator. The most probable answer is that sometimes it is, but that other forms of recognition can be more important in specific instances. A pay increase most often has a motivational impact at the time it is given. The problem seems to be that we soon translate this reward into something which is expected, is owed us. Something which we feel is owed us has no real motivating power. Also if pay is to meet our criteria for a good reward, it needs to be in response to the particular activity we wish to reinforce. It is on this concept that incentive pay programs are based. Under such a program pay is incrementally increased in response to improvements in quantity, timeliness, or quality. If we as managers wish to use pay to motivate performance, we must pay in a way that fits our recognition model. For the moment, therefore, let us leave the debate about its motivating value behind because paying properly, responsively, and fairly is an important human resource function of the manager.

The classic pay criterion is a "fair day's pay for a fair day's work." But such a broad criterion does little to help you and me as managers since the fairness on both sides has many determinants and can be seen in several perspectives. The function of pay is to provide a tangible return in exchange for services. In a totally free market (which exists only in the imagination) fair is thus determined by what the employer and the employee agree to as fair. To the recipient pay has two values. First it contributes to a feeling of personal worth. If I am paid twice what someone else is for the same type of activity then I and my services are worth more. Employees seem to react more to the difference in pay between themselves and others than to the actual increase. Thus two employees starting with different pay levels who both receive a 10 percent increase might react differently. One might react that it was unfair because his or her increase was smaller in actual dollars.

Second, my pay buys food, clothing, and shelter. If I am badly in need of any of these, I will view fairness in respect to the level of my need. The contract between us becomes one of quality and fairness only if I am free to reject the pay offer. Fairness in the modern working world becomes what the market value of the services is or often what employers pay on the average for a specific level of experience and type of responsibility. Again the difference becomes critical. If employees at company X are earning $12.50 an hour and in our organization we are being paid only $11.50 an hour, we focus on the $1.00 we are not getting.

Pay is further complicated in today's world in that most organizations provide benefits in addition to dollars. These benefits, ranging from time off for holidays and vacations to medical benefits and retirement income, are part of the organization's compensation costs. In many organizations the dollar value of these approximates one-third to one-half of the total pay. Thus in looking at the concept of fairness benefits must be taken into account. The employer's view of these and the employee's view will undoubtedly be different. One difference comes about because the employee is given these benefits and usually has little choice about what kind of benefit is given. Another difference has to do with the fact that insurance benefits represent cost avoidance to the employee. One who is not sick doesn't feel he or she got much from the company's medical benefit.

For the manager fairness is even more specific. To be fair means to pay two people performing at the same level the same pay for the same work. This is difficult because in most jobs there aren't generally two people performing exactly the same tasks at the same level. This is also difficult because we as managers evaluate and measure performance subjectively.

Fairness is further complicated by the fact that to some extent all pay is affected by seniority. For the college-graduate engineers, although there is usually a considerable range of salaries, there are maturity curves. These curves reflect years since graduation, are published by professional societies, and document the relationship of experience and age to pay. You may think of salary in this sense as a career salary, one that is based on experience and the sequence of positions one has held. For the nonprofessional, pay also relates to age and experience. In some unionized organizations, this becomes even more specific because paying for seniority is built into the contract.

Fairness is further circumscribed by the fact that in most large organizations pay ranges and policies are established by a central professional staff. In the best sense this central planning aids the manager in determining what is fair. The staff professionals assure that rates are compatible with the world outside. The staff professionals assure that older employees are not penalized for market fluctuations that cause new employees to come in at higher rates. The staff professionals assure that two managers in different departments treat people performing at the same level similarly. Despite the positives this central planning and control is liable to encourage the manager to feel he or she does not really establish pay. This may allow the manager to sidestep a real human resource responsibility, give the impression of powerlessness, and spread the impression that salaries are all determined by the computer.

One new variation in pay systems has emerged as the result of experiments in the improvement of quality of work. In plants where self-managing teams have been tried, where the workers determine who does what and often who is qualified for an increase in pay, a new basis for pay is necessary. The evolving concept is that pay should be determined by what people know, what skills they have, and what they are prepared to do rather than what assignment they are on. Thus in one such experiment the base rate was determined as the amount paid to a member of the team who could perform one task. When the person could perform all the tasks covered by that team the person was entitled to a team rate. When the person could perform tasks beyond the team additional compensation was added. Such a scheme has the advantage of providing a way of measuring underutilization or underemployment. The career salary is the salary based on what the person is capable of doing. If this exceeds what is normally paid for the function the employee is performing, then the employee is underutilized.

Considering the variability of organization policies on pay, both union and nonunion, and the differences between professional, skilled, and unskilled pay systems, what general principles can we state? Are there any?

Before trying to state general principles, it should be helpful to look at some of the complaints about pay from the employees' perspective.

These were gathered from many personal reviews of employee grievances where pay was a central issue. The organizations based pay on merit rather than a job rate or fixed pay. In a unionized organization where pay is fixed for a specific job and generally does not respond to performance or merit, the second and third examples would not exist.

· *Size of the incremental change in salary for a promotion relative to a previous change.* A classic type of complaint is the one where the employee's prior several raises were larger for merit (performance quality) changes than the most recent one associated with a promotion in status. No amount of explanation of ranges and position in ranges will alter simple logic. In the eyes of the employee the size of the increase for a promotion should be larger than a normal salary change. Fundamentally I feel the employee is right.

· *Size of incremental change relative to the change someone else got.* Although management likes to feel that salary information is private, employees do share it. If as an employee I believe my performance is better than someone else's, any manager will have difficulty in explaining why my salary increase is smaller. In such a case even the fact that my overall pay may be higher is easily discounted by me since in fairness I feel I should stay ahead.

· *Size of incremental change relative to previous change when performance has been acknowledged as improved.* If on a scale where 1 equals top performance I receive an increment of $10 when rated a 3, how does it make sense to get $8 when rated a 2? No amount of explaining about closeness of my pay to pay for this level of performance really fixes this one either. The technical explanation is that merit salary systems give the person who is paid much lower a larger increase than one who is being paid at or near the appropriate level.

· *Relative pay for responsibilities when compared to someone else in the organization who is perceived as having lower responsibilities.* Pay is usually determined by the level of the job's responsibilities in the salary system. That is, a job with greater financial or higher level technical responsibilities will generally be placed at a higher salary level. Employees do not understand these rating schemes since in general they have not been explained to them. Also regardless of the system or scheme, it is the perception of responsibility on which the employee bases the assessment of fairness. Thus one employee who perceives that his or her responsibilities are greater than another's will never understand why the other person is paid more.

· *Relative pay for responsibilities when compared with someone outside the organization.* This is the same as the above example except that the person with whom the comparison is made is outside the organization. It is even more difficult in this case to understand true responsibility and appropriate or true pay.

These problems are primarily salary problems of the nonunion organization. In the union situation the employee has someone other than management to check on fairness. In the union situation salary changes are negotiated and are generally the same for a particular skill level. Thus a given employee accepts as fair that all are paid the same by the act of supporting the union. The manager's ability to differentiate pay based on performance is lost unless the union agreement includes some type of merit or incentive pay. However, union or not, these pay grievances make a significant point. Feelings of unfairness are generally associated with incremental differences rather than absolute amounts. If a new union settlement down the street provides more vacation, then that becomes the issue even though the pay may be better here. If in a nonunion situation the individual feels he incremental change is not fair, then the fact that the individual's overall pay is high is temporarily set aside while the difference becomes the issue.

General Pay Principles

As a manager, regardless of what pay system we find ourselves operating in, we can use the following principles as guides:

· Take responsibility for paying your employees properly and fairly and do not hide behind the system, the ranges, or the failure to get higher-level approval. It is your responsibility to fight the system if necessary.
· Examine the logic of changes in the eyes of the employee. If the pay schedule calls for an increment that is smaller for a promotion than a nonpromotional change, get an exception since this doesn't make sense to the recipient.
· Try to make pay responsive to performance. Diligence and creative achievement should pay off.

· Be particularly sensitive to and avoid inherent discrimination in salary based on age, sex, or race.

Promotions

Promotions in status and responsibility have come to be valued as one of the primary sources of recognition in the world of work. A person's value in the community, across the back fence, in organizational dealings, and in conversations with fellow employees is often determined by work title. For this reason, perhaps in your own career, certainly in mine, there were times when I would have traded money for a specific position or title. The authority to change status, to promote, is thus a powerful recognition tool in the hands of the manager. However, there are real promotions, and there are changes in position that are sometimes made to look like promotions. It is the former, obviously, that we are talking about.

Promotions come about for two primary reasons: (1) to fill a position at a higher level in the organization, (2) to recognize professional accomplishment and maturity. Scientific and technical organizations attempt to view these two reasons as separate. Usually called the dual-ladder system, promotion is provided through a series of positions in nonmanagement ranks in recognition of increased levels of competence. Promotion up the other side, managerial positions, is much more in response to openings and needs. Promotions to openings are easy to defend. Promotions in response to capability without an opening must be fought for by the manager. In the sense of recognition this second kind is extremely important.

Much difficulty in the perception of responsiveness of recognition and fairness of recognition is rooted in these different reasons for promotion. Highly structured organizations like manufacturing usually stick pretty close to the hierarchical-opening concept. The rate of turnover or growth, not employee readiness, is generally the determinant of promotion timing. This tends to depreciate the promotion as a recognition tool. In an organization of slow change it is almost impossible to be appropriately responsive to the growth of the employee in this manner. In an organization of rapid growth promotions are also more often responsive to need than to employee readiness. In the organization that is growing and changing rapidly, however, there is a greater chance the promotion will approximate the right timing for the individual than in the slow-moving one. However, creating a dual-ladder technique for being responsive often adds new problems as well as solves old ones. One of the problems is that it is hard to define job and task differences that correspond to the created status differences. Thus we have engineering organizations where engineers at several competence levels are actually performing the same kinds of tasks, at the same responsibility level. The challenge in making a dual ladder work is thus to create competence levels that represent real differences in level of technical performance.

In summary, promotion can be a real form of recognition when it comes either through additional responsibilities as represented by a hierarchical change in position or through a real change in competence status. If a position opening in the hierarchical sense is available at the right time, this can be recognition. If a competence or level change without managerial responsibility can be created that is real, this has a better chance of being perceived as a real change. The latter has the better chance of being timely and in response to change in the capability of the employee. Recognition as promotion is valuable when it meets the following specifications:

· It represents a real change in level of responsibility in the nature of the job, and in job requirements.
· It is timely in that it corresponds to a change in the competence and capability of the individual.
· It is perceived by the members of the organization as being real and not a manufactured change or change of convenience.

SUMMARY

Recognition of performance is a meaningful way of rewarding the individual, motivating continued performance, and establishing the base for individual development. Recognition must meet the values of the individual being rewarded. It must also meet the general criteria of fairness held by other members of the organization. Recognition is best when it comes within the expectations of the individual involved. If we reward out of proportion to the effort and the achievement, it will be received as unreal and unauthentic. If we reward in a timely fashion, timeliness aids in associating what the individual did to what happened. If we reward in a delayed relationship, the motivational impact will be smaller.

Whether we use the simple "thank you" or pay or promotion it must fit the work environment and culture if it is to be of value. Managers have a broad range of reward techniques. The challenge for the manager is to pick the right form to fit the circumstance and the individual. The challenge for the manager is to use rewards and recognition in ways that cause the employee to strive to increase personal effectiveness, not to win against someone else. The challenge for the manager is to use rewards more to spur individual development than to meet specific performance goals. The challenge to the manager is to use a variety of recognition approaches so that no specific recognition becomes owed in the eyes of the employee.

Recognition and Reward, Pay and Promotion Checkup

1.   Which of the following statements best reflects your personal view about recognition and reward?   ( )

     a.   Pay and position are a base; all recognition and reward is represented by additions to base pay including financial extras, personal attention, and unique rewards. These additional rewards are necessary to get anyone to work above a minimum level.

     b.   Recognition over and beyond pay is both desirable and necessary as a technique for motivation but should be used with discretion and kept in reasonable bounds.

     c.   I've never really thought about it, and I don't have a theme and set of beliefs about recognition.

     d.   Discrimination and differentiation between people and groups by recognition and reward accentuate individual differences in performance and are generally unnecessary and poor.

     e.   The pay and the job with our company policies and good working conditions represent the best recognition and reward system. There is no need for extra recognition beyond normal pay increases and promotions.

2.   With what frequency do you feel you use the following broad categories of recognition and reward with the people you manage? Try to look back over the last year or so. Assign the appropriate letter representing frequency: (a) once a month; (b) once in six months; (c) once a year; (d) once every several years; (e) very infrequently or not at all.

     thank yous and private personal praise   ( )
     public acknowledgement, publicity, etc., for accomplishments   ( )
     special benefits, time off, extra travel, moderate monetary rewards of a non-
     regular type   ( )
     large once-in-a-lifetime dollar rewards   ( )
     the opportunity to pursue a task or assignment which really fits, really allows
     the individual to work toward personal goals   ( )

3.   How do you judge which is the appropriate reward for a specific performance? Here are some statements reflecting different approaches. Put the appropriate letter after those which you feel represent your behavior: (a) strongly; (b) moderately; (c) not at all.

     I reward and recognize accomplishment when it is definite, definable, and measurable with one of the many forms of recognition available.   ( )
     I recognize and reward accomplishment when I feel that it should be recognized. That is, I take a risk on the side of reward, using the many forms of recognition available to me.   ( )

I recognize and reward accomplishment generally by using the standard forms of pay increase and promotion when it is evident in my group.   ( )

I use unique, single recognitions only for once-in-a-lifetime performances because I am fearful of the backlash that employee grievances can cause.   ( )

I have an open, variable style, recognizing and rewarding in no particular pattern and without noticeable consistency.   ( )

4. Are you creative in recognition and reward? Put the appropriate letter after those which you have used: (a) frequently; (b) occasionally; (c) seldom.

precommitted rewards specified for given levels of behavior (incentives)   ( )
increases in pay   ( )
one-time dollar recognition, evenings out, or trips   ( )
promotions in status   ( )
promotions in responsibility   ( )
unique forms which fit the individual and the specific situation   ( )
certificates, paper weights, and memory joggers   ( )
unique forms which I have created   ( )
jewelry and prizes provided by the organization   ( )
group recognition in the form of dinners and events   ( )

5. Which of the following statements best describes your operating philosophy and approach on pay?   ( )

a. I pay people as I believe they should be paid without sticking absolutely to the pay plan or program and suggestions of the salary professionals.

b. I occasionally pay people as I believe they should be paid, and I fight for the exceptions with salary administration, occasionally winning my fights.

c. I pay people in accordance with the guidelines and the rules with minor deviation in special cases.

d. I pay people as the guidelines suggest and do not deviate except within ranges of timing and size as allowed.

e. I am really not involved since pay is determined by negotiated rates or computer formula and programs.

6. Which of the following statements best describes your personal philosophy with respect to pay? (Try to answer this as *you* feel, not necessarily as the organization administrates pay.)   ( )

a. Generally the manager should be free to pay what he or she believes is right based on information about how others are paid in and out of the organization.   ( )

b. Generally there should be a significant (50- 100 percent) but structured range to reflect pay for performance, and the manager should be free to use it.

c. A given job is worth a specific amount, but there ought to be a range within which I can recognize performance differences.

d.   A given job is worth a specific amount dependent on market and is not affected by individual performance.

e.   The manager should not generally be part of the salary determination; we should leave it to experts.

7.   Which of the following statements best reflects your outlook on promotion?   (   )

a.   Promotion should come at a time when there is some risk that the individual may fail and significantly before the individual has demonstrated ability to operate at the higher level and before one can create an opening.

b.   Promotion should involve some risk, but there needs to be an existing not a created opening.

c.   Promotion should occur based on openings at the individual's readiness.

d.   Promotions should come only when the individual has demonstrated some performance at the higher level and there is an opening.

e.   Promotion should come only after the individual has demonstrated ability by operating at the higher level for a significant period.

8.   Which of the following statements best reflects your feeling about how you as an individual have been treated on the issues of pay, promotion, recognition, and reward?   (   )

a.   I really feel my management has taken frequent risks in promoting and paying me and has more than occasionally used ingenuity in appropriately rewarding me. I feel I've been treated very well and uniquely.

b.   I've been uniquely and well rewarded and paid with some adherence to rules and the system.

c.   I've been treated fairly and generally well, but unique recognition has been the exception.

d.   I feel that generally I've been paid and rewarded within the system and not in unique response to my performance. I don't feel badly, but I don't feel uniquely recognized.

e.   I don't feel that my pay or recognition has ever really reflected my unique contributions or performance. Generally it has been too little, too late, or not at all.

Note: Your outlook and how you treat others is usually shaped in part by how you feel you have been treated. Check back to prior questions.

9.   Pick what you consider the most appropriate reward from the following: (   )

   a.   The highest recognition for me is to be given the challenging assignment I want and the freedom to pursue it in my way and get appropriate recognition and a personal sense of accomplishment.
   b.   The highest recognition for me is to get promoted to a position of significant importance and responsibility with a significant increase in pay.
   c.   The highest recognition for me is to gain the promotion and position which represent power and influence, but pay is definitely a secondary issue and not so important.
   d.   In being promoted to a higher position the pay and benefits are more important than the position.
   e.   Pay, promotion and freedom to do my own thing are not that important; more important is that I am accepted and belong as part of an organization with an important mission and that I have a meaningful job within the organization.

Ideas for Action: Improving Your Recognition and Reward Performance

		Something to try

1. Actively explore with your fellow managers the wide variety of rewards and recognition, and experiment with trying to increase your range.   ( )

2. Set up a discussion of rewards and recognition with your group. Ask for their suggestions and experiment with some.

3. As a part of each appraisal interview, make it a practice to discuss rewards and recognition so that you learn what each employee sees as a personally valuable form of recognition and then try to tailor rewards to fit the particular employee's values.   ( )

4. Take a course inside or outside the organization with explores motivation, reward, and recognition.   ( )

5. Read additional references on this subject such as:
    W. F. Dowling and L. R. Sayles, *How Managers Motivate* (McGraw Hill, 1978).
    S. W. Gellerman, *Motivation and Productivity* (AMACOM 1963).   ( )

6. Experiment with recognition for outstanding performance and offer the employee greater freedom in choice of the next assignment.   ( )

7. Try to make your recognition, whatever form it takes, as immediate as possible so that it is clear what action caused what reward.   ( )

8. Arrange to give each employee some private time, your full attention and interest, in recognition of some general positive performance or outlook.   ( )

9. Establish some group objective which will require greater cooperation, and reward the accomplishment by group attention.   ( )

10. Provide opportunities for your employees who have performed well to make presentations to members of management at higher levels. Reward with visibility and see what the reaction is.   ( )

11. Read, discuss, and debate pay and promotional policies with other managers and staff professionals.   ( )

12. Try to identify a pay or promotion exception and fight for it. Test your ability to deviate from rules in order to be responsive to individual situations.   ( )

13.   Ask the personnel professionals to provide you with statistics which help you to do an audit to assure that you are promoting and paying fairly with respect to timing, performance requirements, experience level, and breadth of experience.   (   )

14.   Work to include pay, recognition, and promotion questions in an attitude morale survey in your organization so you can see how the organization does on these issues. If you have such a survey, study these questions carefully for what clues they may provide. If you have such a survey, use it with your group to form the base for an open discussion of these issues.   (   )

15.   Talk to some managers in other organizations to discover how your feelings may have been shaped by the culture, environment, and policies of your organization.   (   )

CHAPTER
11

Basic Discipline

Creative Discipline

Types of Discipline

Dismissal

Rocks and Shoals

Dealing with Inadequate
Performance:
Discipline and Dismissal

Just as the last chapter on recognition and reward represents the fun part of management, so this chapter's title no doubt sends waves of anxiety through each of us as managers. It is just as important to weed out inadequacy as it is to reward competency with promotion. It is just as important to discipline as to reward performance. Good management is a healthy dynamic balance of dealing with both ends of the spectrum. Yet the manager's unease and expectations of personal punishment for failure are almost all on the side of discipline and dismissal. New laws and discrimination suits have increased the fears of the manager on this subject.

In addition to these fears we have a general cultural bias against discipline. This bias has been brought on at least in part by the last thirty years, which have been characterized by permissiveness in raising our children. The behavioral psychologists have also encouraged us to use positive rewards for those activities we wish to reinforce. Although the behaviorists also use punishment with the rats they study, many of us have been discouraged about punishing human beings. If these challenges are not enough, we've been through a rapid growth period in many organizations lasting over extended periods of time which made person power scarce and allowed us to cover up or transfer to someone else the less-than-satisfactory performer.

Yet as I start to write this chapter I am mentally reviewing case after case of employee grievances that I have investigated and tried to settle. One cause of serious disagreement, of pain for both management and the employee, has been the failure of the manager to be honest and forthright about failures. Most of these cases have been people, who although inadequate in performance, were gently and forgivingly appraised or given satisfactory ratings because the manager could not face the trauma of telling the person he or she had failed. What happens in many of these cases is that years later the inadequate employee arrives under the management of a manager with guts. The new manager gives an honest appraisal of the inadequate performance. The employee holds up many past satisfactory or even very good appraisals as defense and indication that the new manager is wrong. Yet careful research shows inadequate performance has been covered up by scared managers. By the time the problem surfaces, management is morally responsible in part for the employee's failure. I suspect this will be an increasing and serious problem as we extend the work life by pushing out or even eliminating forced retirement. Unless we learn how to be more forthright, the social cost, for the organization and the nation, of dismissal of senior employees whose inadequacy has not been faced over long periods can become very great.

Basic Discipline

The prime function of discipline is to avoid repetition of a mistake or improper activity. The effectiveness of discipline can be measured by whether or not it does avoid repetition. The effectiveness of discipline has nothing to do with the severity of the punishment. In fact, if the error can be addressed without the individual ever feeling that he or she was punished this is the best way. A broad criterion for good discipline is thus that it avoids punishment.

The next principle of basic discipline is that it should begin with a review of the understanding of the assignment, instructions, and the psychological contract. Very often the early failure to perform is a failure to hear and understand the assignment in the first place. This failure may result from language difficulties, the absence of an experience base on which to build understanding, or the lack of self-assurance sufficient to question instructions not understood. Clear communication requires that the sender (manager) think of the position of the employee, that there be shared experiences and information bases, and that the employee listen. Thus failure to understand the assignment may not be a one-sided or employee failure. The manager should reexamine, question, and search for evidence that there was understanding. Understanding is a part of the content of the psychological contract.

Next the manager should objectively examine the quality and clarity of the instructions. Were the instructions complete? Even if the employee understood the instructions, could a satisfactory job have been done? And in this prediscipline review, the understanding of expectations, the psychological contract, must also be reviewed. Here it is important to look for emotional loading and prior employee understandings which may affect the relationship.

One case comes to mind to illustrate this. An employee in the hiring interview thoroughly questioned and probed company attitude about legitimate reasons for absence. A serious question the applicant expressed was: Were people dismissed for absences? The interviewer was sensitive to the fact that there was probably something in prior work history that made this person overly sensitive on this subject. The interviewer hastened to describe illness as a legitimate reason for absence and was reassuring. This exchange was unfortunately not passed on to the manager. The manager had a department where absenteeism for all reasons, excessively long lunch hours, apparent wasting of time in casual conversation, and frequent, possibly work-related, absences from the work station were a problem. The manager therefore laid down rather specific rules and created a situation of pressure for presence at the work station, proper work attitude, and attendance. The new employee had reasons for legitimate absences, and the employee's performance when present was good, although the person did not feel challenged by the job. The continual review of absenteeism by the manager left the employee with the impression that the manager was trying to build a case for, at a minimum, discipline or, at a maximum, dismissal. Communication broke down, misunderstandings multiplied, a grievance developed, and the employee claimed discrimination. In this case prior experience and an incompletely understood psychological contract interfered with clear communication and led to a breakdown of manager-employee relationship. This breakdown eventually negatively affected other aspects of performance. The lesson is that *really* understanding the background and searching for uncommunicated issues affecting the relationship should precede even the appearance of the intent to discipline.

Positive discipline should be responsive to early signs of misunderstanding or impending failure and should quickly but gently create a feedback opportunity. The approach should be one of query and should transmit the manager's sincere desire to help, not to punish, as the first reaction. The tone, the timing, and privacy are all important. In fact, the tone may be even more important than the content. But the most important part of this principle is not to save problems, only to later drop them as a "big bomb." Don't add up a series of presumed failures or offenses. Deal with the small indications of a problem as they come along, as immediately as possible.

The next principle is to focus on behavior and performance, not personal attributes. "You don't seem to understand what is required" attacks the person. By contrast, say to the employee, "Satisfactory performance means completing the assignment on schedule. What can I do to help you achieve the objectives on schedule?" The second approach provides the employee opportunity for saving face and does not start with the assumption that there is something wrong with the quality of the employee.

Our next principle is consistency: Consistency in what causes us to take action and in the type of action we take for similar failures. In review of charges of discrimination, the reviewer looks for consistency. If for whatever reason it can be shown that some people are treated one way and others more leniently, then discrimination is suspected. A reviewer searches for evidence of uncaught violations or problems. The manager is challenged by the need to be both personally consistent and to make his or her actions consistent with other managers in similar situations. The organization through its personnel professionals, its policy, management training, and communication bears some of the responsibility for manager-to-manager consistency.

These principles are basic and emphasize fairness more than creativity. They represent the caveats, the underlying necessities. The following principles or concepts are more specifically addressed to the "how to" of creative discipline.

Creative Discipline

Creative helping is thus our next principle. When the manager recognizes poor performance or failure to adhere to rules, the first approach, rather than appearing and sounding like discipline or negative action, should be based on the desire to assist. Creative helping or assistance is based on the following principles:

- Be empathetic; put yourself in the other person's shoes.
- Provide training, information, materials, or facilities that will assist the person in performing the job in a satisfactory manner.
- Provide attention and follow-up by increasing the frequency of manager-employee contact and changing the nature of interchange from generalities to specifics.
- Listen and be supportive; provide the opportunity for the individual to create his or her own answers to why he or she is doing certain things.
- Compliment and reward improvement and positive accomplishment, however small.

· Provide clearer and more specific statements about requirements for satisfactory performance.
· Adjust and redesign the assignment to open the opportunity for different learning modes (that is, doing versus being told or pictorial representation rather than words), and allow for a longer learning period.
· Explain the consequences of continual failure and describe the nature of the discipline which you believe will be warranted. This means achieving a careful balance between scaring the employee and factually letting the employee know the ultimate consequences.

Avoiding the no-win assignment or work situation is the next principle or concept. Often the reaction to inadequacy is merely to construct a situation which exactly duplicates the one on which failure occurred or sometimes even to create a more difficult assignment. Creating a more difficult assignment as a measurement and as a discipline is not constructive or creative. If you are unsure whether a change in assignment is fair, it is often desirable to discuss the measurement assignment with another manager or a staff personnel specialist.

Being supportive without taking over is the next creative concept or principle. If the energy and attention that you provide is enough or nearly enough to do the assignment, then you, not the employee, are performing. If you do this then when you withdraw your attention and assistance the individual will again fail because the individual has not been taught to stand on his or her own feet. Simply put, the manager must multiply his or her power through the effective use of people. If there is no gain, no amplification of the energy put in, then we do not have a productive process, and we are not effectively using the power of the employee.

The last of the creative principles has to do with the chemistry of the second chance. Find out what is important to the employee and use that value, need, or goal to motivate for a more successful try. Often the reason for failure was poor job/person fit or poor chemistry. That is, doing whatever was required on the job was not important to the individual. You should try to discover what will make it important and thus improve the odds for success the second time around.

Types of Discipline

If the positive, supportive approach fails, what does one do? Continued failure to obey rules or to meet performance standards must be addressed both for the long-run benefit of the employee and for organizational viability. One category of discipline, dismissal, will be addressed in the next section. First we shall discuss the alternatives one may consider for failures that do not require the ultimate action of dismissal.

The following classification of types of failures may help us to review and judge the appropriate disciplinary actions and assist in choosing the one which will work best. Because individuals and organizational contexts and environments are different, these categories will not have the same values in all organizations or work situations. Also the types of disciplines which can be used successfully will vary with organization policy and climate.

1. Failure to meet the requirements of the task assignment in time, quality, or quantity. This category assumes repeated failure after clarifying the assignment and giving all possible aid and support. This category applies most specifically to the new employee.
2. Failure to meet the requirements of the assignment as in (1), but here the assignment represents a promotion or change based on prior successful performance by the employee. This category applies to the long-term employee who has been successful.
3. Failure to adhere to basic requirements for employment such as attendance and punctuality, sobriety, dress codes where required by the work, and safety requirements.
4. Illegal actions including theft and unethical business practices.
5. Disruptive and negative activities interfering with the work of others in the group or organization. This category includes poor attitude, one of the most troublesome situations to deal with.
6. Disorderly behavior such as fighting with fellow employees, abusive behavior, and unsafe behavior. These are more severe and usually precipitous as compared with incidents classified under (5).
7. Failure to stick to a prescribed remedial program as in the case of alcohol or drug addiction.

With these types of failure it should be possible to describe types of discipline and see how each may or may not apply. One of the simplest types of discipline is to send the person home. This may or may not prove to be disciplinary depending on the individual, the context, and whether it is with or without pay. It could be disciplinary and positive. For example, where the activity of the individual has been disruptive, you have indicated it was wrong, and you want some cooling off time before addressing it

further. In this case the seriousn[...]
there was no loss of pay. Sometimes [...]
provide for interviewing others, gathering [...]
facts so that discipline can be fair. In some org[...]
hourly paid workers, time off without pay is used to ge[...]
individual to the necessity for a change in behavior. The pr[...]
type of discipline is that it usually does not change anything[...]
maximum benefit is usually that it provides investigative time or reflec[...]
time. It is most often used in failure types 3, 4, 5, and 6 above. The ability
to use this disciplinary form depends on organization policy and often on
union contract agreements.

The second form of discipline one might consider is a reduction in
pay. This can be either temporary or permanent. Even a small cut can be a
strong punishment especially with someone who has commitments for
total income. Although the concept gets attention, it is private and allows
the person to stay on the same job; thus there is usually no loss of face with
fellow employees. Organization policy, consistency in use, and union
agreements can affect the manager's ability to use this. It is not applicable
to failure types 4 and 7, but could be used for other types.

Downgrading of the employee's role or type of work without status
or pay reduction is the next type. This type of discipline makes the failure
public and is generally utilized when one wishes to use peer pressure as a
positive motivation for improvement. It can, of course, cause the reverse. I
can remember a case, for example, when an employee was judged to have
failed in the role of assistant to a manager, and these duties were taken
away. In this case the group rallied around the employee and felt the
manager had been unfair. On the other side it does provide an opportunity to recoop, to try again with somewhat lesser stakes. It is most applicable to failure types 1, 2, 5, and 6.

Demotion, actual change to a lower status job with or without pay
reduction, is the next type of discipline. After failure to improve on
performance-related problems, this type of action can be a healthy and
positive type of discipline. It transmits a clear message of the price of
failure to the individual and to the group. It provides an opportunity for
the employee to perform where the stakes are lower. An experienced
employee could be returned to a level where success had previously been
achieved. Whether there is a pay reduction or not depends on organization policy, culture, and the presence or absence of rules negotiated with a
union. It is most applicable to type 1 and 2 failures.

Still another discipline category is to reduce freedoms. This is the
sort of action we may remember from early school days. Except in a very

...applicable in the organizational en-
...our desire to create an adult work
...take responsibility for their actions. It
...where the work has been done unsuccess-
...from the supervisor and now is tried again
...chful eye. It has very limited usefulness but
...ure types 1, 2, 5, and 6.
...of moderate and private discipline is to down-
...performance appraisal rating. This can be effective
...here the appraisal program is well accepted and where
...stood that appraisal ratings can affect future pay and
...sideration. It seems most applicable to failure types 1, 2, 5,
...use depends on policy and culture.

Dismissal

Like other forms of discipline, dismissal must be applied consistently and fairly. In one sense it is the ultimate disciplinary action. In another sense, when you are separating someone early in their career, it may provide the shock or crisis necessary to cause changed behavior and therefore may be a very positive action. Organization policy and practice must establish the ground rules for deciding what infractions are important enough to warrant dismissal.

The most obvious causes for dismissal and ones which require little discussion are failure types 3, 4, 5, 6, and 7. If the employment contract, either written or understood through practice, supports some required behaviors in order for the employee to maintain the right to employment (type 3) and the employee fails without a supportable reason, then dismissal may be appropriate. In the case of type 4, illegal actions, it is usually necessary to suspend the person and await a guilty finding in a court of law. This is true when the act in question is external to the organization or when the act is internal but of a level to also involve police and the courts. If the investigation and the proof of guilt are all internal to the organization, the organization chooses not to take legal action, and dismissal is consistent with policy and practice, then dismissal can be immediate. Perhaps an example will clarify this. Most organizations have clearly spelled-out rules of acceptable employee behavior in relation to suppliers and vendors which make accepting entertainment from vendors unacceptable. In such a case an employee who does accept unique entertainment can and should be dismissed if this outcome had been communicated and dismissal has been the practice in the organization. Such an infraction does not involve the police or the courts. The word *unique* has been used to assure that the employee is not dismissed for something clearly acceptable to all, for example, accepting the discount on automobile rentals often offered to all employees of a company, even for personal use, as a provision of a corporate contract.

Type 5, disruptive activities, actual interference with the work of others, if severe and repeated despite counsel, is certainly a real cause for separation. When an individual, after duly understanding the requirement and warning, continues activity disruptive to others, management must dismiss or face loss of respect on the part of the other employees. However, it would be unfair to suggest this case is easy. There are many shades of gray, and it is highly probable that management would not see every infraction of this type.

A type 6 incident, where an employee strikes another or threatens another with a weapon, is most often a cause for dismissal. To support the action the organization will have to show consistency in applying this discipline. The employer's action may also be affected by whether and what type of legal action is taken by the wronged employee. If, for example, a court clears the attacker, the employer is in a weak position to support dismissal on that incident.

Alcoholism and drug addiction (category 7) are illnesses. However, these illnesses affect performance, attendance, and often interpersonal behavior. As in other cases of inadequate performance before dismissal, there should be a management-supported attempt to get the employee to change behavior and improve. If, through referral to AA or some outside agency, continuation of a corrective program has been made a condition of employment, then failing to pursue it can be cause for dismissal. The real tough areas for applying dismissal as the discipline are job performance categories 1 and 2. They are tough because in order to be fair the message about the job requirements must have been explicit and clear. It must also be demonstrated that it was fair to expect that level of performance based on employee qualifications. In this case it will normally be necessary to show that others with similar background can successfully perform the same activities. It must also be demonstrated that the measurement was fair and unbiased. These requirements mean that the type of helping activities discussed in the early part of this chapter must have been tried. And in our litigious times, demonstrating all these things may take many documents and records. I know managers who consider the required paper support of communication and counseling to be excessive. The organization's case will also be stronger if it can demonstrate internal review by a third party. The third party may be a counseling or an investigating arm of management or in some cases a union representation. Union review most often takes place after the fact of dismissal.

The measurement assignment is most normally the central factual basis for a dismissal for performance failure. This assignment is usually created for the specific purpose of testing the employee's ability to perform. Usually this occurs after a series of failures at normal assignments handled in the usual manager-employee relationship. A measurement assignment is one which has a defined beginning and ending. It is an assignment that the employee can, based on training and experience, be clearly and fairly expected to perform. It is generally not just a repeat of the type of assignment where previous failure has occurred. It is an assignment that has most often been reviewed prior to instituting it by a fellow manager, a technical expert, or a human resource professional. It is an assignment that can be clearly described and laid out for the employee, usually in writing. At the outset of the assignment, the purpose of the measurement and the price of failure must also be discussed and understood. In essence, therefore, dismissal for performance is usually not for the first performance failure but for a failure where communication was complete and the assignment was designed to measure competence. One special case of dismissal for performance failure should be mentioned: A training program is sometimes considered the first job assignment, and failure to successfully complete it is understood to disqualify people for employment. This can be considered a type 3 failure.

In some cases where there is a meeting of the minds and the employee is in agreement, the dismissal is replaced by a mutual agreement resignation. This is better for both parties and happens most often with professional employees and members of management. It is better because it casts the separation in a more positive light. Usually, for example, the employer supplies transition money of some sort and sometimes job-finding assistance. It is better because the record shows a resignation, not a dismissal. It is better because it reflects the mutuality of responsibility for failure. It is therefore possible for the employee to seek other employment without some aspects of the negative aura of dismissal. It is better for the employer because it safeguards against some type of fight over separation.

Rocks and Shoals

Clearly the twin rocks or shoals in the area of discipline and dismissal are fairness in measurement and the need to avoid discrimination on age, race, or sex. The best proof of fair measurement is that others with like backgrounds, experience, and training can perform or meet the requirements at which the disciplined employee failed. The best proof of nondiscrimination is the ability to demonstrate that all people are treated in the same way. The more subtle rocks and shoals, which have been mentioned or can be drawn from earlier discussions, are as follows:

Discipline Issue	*Remedial Action, Defense, or Demonstration of Fairness*
1. Managerial inadequacy	Demonstrate that the manager is appraised well in managerial performance, has been successful in helping other employees with problems, and that there were third-party reviews, which assure this action was fair.
2. Unfair measurement assignment	Demonstrate that other employees have and can meet the requirements represented by the measurement assignment. Demonstrate that the measurement assignment was reviewed by others and that this person could be expected, based on experience and training, to perform at that level. Demonstrate that the assignment was clearly and completely spelled out and the consequences of failure understood.
3. Inadequate documentation	When the dismissal is challenged and there is inadequate documented evidence to demonstrate that the employee knew the consequences of failure or understood the assignment or requirement, then the only answer is to provide a fresh opportunity without prejudice.
4. Inconsistency	There is no defense for treating employees differently in response to the same offense.

177

5. Inadequate help, assistance and support by the manager

The manager should document the assistance provided and discussions about needs and job requirements when dealing with inadequate performance or when in a measurement situation. If the help has been inadequate, then a fresh opportunity under a new manager should be created.

6. Inadequate understanding and communication of requirements

Clearly stated policy and written job requirements can in most cases avoid this problem. If such was not the case, then the only answer seems to be to start fresh with clear ground rules.

SUMMARY

Despite the fact that we as managers do not like to take corrective action for inadequate performance, it is our responsibility. In fact, not doing it early in an employee's work experience can make us morally responsible for later failure. The worst thing we can do is to avoid responsibility and overrate performance. We are not doing the employee or the organization a favor and we are not even making our lives easier, as we might think we are.

In facing inadequacy it is important to assure that there has been open and clear understanding of what was required at the outset. If this was not the case then starting over on a clear basis, not discipline, is what is required. Next, the first actions should be supportive and helpful. They should not be cast in a form which assumes that the employee is wrong, but rather that assistance is needed. When this fails, it is possible to take disciplinary action or to establish a measurement assignment. The effectiveness of the action is measured by its avoidance repetition, not by its severity.

The nature of the special performance measurement on which to base dismissal and the types of discipline must fit organizational policy and culture. Discipline, to be fair, must be consistent. It must be able to be reviewed by a third party in case of disagreement. This means there is a necessity for documentation. Good disciplinary and corrective action always withstands the review of the third party.

Dismissal, the ultimate organizational punishment, must be based on fair measurement where the consequences of failure were clearly understood. Dismissal can often be the crisis which shocks the person into personal change for a better, more successful, life.

The subject of discipline and dismissal will become more critical as we extend the work life and make retirement an individual choice. The reasoning behind this is that the organization will no longer be able to carry some of the inadequate performance of the past. This need will force all managers to sharpen up on their skills of weeding out inadequacy early. It will also increase the probability of discrimination suits based on age and inadequate or unfair performance measurement.

Inadequacy, Discipline and Dismissal Checkup

1. Pick the most applicable statement from the following.   ( )

    a. I am successful in dealing with inadequate performance and disciplinary situations despite my discomfort with the activity.
    b. I am occasionally successful in dealing with inadequate performance and disciplinary situations.
    c. I tend not to focus on or identify inadequacy and deal only with reinforcing positive performance.
    d. I avoid dealing with inadequate performance and situations requiring discipline.
    e. I have no employees who are inadequate or require discipline.

2. Review your activities on the most recent case requiring that you take action of a disciplinary type. Answer the following questions.

		yes	so/so	no
a.	I spent a lot of time and energy trying to clarify the instructions and assure understanding of the requirements.	( )	( )	( )
b.	I investigated to see if there were prior conditions or experiences which affected the employee's outlook.	( )	( )	( )
c.	Clarification of the instructions led to performance improvement.	( )	( )	( )
d.	The discipline I used was effective in avoiding repetition of the problem or error.	( )	( )	( )
e.	The discipline techniques I used seemed in proportion to the infraction.	( )	( )	( )
f.	I kept my attention and discussion focused on the required behavior, not personal attributes.	( )	( )	( )
g.	My approach was consistent with other similar cases I have had.	( )	( )	( )
h.	My approach was consistent with other similar cases in the organization.	( )	( )	( )
i.	I judge that my approach was creative.	( )	( )	( )
j.	I believe the outcome can be judged as successful.	( )	( )	( )
k.	I feel sure there are no unidentified and unaddressed similar cases.	( )	( )	( )

3. Do you have any cases of employee inadequacy or incidents requiring discipline at the present time?

    (   ) yes   (   ) no   (   ) don't know

4. If your answer to 3 was positive respond to the following.

	yes	so/so	no
a. I have embarked on a corrective program.	( )	( )	( )
b. The program seems appropriate when reviewed in the light of this chapter.	( )	( )	( )
c. I have not embarked on a corrective program because:			
I am unclear about organization policy.	( )	( )	( )
I don't know what to do.	( )	( )	( )
I am unsure or afraid.	( )	( )	( )
Other_____			

5. I have now or have had employees whom I believe were overappraised by prior managers and the problems seem to have grown more serious over time.

    (   ) yes   (   ) perhaps   (   ) no

    When I indentified such a case I took corrective action despite the difficulty and moral involvement of management.

    (   ) yes   (   ) partially   (   ) no

6. My assessment of the climate for discipline in our organization is that it is:

	yes	partially	no
a. Confused and unclear.	( )	( )	( )
b. Well stated and communicated.	( )	( )	( )
c. Discouraging to the manager who wishes to take action.	( )	( )	( )
d. Accepting of coverup of inadequacy.	( )	( )	( )
e. Inconsistent and somewhat unfair.	( )	( )	( )

Ideas for Action: Dealing with Inadequacy

Something to
try

1.   Identify your poorest performer, personally review the history, decide on appropriate action, and then review the case with your manager for comment, suggestions, and support.   (   )

2.   Audit your techniques for establishing assignment expectations, communicating the expectations, and describing the consequences of success or failure. Try to improve your clarity and check on your performance by requiring feedback from the employee as to what he or she understands.   (   )

3.   Review all cases of inadequacy in your group and establish plans of action based on the principles presented in this chapter.   (   )

4.   Search out policy statements and gain insight into practice through discussion with fellow managers and personnel professionals to assure that you understand the disciplinary expectations in your organization.   (   )

5.   Request a workshop on discipline from your personnel professionals.   (   )

6.   Use this chapter as a discussion base with a group of fellow managers. In other words, create your own workshop and invite an appropriate personnel professional.   (   )

7.   Take part of one of your group or department meetings to engage your employees in a discussion of the appropriate use of discipline. This session should be primarily aimed at eliciting their views but you must be prepared to state yours.   (   )

8.   Analyze your group operations to determine if there is any regular repetition of a specific type of mistake. If there is, devise a program for dealing with elimination of that error starting with clarification of expectations.   (   )

9.   Work to establish disciplinary policy, consistency of approach, and communication about it wherever you find that there seem to be inadequate directions in your organization.   (   )

10. Review the adequacy of your past corrective activities by sitting down with an employee who has improved, and sincerely ask how you could have been more helpful or supportive.   (   )

PART III

The Positive Thrust

To make progress we must choose goals and create strategies for achieving them. Here are some components from which you can create a forward thrust for improving your management of people.

CHAPTER
12

What You Need

What to Expect

When to Ask

How to Judge the Quality of the Advice You Are Given

Creative Use of The Staff Professional

Support from Staff
Professionals

In any but the smallest organization there are professional people in departments with personnel and human resource labels who are there to help us as managers. There has been and there will be a growth in personnel specialization for several reasons. First, because of the complexity of benefits interpretation, it is no longer rational to expect the line manager to be able to interpret payment schedules under complex medical benefits programs. Second, there are many human resource activities that are more effective and cost less when they are done centrally. Much training and education fits this category. Third, some functions, such as recruiting college graduates, require extensive external contact, and efficiency and effectiveness suggest specialization and centralization. Fourth, there are aspects of human resource management such as attitude and salary surveys, that can only be meaningfully analyzed on an aggregate basis. We as managers need the support and assistance of trained personnel specialists.

It is reasonable, therefore, for the line manager to expect and receive quality advice and counsel in specialized human resource areas. This chapter is designed to help you become a good judge of when and what to ask and how to determine when you are getting quality support. The chapter is also designed to help you avoid the pitfalls of too much staff support: to assure that you stay in control and make the decisions, that you don't abdicate your line management human resource responsibility, and that on crucial personnel issues your employees see you as their manager, not just as some information referral service.

What You Need

A manager has only his or her experience, the written policies and guides of the organization, and the input from applicable management development courses on which to base decisions and build a human resource practice. The first broad category of managerial needs, therefore, is a supplement to this experience and knowledge base to assist in special situations. General examples range from employee problems requiring medical or legal expertise to those requiring a special understanding of pay, industrial relations, benefits, education, employee placement, and recruiting. In each of these categories the manager needs the lessons or principles that come from review of multiple cases involving a specific type of problem as a supplement to his or her personal experience with but one. In addition the manager is searching for a specialized depth of information which it is not normal to expect the line manager to have. Specific examples in this category are (1) handling performance problems where the employee is under a doctor's treatment, (2) transferring an employee to an area in the business where the manager has no specific information, and (3) interpreting benefits payments in complex medical cases where the manager has no experience. In these special situations, the manager must determine when the problem is sufficiently unique to require specialized knowledge. This judgment is difficult because problems that initially seem to be within the scope of normal managerial attention later grow. When we are in the middle of an employee problem, it is hard to determine when the problem becomes critical enough to require help. Also, it damages our pride to ask for help. I have never criticized a manager for seeking specialized advice. I have criticized managers for not seeking it, especially when the problem later became a major organizational challenge, a serious issue.

A second category of advice the manager may need to seek from specialists is trend and statistical information drawn from the whole organization or the world outside. An example might be determining how well you are paying your employees with respect to all the employees in the organization who are in the same pay level and are of similar experience, preparation, and time at that level. This is not highly specialized information but it is information only someone with data about the whole organization can generate. And the need for it is not generally created by a problem; rather it is created by the manager's desire to avoid a problem. This information is useful primarily in assuring that your judgments are in the proper range and that you are being fair to those under your direct supervision.

A third broad category where the manager needs help is in counseling and support services. Sometimes this means that you need a friendly critic or general advice. An example might be assistance on how to gain employee participation in improving the effectiveness of the department or group operation. Here the manager is looking for input on what has worked for other managers, and some input as to the degrees of freedom he or she has. One way of differentiating these issues from those in the first category is to remember that the prime purpose here is usually improved management of the group, learning for the manager. This does not mean that seeking help on how to deal with a particular employee situation might not fall in this category but that, if it does, it tends to fit a general category of problem and does not result from a critical issue with a specific employee.

From time to time especially in large organizations, the organization may decide to offer or sometimes require the use of a particular kind of human resource assistance. This is unique because the organization, not the manager, initiates the action. For example, most organizations created such a category of staff help to address their equal opportunity programs. From time to time such action also results from the introduction of new salary practices or new appraisal programs, new laws, or other major changes in human resource policies or practices. Most generally these support activities for the manager represent some combination of training and individualized counsel.

In summary, the following list of areas where you may ask for advice of staff professionals is offered:

· Ask for data about employees in general to understand how well you are treating those you manage.
· Ask for data about how other employers are treating employees of a category similar to your employees.

- Ask for advice where specialized information is needed, as in medical, legal, benefits, employee relations, and salary.
- Ask for advice in the interpretation of policy.
- Ask for advice on how to handle a particular employee with whom you are having difficulty.
- Ask for information about skill needs and recruitment in other parts of the organization.
- Ask for advice where information is needed about how a broad class of employees or issues, such as tardiness, is handled.
- Ask for advice when broad statistical analysis of many cases is required.
- Ask for advice when you need another perspective, a different point of view.
- Ask for advice when the issue represents a general class of problems, such as issues concerning minorities or safety.

What to Expect

"Competent advice" is what comes to mind as I start this section. And yet I have no clear, direct way to tell you how to judge when you are getting it. As in seeking advice of any kind, in any aspect of life, you, as the buyer, must set the standards. Just because the specialist works for your organization is not sufficient protection. The staff specialist is measured by different performance requirements. Doing what satisfies your measure of performance versus doing what will earn outstanding ratings on his or her appraisal, or what he or she believes is expected by the organization may create conflict. A good staff specialist lays this conflict of measures on the table and explains it. For example, most human resource organizations are measured by their ability to keep management out of trouble. Such a measurement is unfortunately not designed to encourage personnel professionals to be innovative or creative. In fact, the conservatism of human resource professionals is, often a key complaint of managers. But we should not be overly harsh because each person's behavior reflects how he or she is measured. The contention between the two measures of performance is constructive and assures that in the pursuit of results we do not misuse employees.

You should probably expect that the advice you receive will be cast in a context intended to protect the employee and to keep you out of trouble. Although you should listen to the advice, you are still responsible for the decision. Generally you are not going to make significant progress without taking some risks. Risk taking is a key element of the manager's role. You should, however, expect the personnel professional to hold the interests of the employee as primary. They are paid to assure that the individual is fairly treated. But you should test to be sure that they do. This perspective can be of definite advantage to you in dealing with a problem employee. The professionals' presence and counsel can go a long way toward assuring that you are neither precipitous nor unfair. They can help to assure that an audit review will not find that you made some gross mistake. Use them, then, to constructively criticize your plans for corrective action.

Expect them to provide interpretation of organizational policies and governmental rules. They can and should be a useful source of in-depth information about organizational intent, often unwritten, behind a particular policy or program. For example, advice of staff professionals is of assistance when trying to interpret the intent of educational assistance policies. In interpretation of rules one of the staff professional's roles is to assist you in adhering to the intent of government laws and programs. The duality of their role is, therefore, to help you understand your degrees of freedom and to assure that you stay within necessary limits. They add a necessary depth of understanding no individual manager can be expected to have.

Expect personnel professionals to aid you in thinking through any personnel issue. The presence and counsel of an experienced human re-source professional should enrich your thinking processes and sharpen your decisions. By reflecting back to you what you say, by suggesting alternate points of view, by referencing other cases or issues, they should help you arrive at the best answer. Use them as your personal management consultants.

Expect central human resource groups to find you at fault when you have been unfair, have wrongly interpreted a policy, or have acted in a way that may set an unfortunate precedent. They should, however, help you to find the right approach to deal with your problem and to protect the organization. Despite the danger of setting a precedent, there are times when you must take action. For organizational policy it is more often better to be faulted for taking action than for failing to take action. For example, it is generally better to take disciplinary action at the time of the incident and later lessen the discipline than to fail to discipline and lose the rational base for action. In failing to discipline you also lessen your effec-tiveness as a manager.

Expect human resource professionals to act as an escape valve when employee-manager relationships are overheated. They should provide a route for review of grievances and differences. They should provide an alternate route when the employee and manager are not communicating effectively.

Expect personnel specialists to alert you to conditions in the outside world or in other parts of the organization that may affect your ability to manage. For example, if there is an employee-management difference in one part of the organization that may spread, they should alert you. When a nearby organization has taken action that your employees may use to try to get you to change or respond, personnel professionals should alert you. When there is a union settlement in another organization that affects the fairness of your pay rates, they should alert you and assist you in making appropriate changes.

Expect personnel professionals to try to help you do the best job possible as a manager. The personnel professional is there to help you and to protect the organization as a whole. Good professionals know that they must protect the relationship between you and those you supervise. But they also know that they are not surrogate managers. They are motivated to help because their purpose is to assure that the organization has good employees, uses them well, and treats them fairly. In the broad sense, their success is your success.

When to Ask

When to ask for help is easiest to determine after the fact. That is, when your problem might have been avoided if you had sought counsel, you know you should have sought counsel. On the other hand, you may feel asking seems to reduce your degrees of freedom when you need the freedom. There are times to do what seems right based on your understanding and experience and times to ask for advice. The tough issue is to decide when to ask and when not to ask. The following checklist may help you to determine when to ask, as opposed to what to ask. Positive answers are generally desirable and lead to the decision to ask. Your threshold for asking can only be determined by your experience in your organization. Thus, it is not possible to say that positive responses to the following questions are always appropriate. Whether or not to ask can only be determined by understanding your capability, the culture of the organization, and the quality of staff professional service available to you. The checklist is representative, not complete.

I should ask for help when:

- there is a question of fairness when my action has the potential for a grievance, union action, or outside review
- there is evidence of conflict and possibly poor communication between me and an employee
- the special situation or problem involves a minority employee
- my decision can be improved by statistical or overall information about how others in the organization or outside are treated
- my decision or action might become a reference base for other employees to ask for similar treatment
- the issue or situation is one where I simply have no applicable experience to guide me
- I simply do not know of any applicable policy or procedure
- the answer requires a depth of expertise in a specialized information area like medicine, law, education, or psychology
- the organization provides a centralized service to assure consistency, or to relate to the outside world in a standard way such as in recruiting or industrial relations
- I simply need someone to reflect my thinking back to me who has employee interests as central and a different experience base than I have
- it appears that the solution to my problem requires response by other parts of the organization

How to Judge The Quality of The Advice You Are Given

Your judgement about the quality of advice lies in your personal integration of feelings and organizational signals. One of the prime criteria is the reputation the staff professional has with your fellow managers for being helpful and giving good advice. A second basis is your own feeling of ability to communicate honestly and openly with the staff professional. You must be able to communicate effectively, and only you can judge this interpersonal chemistry. Only if you feel you have been told the whole story can you feel you have quality advice on which to base your decision. Another base for evaluating advice is your own prior experience. Has past advice stood up over time? The reputation of the staff professional outside your organization is also important. Is this person active professionally? Is this person giving papers or teaching or continuing his or her professional education? In short, is the person acting like a professional? Lastly, your judgment depends on your answer to the question, Is the person able to understand and admit the limits of his or her own advice? Does the person tell you when he or she believes they do not really know the answer?

Creative Use of The Staff Professional

Creative use means amplifying your capability as a manager by supplementing your fund of knowledge and experience by using the staff professional to sharpen your own perceptions. Creative use starts with knowledge of your own strengths and weaknesses in managing people. Use the professional in areas where you are weak. Use the professional to enhance your learning. Use the professional when knowledge of what is happening outside your own area is needed. Use the professional where specialized knowledge or experience is needed.

Set limits on what you are asking. That is, you should define the territory and the range of assistance you require. If you fail to define the limits, you may get unfocused and useless advice. The more specific you can be about your need, generally the better the advice you receive will be.

Search for the right person. Especially in large organizations, the most obvious person may not be the right person. The right person is the one you can relate to and with whom you feel you can be totally open. The apparent right person is the specialist in the area of your question; yet if you relate poorly to this person the quality and usefulness of the advice is limited. You must understand that your perspective is a definite part of the usefulness of the advice.

Do your homework before you ask for advice. That is, go to the professional when you are fully steeped in the issue. The more you know about your problem or challenge, the more qualified you are to measure the quality of the advice you are getting. Establish personal limits on the time you will invest in the process of seeking advice. If you do not you may waste a lot of time getting advice but make little progress. Another way to say this is that you, the manager, should stay in charge of the relationship with the staff professional. By doing so you can determine best when to stop seeking advice and when to make the decision. In the end you are responsible for the decision.

Use the staff professional as you would a management consultant. Probe and get as much as you can for your investment. Plan your interview by listing the questions you wish to address. Demonstrate your ability to manage the situation, and the professional will rise to the quality standard you have set.

SUMMARY

Organizations vary considerably in the level and quality of their professional personnel staffs. Some provide very complete services and assistance for the manager, others very little. Whatever the level, it is your responsibility as a manager to make proper use of their expertise to supplement and enhance your own capability.

In considering asking for assistance, it is necessary to understand the staff professional's special perspective and to use it to supplement and complement yours. Staff professionals are rewarded for keeping you and the organization out of trouble. This generally means their perspective is conservative. They are paid to represent the employee's interests and thus assure fair treatment. Because of these factors the manager should generally expect that the personnel professional will take the conservative route. It is incumbent on the manager to make effective use of the staff professional by understanding his or her perspective in the organization.

Determining when to use the professional is a difficult decision because the process of asking may indeed seem to limit your degrees of freedom. This may reflect the professional's need to protect the organization and the employee. It is difficult to decide when to ask because failing to ask early may expose the organization to difficulty with other employees or outside organizations. Also difficult is judging the quality of the assistance you have been given. Because of their greater depth, broader context, and expertise, their advice is valuable. You have only your own experience as a reference base, and this may be inadequate. One way to check out when to ask is to talk to your fellow managers.

Creative use of staff professionals can enhance your learning and improve your ability to manage effectively. The most important subjects to seek advice about are those where supplementing your perspective with a view of the total organization may help. This is particularly true in salary, employee relations, and benefits areas. It is also important to use staff professionals as management consultants on special situations and individual employee problems. Often the most important of these are employee performance problems that need corrective action. Finally, use the professional when you need someone to take the employee's perspective to assure that your actions are fair.

Effective use of Professional Personnel Staff Checkup

1. How recently have you used professional personnel staff to assist you in each of the following areas? Check the appropriate response.

		in the last month	in the last six months	in the last year	never
a.	determining a proper salary increase	( )	( )	( )	( )
b.	assisting you in finding a growth and development opening for one of your employees	( )	( )	( )	( )
c.	recruiting potential new employees for your interview and hiring decision	( )	( )	( )	( )
d.	assisting you in dealing with an employee performance problem	( )	( )	( )	( )
e.	providing specialized information on benefits	( )	( )	( )	( )
f.	providing you with educational assistance	( )	( )	( )	( )
g.	providing you with opinion or attitude information	( )	( )	( )	( )
h.	assisting you in dealing with an employee grievance	( )	( )	( )	( )
i.	providing you with medical, legal, or industrial relations counsel	( )	( )	( )	( )
j.	providng you with career counseling assistance or career help for an employee	( )	( )	( )	( )
k.	assisting you in organization development (improving group learning and work relationships)	( )	( )	( )	( )

2. Pick the statement which best describes your threshold for asking for professional staff assistance.   ( )

    a. I never ask for it.
    b. I ask for it only when I'm in serious trouble.
    c. I ask for it when I feel my actions may affect the whole organization.
    d. I ask for it only when I need their services to provide me with specialized expertise.
    e. I ask for it selectively when I feel the need to think through and understand a special case more completely.

3. What is your knowledge of the services provided by your professional personnel staff? Check the most appropriate response. Then check your answers against (1) where appropriate.

		good	fairly good	uncertain	inadequate
a.	educational programs and specialized assistance	( )	( )	( )	( )
b.	recruiting	( )	( )	( )	( )

c.	benefits	( )	( )	( )	( )
d.	salary	( )	( )	( )	( )
e.	employee problem issues	( )	( )	( )	( )
f.	career assistance and transfer	( )	( )	( )	( )
g.	grievance handling	( )	( )	( )	( )
h.	legal assistance	( )	( )	( )	( )

4. How do you feel about the overall quality and quantity of the professional personnel services available to you? Check the most appropriate response. Then compare your responses with those to (3) to see if your lack of information about these services may be affecting your evaluation of them.

		good	fairly good	uncertain	inadequate
a.	educational programs and specialized assistance	( )	( )	( )	( )
b.	recruiting	( )	( )	( )	( )
c.	benefits	( )	( )	( )	( )
d.	salary	( )	( )	( )	( )
e.	employee problem issues	( )	( )	( )	( )
f.	career assistance and transfer	( )	( )	( )	( )
g.	grievance handling	( )	( )	( )	( )
h.	legal assistance	( )	( )	( )	( )

5. Assess your performance for evidence that you have failed to seek professional assistance at the appropriate time or failed to receive useful advice when sought. Pick the most appropriate answer.   ( )

a. I have no negative evidence in the form of grievances, prolonged and serious employee problems, loss of key employees, morale problems, or court cases that I have failed to take appropriate action.

b. I have evidence in one case that I may have missed the time and place to seek advice and counsel in order to avoid more serious problems.

c. I have evidence in several cases that I may have missed the time and place to seek advice and counsel in order to avoid more serious problems.

d. I have sought advice and counsel, used it as I felt I could, and have nevertheless ended up with problems.

e. I have sought advice and counsel, feel I've received inadequate help, and ended up with problems.

6. Assess the following personnel roles to try to determine which aspects of the personnel function need improvement.

		very good	adequate	needs improvement	don't know
a.	policy making (rules, principles, employee support, approaches)	( )	( )	( )	( )
b.	policy remaking (updating for change)	( )	( )	( )	( )
c.	general advice and counsel for decision making	( )	( )	( )	( )
d.	services (benefits, salary, records, recruiting)	( )	( )	( )	( )
e.	employee or organizational improvement (education, organizational development, proactive services)	( )	( )	( )	( )
f.	problem solving (assistance with critical employee problems)	( )	( )	( )	( )
g.	mediation (third-party review of manager-manager differences)	( )	( )	( )	( )
h.	grievance and appeal handling (employee centered)	( )	( )	( )	( )
i.	management training	( )	( )	( )	( )
j.	personnel research (attitude surveys, studies of human relations trends and changes)	( )	( )	( )	( )

Ideas for Action: Improving Your Use of Staff Personnel Professionals

something
to try

1. Make an appointment to visit and understand each of the key functions in personnel and get acquainted with the people involved.   (   )

2. Find out which of the staff professionals are prepared to talk about their services with your employees and invite them to one of your group or department meetings. (Discussion of benefits are especially important topics.)   (   )

3. Ask for a salary review of your group with statistical data on how your employees rank in the organizaton and outside.   (   )

4. Single out your most difficult employee problem as a test case, go and describe it to the appropriate professional, and see what type of help they are prepared to provide.   (   )

5. Determine what type of specialized training or education would improve your group's performance, and go to the education staff or appropriate personnel person to see what kind of assistance they can provide.   (   )

6. If you have questions about how your employees feel, find out what opinion survey or other type of feedback service might be available.   (   )

7. Ask for or enroll in whatever employee relations training is provided, or request a recommendation on what outside programs to consider if there is none in the organization.   (   )

8. Identify your most outstanding performer, someone ready for a broadening growth experience or promotion you can't provide, and approach the appropriate personnel person to see what they can do to help this person get a development opportunity.   (   )

9. If you feel your personnel services need improvement, get together with your fellow managers and check their reactions. Try to agree on an improved service you need and ask for it. If necessary go to higher management, but only after trying the direct approach.   (   )

10. If you feel personnel services in your organization need improvement and the approach in (9) doesn't work, see if your personnel professional can hire outside consultant services to provide training or enhance the available support.   (   )

CHAPTER
13

Leadership and Authenticity

Why another chapter on leadership? It would seem as though this chapter overlaps both chapter eight, "Leadership and Coaching" and chapter five, "Who Are You?" However, there are many ways to look at leadership, and it is one of the most difficult aspects of management to discuss and to communicate. The emphasis in this chapter will be on authenticity, the performance of the leader, differences in values which seem to differentiate leaders, and some of the principles that may be important. There is a strong need to be yourself and to develop your own leadership style and strategy. An authentic leader is one who has his or her act together. This does not mean conforming to someone else's prescription. Therefore, take the ideas in this chapter with a grain of salt. Use the ideas, not as prescriptions, but as experiments you might try in developing your leadership thrust.

Authenticity

To be authentic is to be real. As a manager-leader you must do what you do because you believe it is right and in a way that fits your personality. If you do these things then others should view your actions as sincere and authentic. Realness on your part encourages others to have the strength to say and do what they feel and believe. It takes strength to be authentic because in doing so we must step out from behind our safety screen. Safety screens are made of the acts (roles) we play to keep people at a distance. By putting forth a persona (a mask) we gain ability in theory to size others up, to have time to maneuver. Safety screens are also made of social norms that set standards for acceptable behavior. Norms and acts are not all bad or negative; rather some should be questioned and reviewed to assure usefulness. Realness and authenticity require that we have the guts to let people know and see who we really are. This should result in clearer communication and greater effectiveness.

One of the sets of questions in my book, *Personal Vitality Workbook* (Addison-Wesley, 1977), deals with this issue. I have also used these questions in workshop discussions about work. Who goes through the door when you go into work? Is it the whole you? How do you change? Behind these questions is the belief that one of the challenges in design of effective work environments is the tendency for organizational social norms to interfere with real authentic behavior. If you must guard against taking the whole you through the door to work, the organization may well be getting less capability than it needs. These norms, in addition to our personal protection instincts, can mitigate against authenticity. And a lack of authenticity interferes with productivity and detracts from the quality of work life. This is not to say that there should be no norms. For example, a norm that says it's not ok to hit the manager when you're angry seems at least to be one that as a manager I'd defend! But a norm that says it is not ok to express anger in any way could make an unhealthy work environment. Such a norm would, for example, contribute to work-related stress. Prolonged stress with no relief leads to potential illness, glandular, and body changes. So a lack of authenticity may mean a loss of organizational effectiveness through misuse of energy in worry, anxiety, and the maintenance of false fronts.

Authenticity in an organization can be encouraged in four ways: (1) the most appropriate way for this chapter is by the leader's being authentic, thus establishing a behavioral model; (2) by removing those negative reinforcements for authenticity, a prime example of which is punishment for experimenting and failing; (3) by engaging in processes such as team building where employees, in a family group, learn about their power to make changes in the work environment; and (4) by establishing rewards for authenticity. In general these do not have to be elaborate or monetarily large. The statement by a manager, "I'm glad you expressed your real feeling, and now I understand why you did or said what you did," is often a sufficient reward.

What is necessary for the leader-manager to be authentic is a willingness to stand up and be counted. This strength is usually made up of self-assurance and a feeling that nothing the organization (upper management) can do will really damage the manager as a person. This power is made up, in part, of the manager's understanding and belief that he or she can go elsewhere and secure as good or even perhaps a better job. Authenticity strength is made up of the feeling that the most important value is to be true to self and not sell out to the system. Authenticity strength is a spirit of independence. Authentic and successful leaders use their power.

It is not enough for the leader to be an examplar of authenticity. Creating an authentic work environment requires that the leader use the other three ways as well. Remember the second was to balance punishment against failures. How to do this is covered in chapter eleven, "Dealing with Inadequate Performance: Discipline and Dismissal." It is the fact that these actions are perceived to fit what happened that makes for authenticity.

Another action to support authenticity is training. Through training it is possible to teach individuals and teams that authenticity leads to effectiveness and learning. That is, it is also necessary to encourage and create a more open adult environment. Doing this requires an active program, working to create a work environment of quality. If people are to gain a sense of self-definition through work, the work environment must be adult and authentic. An authentic environment is one where being yourself is expected.

Last, it is necessary to reward authenticity to create authenticity. This means, for example, recognizing the constructive use of differences, of conflict. A person who uses his or her impatience to create the pressure for negotiation is doing so. It means rewarding the person, maybe just by acknowledgment, who drops the protective front to improve communication. Such would be the case when an individual reveals the basic values that motivate what he or she is trying to do. It means recognizing the manager who has the guts to fight for what he or she believes when higher management takes a stand or directs action which he or she believes is wrong. However, one should reward the manager only when he or she also knows when to quit arguing and do what management has decided to do, in this case executing the action with belief and sincerity. These are but a few examples of what is meant by rewarding authenticity. Rewarding in these cases is not the use of some system of dollar prizes. Rewarding in these cases means encouraging, supporting, and acknowledging.

Behaviors

For many years management literature was replete with lists of traits required by the successful executive leader. It now seems evident that, although there is overlap in these lists, the characteristics of the good leader vary with the situation. That is, the successful leader is the one whose behavior fits the culture of the organization, the needs of the group, his or her authentic style, and the challenge of the time. A desirable behavioral characteristic of the leader is thus flexibility. The successful leader is the person who is able to be in tune with the times, the situation, and miraculously does the right things. Flexibility, being able to suit the method to the need and the situation, is a characteristic on which there is emerging general agreement among those who study the work of managers. But in order to take the right action at the right time, to be timely and flexible, the leader must listen for the winds of change. Good leaders seem to develop a third ear, a sense of what is about to happen. One of the central aspects of leadership, the ability to set out in one direction and motivate others to follow, requires this anticipatory sense. Determining the direction requires making a decision about the flow of events and taking advantage of the prediction rather than letting events grow into problems.

Listening for change and taking anticipatory action leads naturally to risk taking. The process of management is a risk-taking process. This is so because the leader-manager must act on partial data. Risk taking is the only way to achieve profit. Profit here is used in its broadest sense to include all forms of organizational success. Generally if one waits until the data is complete, until the course seems clear, one has missed the opportunity to lead. No risk, no profit; no risk taking, no leadership.

Risk-taking behavior suggests the need for intuitive or right-hemisphere (brain) capability. To assess and take action on partial data requires imagination. When one outruns the logical, rational, linear data base one must utilize feelings. Thus a leader should be able to use both halves of the brain for the unique contributions of each and must be comfortable in shifting to the right hemisphere at the times when intuition is needed. This is another aspect of the need for flexibility of behavior. This flexibility is based on understanding one's thinking style and processes and taking advantage of them.

Another leadership characteristic is a sort of restlessness or a greater than normal need for change. All of us are ambivalent about change. For in change there is risk, and we must leave the safety of the status quo. However, when we look at change rationally we know that it is the vehicle for personal development and growth. Change is also the stuff of leadership. Our tolerance for change and our need for change as a stimulus is a very personal characteristic. Leaders generally thrive on change and desire it as others might value money or status. To lead, to create change, requires wanting it and being at home with it.

A tendency to be independent, to be one's own person, is another characteristic behavior of the leader. Although this includes authenticity, it goes beyond it to never giving up one's self totally to the organization, yet giving to the point of successfully engaging the organization and its purpose. In a personal way perhaps I can explain this better. While working in organizations, I have developed a personal formula for this: whenever I cannot accept the principles, policies, and practices of the organization to an extent greater than 50 percent it is time to get out. Several times it has been close for a short time. Managing this sort of formula requires understanding who I am and what I value. Since neither I nor the organization is unchanging, it requires developing some monitoring techniques. One of the characteristic behaviors of the leader is a self-identity which others react to as independent.

Leaders generally are able to develop empathy. That is, they are capable of reaching out to other people in a way that transmits the feeling that they understand what the other person feels and values. This does not mean leaders cannot or should not at times be ruthless and override the feelings and needs of others. Rather, it means they have the capacity to know the other person. If they override the other person's desires they do it in a way that lets the other person know they are doing it knowingly. If they support the other person's needs and values, they do it in a way that the other person knows they know. Thus the leader demonstrates a capacity for empathy balanced against what must be done to reach the organization's goals.

Challenge is a work attribute on which the leader places a high value. Challenge is a measure of the amount of risk and competition. Higher risks mean greater challenge. Outpacing someone else or some other organization represents winning a challenge. For each of us there is a level of challenge that provides motivation. If the challenge is so big that we are sure we cannot do it, it is not motivating. But if it is too small, it is also nonmotivating. The leader is generally capable of tolerating, even enjoying, a higher level of challenge than the nonleader.

A leader understands that he or she works in a network of systems. This means that the leader knows no action he or she takes exists by itself. Playing the system, understanding the dynamics and the interactions, are necessary parts of success. The effective leader uses the system pressures, the modulations and pulses of the systems in which he or she is imbedded, to amplify and reinforce managerial actions. Fighting system pressures reduces leadership effectiveness. Using the system, by contrast, amplifies the leader's effectiveness.

A leader understands the need for a balance of giving and taking. That is, both the leader and the followers need to give and to take. Even the strongest of leaders needs to take input from his or her followers. Each human being needs a balance of receiving and telling, of listening and talking, of doing and resting. Successful leaders use this need for balance and step up to the follower's need for input.

A leader demonstrates the ability to delegate, to let go and let someone else take over. There are two important aspects to the art of delegation. First, it demonstrates the ability to take risks. This is the risk of letting someone else's performance be counted as yours. Second, it requires choosing those things that are important to do yourself without trying to do everything. The trust demonstrated by the leader causes delegation to become a technique for helping other people to grow. The leader uses delegation as a tool to accelerate the development of others and thus strengthen the team and the organization. The leader delegates to maximize his or her impact. Making right choices about who to give assignments to is a key element of the observable behavior of the successful leader.

Other observers will identify other elements of behavior and other leadership characteristics. However, these examples should be sufficient to establish the important thesis that leaders do demonstrate characteristic behaviors. The difference that makes people leaders lies not in the fact that they have different attributes and values from other people. Rather, the difference lies in the relative importance they put on specific values and behaviors. For example, most of us say we enjoy challenge. The difference between the nonleader and the leader is the relative importance the leader puts on the need for challenge. The difference between the nonleader and the leader is also in the personal price the individual will pay for the opportunity to achieve that challenge.

Performance Requirements For Leadership

The following leader's performance plan assumes that we are managing a leader. You and I are drawing up the performance plan and specifying how we will measure leadership performance. Necessarily our specifications are general. In real life they would include specific goals relating to the mission, the objectives, of the organization. Our performance plan is directed to a manager who manages managers and who is thus part of the middle to executive level in some organization. The following performance plan would, of course, be worked out with the manager.

1. Translate, interpret, and communicate the goals of the organization (which you have participated in setting) into meaningful, exciting, and stimulating goals for your segment of the organization. Measured by: Demonstrated measurable performance of your team in achieving their part of the organization's goals and by feedback that shows that your managers and employees both understand and accept these objectives as their own, and enthusiastically support the organization's goals.
2. Through improved (measurable) performance and increased capability you will demonstrate that you have supported, encouraged, and elicited performance from your managers that results in achieving success in reaching and exceeding the goals

of the organization. Demonstrated by: Measurable output of the group and documented improved performance of the individuals as measured by your appraisal of their performance against planned objectives.

3. Through growth and development of the employees and managers reporting in your organization, you will demonstrate that you have nurtured capability, encouraged personal development, and supported growth. Measured by: The numbers of people you have been able to promote or move to increased responsibility in and out of your immediate organization, your ability to take on additional special assignments and delegate, and the participation of your employees and managers in extra activities and educational experiences.

4. Through meeting and exceeding objectives 1, 2, and 3, you will demonstrate leadership capability, and in addition you will contribute to:

· enhancing the organization's ability to attract and utilize top talent
· enhancing the reputation, image and achievements of the organization in its field of special service and product
· creating breakthroughs that expand the capability of the organization to lead and succeed
· anticipating and taking action on trends, social, business, and technological changes that the organization can utilize to improve its penetration of the market and general success
· experimentation in the improvement of quality of work, including improved matching of employees to work and increasing the satisfactions achieved through work
· improved effectiveness and productivity

Measured by: Appropriate measures of the many categories.

5. Through participation in business, industry, professional, and community activities, you will demonstrate the commitment and contribution of the organization and yourself to good citizenship and the general quality of life and business environment. Measured by: Achievements in outside activities.

6. Through the establishment of personal goals for improvement and personal involvement in new experiences and education, you will demonstrate your personal commitment to growth and de-

velopment. Measured by: Achievement of personal improvement goals and preparation for increased responsibility.
7. You will demonstrate your understanding of and mastery of the many roles of the manager. For example, you will put the appropriate emphasis on the following activities:
· managing work flow
· establishing, monitoring, and managing interfaces (boundaries) with other parts of the organization
· managing vitality and assuring that today's activities lead to an increase in adaptability energy
· auditing relationships where your role is to measure the performance of others.
· teaching your employees the lessons necessary to perform and improve

Measured by: Appropriate measures for each function or role.

Developing Your Leadership Ability

One might give up and say, "I was not born to be a leader." Or at the other extreme, one could try to develop all the leadership attributes. For most of us in management the answer is undoubtedly somewhere in between. We want to take advantage of the capabilities we have—and we all have some leadership characteristics—and we don't want to push ourselves into some nonauthentic mold or idealistic set of specifications. What we need is a positive program of personal development of our capabilities and improvement without artificiality. Too many times what the student of management infers from a discussion of leadership, a management training program, or an article is that there is one right way, one right behavior style. There is no one right style or leadership pattern. It is much more useful to add those new skills and new approaches which can work for you, enhance the ones which you already have, and leave the leadership characteristics and techniques to other people.

Any program of improvement must fit you. Therefore, the true value and meaning of the next few suggestions will come only through your interpretation and tailoring of them to your motivations and interests. There is no universal prescription for improvement, just as there is no universally correct leadership pattern. Improvement comes only through personal attention to what is happening. This means paying attention to the feedback from what you do. And it means expecting improvement of yourself. In other words, outlook is important. It also means giving yourself permission to change, and then experimenting with change. Some suggested steps for building your personal leadership improvement program follow:

- Assess how you are doing. Identify your leadership strengths and weaknesses and ask for some assessment from other people.
- From the weaknesses you identify pick one to improve. (Some action areas are suggested at the end of this chapter.)
- Next, read and ask questions until you become more expert at understanding the aspect of leadership that you have picked to change.
- Next, work out some technique for experimenting with new ways suggested by your new knowledge, and carefully measure the results.
- Last, the process of personal change, of improvement in leadership, is aided by making a game out of your experiment if you can do so. Fun is important in improvement.

SUMMARY

Leadership is an art. Leadership is using the characteristics and skills you have to best advantage. Practicing the art is best done by being yourself and welding on those few additional techniques that may offset any weaknesses. Being authentic is the first step toward building an effective work environment and improving your leadership strengths. You encourage others to be authentic by your own willingness to take the risks of being yourself. Creating an authentic environment contributes to organizational success. In addition, managers should take positive steps to set leadership goals which support and encourage their authenticity and enhance their leadership impact.

There are many managerial traits which make a good leader. Successful leadership behaviors are flexibility, fitting one's style to the organization, matching group needs, and matching action to the problem. The difference between the leader and someone else seems primarily to be the importance the leader ascribes to certain values, personal characteristics, and behaviors. Some of these differences discussed in the chapter include independence, risk taking, listening for the winds of change, empathy, and restlessness, or the personal need for change.

Leadership and Authenticity Checkup

1. Which of the following statements best describes your feeling about yourself?   (   )
    a. I have a sense of direction and self which causes me to fight for my way, and I can often win others over to my outlook.
    b. I often fight for my way and am moderately successful in encouraging others to follow.
    c. I find it generally difficult to identify and state my outlook and beliefs, so most often I am the sponsor of ways defined by others.
    d. The organization way is the right way, and I am a good soldier.
    e. I have no real interest in what the organization believes is its leadership thrust, so I can generally stay uninvolved and unmoved.

2. Pick the most applicable statement.   (   )
    a. I set high standards of personal performance through my behavior but delegate as much as I can to help others to develop and grow.
    b. I set high standards of personal performance, put in long hours, give heavy assignments, and appraise to a great extent on the basis of effort.
    c. I set reasonably high personal performance standards, and I encourage others to do so but expect each person to find his or her right level.
    d. I do not believe that the manager should demonstrate standards by his or her own performance, and I leave work effort decisions up to the individual.
    e. Performance is not a matter of effort but of quality, and all my emphasis is on results of quality.

3. Pick the statement that best reflects your leadership approach.   (   )
    a. I am open, friendly and easily approached with deep interest in and appreciation for each person as an individual, and I say and act as I really feel.
    b. I am generally open, friendly, and frank, but I believe in sticking to business and generally close off nonbusiness discussions. I believe there is a right code of behavior in business.
    c. I am open and exchange information about work easily with my subordinates but feel the manager should be aloof, not one of the gang.
    d. I am often available for employee contact, but much of my energy goes to dealing with those above me.
    e. I feel I am open but have quite limited exchange with employees. My personal safety generally depends on spending most of my energies upward.

4. Your personal attitude about change affects your ability to implement change. Select the statement that best reflects your attitude about variety and need for change in jobs and careers.   (   )
    a. I thrive on change; it provides job stimulation. I am quickly turned off by routine, and therefore I seek change.
    b. I am good at managing change in job and life and have a reasonably high need for change.

209

    c.   I am generally good at making changes and manage change well but feel there are quite a few things we ought not to change.

    d.   I generally tolerate change but don't enjoy it.

    e.   I generally fight change and am fearful of it.

5.   Select the statement that best reflects your method of convincing others of the direction to go.   (   )

    a.   I create a crisis and then paint a picture of how exciting it will be to solve it in the way I suggest.

    b.   I define the problem and use logic to convince others of the need to solve it my way.

    c.   I identify the problem and call a meeting to brainstorm a solution, but I bring them around to my way.

    d.   I call a meeting asking each person to describe the problem as he or she sees it, and then we brainstorm a solution, arrive at a consensus, and go off together to solve it.

    e.   I wait for others to bring me the problem, and then I decide how we will solve it and assign tasks.

6.   Pick the statement which most nearly represents the type of feedback you get from your associates.   (   )

    a.   My associates tell me they can generally accurately predict what I will do by observing my behavior prior to a decision or action and understanding my pattern or theme.

    b.   My associates tell me I am generally predictable in my behavior since I project many clues and they understand my beliefs and goals.

    c.   My associates tell me I am somewhat inconsistent, and they are only able to predict my actions about half the time.

    d.   My associates tell me that I am very difficult to predict and seem to work in the organization as a good poker player.

    e.   My associates are generally unable to predict my decisions and actions and are unable to discern my pattern or theme.

7.   You believe that a person should be: (   )

    a.   open about feelings, attitudes, and beliefs

    b.   generally open about feelings, attitudes, and beliefs

    c.   open about feelings, attitudes, and beliefs only about half the time

    d.   very cautious in sharing feelings, attitudes, and beliefs

    e.   unsharing of feelings, attitudes, and beliefs

Ideas for Action: Improving Your Leadership Authenticity Quotient

something
to try

1. Work on becoming a more authentic person. This includes self-assessment and definition of the values and goals important to you. This also includes practicing at being more open, more direct, more frank in your contacts with others.   ( )

2. As you face issues and make decisions, test the decisions as to whether they contribute to employee dependence on you and the organization or whether they move the organization toward an adult environment. Try to make more decisions which support adult independent behavior within the context of organizational goals.   ( )

3. Practice listening for the winds of change in your endeavor. If you manage in a technical area this means becoming sensitive to technical trends. All of us must become more sensitive to social and business changes. Pick one out, for example, the change in attitudes about work, and make a hobby of reading and exploring the topic. Get on top of at least one trend of change and become expert about it.   ( )

4. One of the best ways to practice flexibility in matching individual needs is to get to know those who report to you. Practice empathy, the ability to get into each individual's shoes, and try to fit your relationship with each person to their unique relationship to work. Learn to deal in their values and their goals, but always in the context of the organization's needs.   ( )

5. Assess your risk-taking tolerance by taking a moment just after you have made a managerial decision to record what happened. It is important to consciously identify the risks involved and to then give them some probability rating for successful completion. In other words, learning to watch your decision-making process can help you identify how you handle risk. If you then determine that you are playing it too safe, you have some idea of calibration. Check up too on how others view your risk taking.   ( )

6. Testing and modifying your restlessness or need for change is very difficult. Look at your recent change history and simply see whether or not you feel and seek and make frequent changes. If you determine that you seem fearful of or reluctant to change, it is best to pick some small change you would like to make, make it, and reward yourself for doing it. Developing the habit of making change fun seems the best way to change this characteristic. Good leaders are able to change themselves and their organizations.   ( )

7. Delegation seems like a good area to consider improvement in leadership. Improving delegation starts with analyzing what you are doing and asking yourself for each function whether it might develop someone else's ability if you delegated it. Think in terms of the benefits for someone else rather than the risks if you don't do it yourself. Try delegating more.   (   )

8. Authenticity is evidenced when what we say and what we do is in alignment. Ask an assistant or an associate to help you become sensitive to the signals you are transmitting by predicting what your action will be before you take it.   (   )

9. Consider a communications (experiential) laboratory training program as a way to improve the clarity of the messages you transmit.   (   )

10. Read some of the literature on authenticity and both organizational and interpersonal communications. Here are some suggestions:
R. M. D'Aprix, *In Search of a Corporate Soul* (AMACOM, 1976).
S. Herman, and M. Korenich, *Authentic Management* (Addison-Wesley, 1977).
M. James and D. Jongeward, *Born to Win* (Addison-Wesley, 1971).

CHAPTER
14

Managing Change and Improvement

Managing change and improvement is for most of us more difficult and more challenging than maintaining a process or function. From my own perspective it is also more fun. A manager's creativity is called upon to manage change. This is partly true because of our mixed feelings about change. The fact that change can mean growth and improvement is often offset by the fear of leaving behind something that has worked. Managing change is a challenge too because it requires a vision, an image or a projection of a different and possibly better condition. To gain participation in change one of the manager's functions is to help each person create a feeling that there is something in it for them. The payoff may be the elimination of a hurt or the achievement of some new desired state. Fundamentally, organizations and people change when:

- they hurt, are uncomfortable, or perceive a difference between internal goals and what is happening
- they are forced by external circumstances which create the need to change
- they perceive that to maintain the status quo is to lose and they place a high value on winning
- they place a high value on the projected or new condition that will result from change
- the risks of change are perceived to be within the range of tolerance
- the change process can be made reasonably comfortable
- they are no longer forced by climate, customers, or friends to maintain the old position (reduction of resistance to change)
- they find a climate of acceptance and support for change from other people (increase of acceptance)
- they have experienced positive results from prior changes

As we explore the change process and the role of the manager, the foregoing list should be helpful. As we review activities for aiding change, each approach should deal with one or more of the categories just listed as necessary for change. For example, in dealing with the mid-life crisis, a transition that, if successfully managed, leads to growth, several of the categories may be involved in the support of the process.

For some people the mid-life crisis actually hurts; and therefore, they are motivated to do something to reduce the pain. Another part of the mid-life crisis is growth, which is necessary to manage one's way through the transition. This growth is represented by the perception that maintaining the status quo is to lose. Improving the comfort in the change process, another item in our list, is supported by activities like counseling and career workshops. Successful aid to the person in a mid-life crisis period often combines activities that make it OK to change an item in the list, and activities that provide support for changes which the person initiates.

Organizational change has all the characteristics of personal change, as well as the additional complexities of the group and the organization. Many forces in both the group and the organization tend to support the status quo, because it represents the known, the safe situation, and because of group norms, unwritten rules, values, and the difficulty of communication within a group. Resistance to change in the organization is also reflected in the desire for independence in a system of interdependence and in each group's need to defend its boundaries. Still further organizational resistance to change is imbedded in the lack of trust of the other party or group's motives. Suspicion about the motives of the person pressing for change gives rise to much debate about when and how to press for change in the organization.

The Preconditions for Change

The recognition of discomfort, of reduced success, however measured, or the expectation of a reduction in future success, or a very strong goal motivation are typical preconditions. Simply put, the need for change must be felt. The person who wishes to create change must, therefore, start by identifying and intensifying the signals that indicate a need for change. This is relatively easy to do when the signals reach a crisis level. Like people, many organizations respond in a crisis mode. An example might be a significant loss of customers and the related profit. A human resource example in the organization might be a strike, a concrete indication of failure in employee relations. An individual example might be the loss of a job. Each of these crises can represent the precondition for change. A crisis makes the organization or the individual vulnerable to change.

The manager's first responsibility in change management is to anticipate the need for change—beat the crisis. But anticipation without the ability to translate and communicate the perception of the need is of little use. Therefore, after perceiving the impending need for change, the manager must convince others of the reality and inspire action. Successful organizations and, by association, successful managers are those who can create the preconditions for change and use them to motivate action.

In the field of human resource management, no creation of preconditions for change is as challenging as the sensing that a currently successful organization must change what it is doing in order to maintain and extend success, for example, the need to change organizational and management practices to maintain vitality. To be motivated to action, management must become convinced that the continuation of today's practices will not bring success tomorrow. Once management becomes convinced, they must design appropriate changes and enlist the support of everyone in the organization in implementing them. The first level of resistance comes from the fact of today's success. Why should the organization give up the practices of success? The second level of resistance to such a change comes from the conflict between short-term and long-term performance measures. Most managers are measured by short-term budgets, schedules, and product or service specifications. Yet maintaining vitality requires investing some of today's energy in preparing for tomorrow. This requires that the manager be willing to take a decrease in effectiveness and a loss of production today in exchange for tomorrow's capability. The level of belief in tomorrow's predicted failure must be very strong for a manager to take this risk. Yet all commitment to investment in increasing employee capability is based on the belief that we must sacrifice today in order to assure tomorrow's success.

What are the ways of creating a crisis that stimulates action when no immediate crisis, of the type to which managements respond, exists? What is required is to amplify or enhance small feedback signals, which can be identified, and extend the feeling of what they portend in a believable way. For example, organizations experiencing an increase in voluntary employee turnover (resignations) can be convinced they need to take action to prevent further increase in loss of people with potential. If people are choosing to leave, there must be reasons. One way to make the crisis real would be to interview those who are leaving to find out what aspects of the work environment are causing them to make the decision to leave. This data, properly presented, may be used to promote action. If, for example, those leaving say they are doing so because they see no long-term growth opportunities, or because they feel they cannot affect the direction of the organization, or because they feel they have worked inordinately long for promotion, something must be done about career management. These employee responses could occur because no one demonstrated the organization cared about these people. This is a meaningful reason for change. But to use it, there must be a desire on management's part to retain valuable human resources. If management believes they can always hire others, highlighting these incidents will not create a sufficient precondition for change. The manager who wishes to create change must therefore pick real feedback, but the data must represent an aspect about the business which others feel is important.

In maintaining the vitality, the power to be successful tomorrow, of scientific and technical organizations, some have used the increasing age of the professional population as feedback on which to base action. Their thesis is that technical creativity peaks at around age thirty-five and therefore an average age of forty for professionals means that there is organizational crisis. The challenge to the manager creating change becomes one of translating this supposed loss of creativity into a positive human resource improvement action. In many organizations this fear of lost creativity has been used to sell investment in continuing education, an investment in change. Incidentally, although I too have used this argument, I do not believe professional productivity has to or should fall off with increasing age. Although it is more difficult than selling increased education, this argument should be used to improve the quality of work life so that the work, not supplementary education, creates continued development of capability. That productivity measures like patent production can be shown to fall off with an increased average age is true. That increasing age of the professional causes a reduction in productivity does not have to be true.

One of the most powerful preconditions for organizational change is increasing costs. These can be demonstrated in measures that management understands. Dollar figures tend to be viewed as real. The challenge here is to turn this loss of effectiveness into motivation for positive change, as opposed to typical cost cutting. It is generally much easier, for example, to sell a change to the use of a cheaper material in the product than it is to sell a change in the way people work or are integrated into the organization's purpose. The cheaper material change appears real and is easier to understand than an innovative change in work organization that harnesses the employee's decision-making capability. Demonstrating the difference requires contrasting the short-run measures with the longer-run developmental improvement.

Figure 9 describes the steps in making organizational change and shows the manager's functions. The diagram starts at the top with preconditions for change. These exist all the time. However, in order to motivate people to make changes, these must be identified and focused so that the improvement is perceived as worth the risk and effort. This is generally the function of the manager or in some cases a change agent. After it becomes evident a change could be valuable it is necessary to involve appropriate people, usually those involved in the change, in planning it and deciding how to implement it. After implementation, it is necessary to assess the results and to feedback evidence of success in order to sharpen the impact of the change.

Who, What, Where, and How

Assuming that you as the manager have uncovered a precondition for change and improvement, and assuming that you can translate this into a real hurt, who should do what, and where should change start? George Farris wrote an article in *Organizational Dynamics* entitled "Chickens or Eggs: Which Comes First?" which expresses the first part of this dilemma. He suggests that in the common situation, the employee is waiting for the manager to demonstrate what he or she wants and will reward change and improvement. And on the other wide, the manager is waiting for the employee to demonstrate the extra effort or ingenuity that is the ingredient for change.

With a reasonably mature work group which seems desirous of operating at an adult level, the place to start is with group identification of problems. Such a group is open to participation and, provided they can see some personal gain as well as organization gain, they are normally motivated in favor of improvement. With this group some of the group process ideas growing out of organization development are undoubtedly useful. In this case the group determines what to change, how, and when. With a heterogeneous group or a group that is immature and dependent and generally desirous of structure and limits, the task falls more heavily on the manager. In this case the manager must first introduce the need for change, sell or persuade the group that change can be beneficial, and then personally introduce the change in a gradual fashion. The manager must

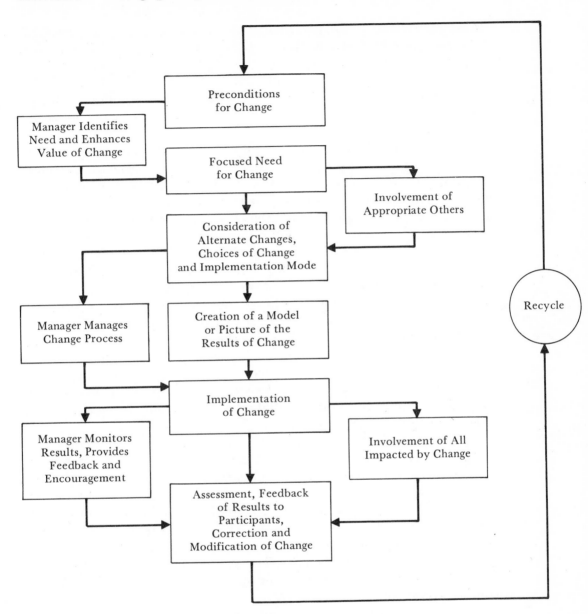

Figure 9. *Managing Change*

219

be very conscious of how it is going, that is, listening for employee feelings and quick to reward cooperation and achievement under the new work form. The spirit of experiment, of a special role for the group, can often be used as an additional motivating methodology. Even in the case of a dependent immature group, the manager should be responsive to learning and growth and provide for greater employee participation as the group becomes ready.

In the two foregoing groups the change or improvement is contained within the group function. In interdependent organizations this is seldom true. Many changes involve reestablishing or changing boundaries between groups and functions to provide for better control and wholeness of function. Some organizational changes actually require elimination of functions or groups. In these cases it is necessary to enter the organization above the group or department level. Here a useful technique is often to start by making a survey. The survey, a collecting of issues, feelings, and problems, has the function of defining the challenges, sharpening the focus on the preconditions. It can be made by insiders or a consultant. Often the consultant, because of fresh perspective, can see and describe what is happening more clearly. Once the survey exists, the ususal next step is to create a task or change committee from the several parts of the organization affected. The committee should be made up of people with sufficient power and authority to decide on and implement change. This committee should function as an adult group, deciding what to change, how to change, and when to change.

It is usually desirable to have a catalyst, process observer or, if you will, change agent as part of the committee. This person, who should not have a position to support or defend in the current organization, can be helpful in assisting the committee to navigate rough spots. He or she can often help by feeding back to the committee its own actions for analysis and improvement or learning as the problem-solving process goes on. Often, too, this person can help by assisting in documentation and establishing agreements and schedules. This process-aid person may be from a neutral part of the organization and may or may not be paired with an outside consultant.

Another place to start change is at the top of the organization. Types of improvements, implemented at the top, most usually start with one or more top executives defining a challenge or problem. At this point the problem identification may be clarified by asking an outside consultant to view it and aid the top management in addressing it. Problem definition may also be moved ahead, where a mature, cooperative top-management group exists, by going off into a retreat, planning, or problem-solving session. Effective management teams use this process regularly. Usually they come back with a mutually agreed upon agenda for change and some follow-up program to assure that changes are implemented.

We have discussed entering the organizational system at three levels: (1) at the department or group level, (2) at a multidepartment or multigroup intermediate management level, and (3) at a top-management level. Which level is appropriate depends on the organizational culture (what has worked in the past), the nature of the challenge, and the role of the person clarifying the challenge. Thus the level of entry addresses the who and the where. The what is addressed by the nature of the crisis, or created crisis, and the committee or group process which sets out to solve it.

The techniques so far discussed are direct and frontal. A less direct and longer-term technique that can be used alone or in combination with those discussed should also be mentioned. Through the use of an educational program it is possible to sow seeds which if properly nurtured, will flower into new values and goals and thus affect the capability of introducing future change. For example, in one organization where I worked, one of the changes which needed to take place was to move employees toward a more adult, less dependent role. Two types of educational programs were used to lay the foundations for this change. The first was an educational program designed for the employee that improved knowledge of the organization and established the expectation that employees could in many ways manage themselves. Career management is an example of the expected self-management that was introduced. Second, the organization inserted into management development programs modules or elements which introduced the manager to a more independent role for the employee. Thus, employee and manager were both exposed to the new expectations of shared responsibility. Later, when new policies or programs were introduced that built on this concept of shared responsibility, there was a readiness on both sides. Even before the change was introduced, many managers and employees experimented on their own and created a more open exchange and sharing of responsibility, both for managing day-to-day activities and for managing careers. This section has emphasized the need to create a need, an openness, a readiness for acceptance before embarking on implementing change. Once the need is established, the culture of the organization and its level of adult behavior set the stage for who, where, and how.

A Model

One of the techniques that is helpful in identifying the characteristics and values of the proposed changed condition is a picture. To make the goal of change desirable we have discussed the creation of the need. The need or hurt pushes us into change. By contrast, the creation of a picture, or a model, works at the other end of the change process. The picture makes the new or desired condition understandable and perhaps real. The model attracts or pulls us into change. Once it becomes real the change has the opportunity to become desirable in our minds. Many people do not have the understanding to create their own picture, so the manager of change should be a creator of pictures of tomorrow. In this sense, the science fiction of the thirties which made landing on the moon seem possible also made it desirable and helped to motivate us to try.

One of the ways this concept of model is used in organizational change has to do with physical layout, office equipment style, color and space treatment. When an organization is anticipating a change of facilities, the architect is often asked to produce a model in the form of drawings or even a mock-up of a room and its facilities. In this way, new arrangements can be experienced and modified. The desirability of the

SINCE i've STARTED JOGGING, i've NOTiCED THAT AGING SEEMS TO SPEED UP THE SLOWING DOWN PROCESS !!

Tom Wilson

©1978 Universal Press Syndicate 10/7

changed condition can be used both to help the group endure inadequate physical facilities and to work to support the change.

To picture, or model, a change in policy, organization, or mode of operation is more difficult than is physical change. The principle, however, is the same. The picture, or model, can help in communicating the desirability of the changes and in fine tuning the change because it makes it possible to discuss how things will operate. It may take the form of a flow chart, an organization chart with activity descriptions, a description of relationships, or even a computer program. In the latter case the value is obviously not in the pictorial aspects but rather in the fact that it is dynamic and can be run again under different conditions. In this same sense, where interrelations of people are involved one could role play the new relationships. This is a three-dimensional model, with actual personal interactions as part of the simulation.

The Nature of The Change

Changes should represent an improvement for people. That is, whether the change is to improve profit or service, we should look at improvement for people. What are the fundamental categories of change in organizations that represent improvement for people?

- any change that improves the process of and quality of matching people's needs and capabilities with the needs and capabilities of the organization
- any change that improves the benefits (in the broad sense) for work. These benefits may range from pay, working conditions, and hours to psychological incomes such as learning, sense of personal worth, or feeling of personal control
- any change that improves communications and understanding so that the operation can be carried out with more open, frank, honest, and adult interpersonal exchange
- any change that increases the opportunity for personal growth, learning, and individual development through work
- any change that tends to equalize the power balance between the individual and the organization, thus moving the organization toward an adult, rather than a dependent, environment

In the broad sense, all these categories of change improve the quality of work life. Quality, however, is an aspect that is in the eye of the beholder. It is necessary to manage human resource changes in ways which make it possible to make gains in areas that are highly valued by the participants. This suggests rightly that part of the change process requires that values and personal measures of work quality be elicited and discussed. When these issues get out in the open, it is easier to relate what is to be changed to what it will mean for the individual or the group. Motivation for change is strongest when both the organization and the individuals are working toward the same ends. So it is up to the manager to manage these forces, to gain congruence of purpose between the organization and the employees.

Job Redesign

For the individual, the place where the action is, where change can make a difference, is in the specific task assignments that make up the person's job. For this reason we will use the job as a focus for some specific suggestions of things to be changed.

The following aspects of jobs are amenable to change and may be important in improving psychic income, personal growth, and personal effectiveness. Not all aspects will be equally important to all individuals or to the same individual at different times or in different phases of life. Also, some jobs are not amenable to redesign because of technical and interface requirements.

The first aspect is *discretion,* or the ability to make decisions about one's work. This factor includes setting one's work goals, schedule, and priorities and having the freedom to determine how and when to do the job. To find out whether this aspect is satisfactory, you must ask the individual; it is the size of the difference between expectations and reality that determines the dissatisfaction. The smaller the difference, the greater the satisfaction. Satisfaction is thus dependent on individual outlook. Discretion can be changed whenever it is possible to allow the individual to take responsibility for decisions. As a general principle we can usually exert more decision-making responsibility than we feel we have. It seems to be a human trait that we set limits on ourselves that are more binding than those imposed by the organization. It is generally not possible to increase decisions when interrelationships mean that these decisions impinge on the freedom of others to control their work.

A second aspect of a job amenable to change is *learning,* or gaining new knowledge and skills. It has been identified as an important aspect of a job by those studying work satisfactions. In determining whether or not the job requires new learning, the manager is not totally dependent, as in the case of discretion, on the reaction of the individual. In this case it is possible for the manager to determine whether he or she feels learning is continually required. If not, the question is, Can the job be changed, increased in variety or scope, so that learning is required? If it can, job quality can be improved, but only if the employee is desirous of learning.

A third factor is *social purpose,* or whether or not the job and the organization contribute positively to the quality of life for all. This can be an important aspect of a job, often increasingly important as we as a population become more quality oriented. The mission of the organization generally sets the social purpose of the job; therefore, job redesign per se usually has little affect on this aspect. For example, those who work in hospitals may feel they have positive social purposes regardless of tasks. Moving from food services to the operating room, however, moves one into the purpose of the institution. But in an organization with a negative social purpose like munitions manufacture, there is little one can do to make the job positive. Little does not mean nothing, however. For example, a person who has a job associated with safety has a positive social purpose even in a munitions manufacturing facility.

Another factor is *wholeness.* This is an aspect of a job that is often amenable to change. That is, a good job is one that is large enough to be identifiable and provide the individual with identity. This factor may include responsibility and ability to participate in planning and overall goal setting. Wholeness must be viewed from both the perspective of the incumbent and the manager. The feeling of wholeness is something the incumbent must help to create. The manager can alter the job conditions to make the aspect of wholeness more probable. Much of the activity in job improvement focuses on this aspect. Having small teams building a whole truck or car instead of individuals working on an assembly line is one such experiment. Wholeness is something that can be redesigned either for the individual or for the work group.

Two other job factors we will use for examples are *closure* and *cycle time to feedback.* These are important aspects of a job for many people. Closure means having a definable end when things are over and one starts again. Cycle time is the time from task beginning to feedback evidence that something has been accomplished. One's personal sense of accomplishment, of doing something, is related both to the nature and timing of feedback. Some jobs provide physical evidence of accomplishment, such as seeing the paint on a wall; others provide subjective or diffuse evidence. In this case input from the job incumbent is very important because only that person can understand his or her tolerance for vague endings and lack of feedback. In one recent example a team of four people managed a process machine. From time to time, the manager would provide feedback saying, this is a good day or a bad day. The people were not able to relate what they did to what happened because of the vagueness of the measure and the delay in feedback. By rearranging the job and job measures so that the team always had real-time feedback of what was happening at the output of the machine, the job was improved. First, learning could take place because they could relate what they did to what happened to output. Second, they felt better because now they felt they were in control. Third, production went up. And fourth, they reported the job was more fun.

These are but a few of the aspects of a job that can be modified. Some other aspects include:

- opportunities for personal development through the job
- social support, the feeling of belonging to a team
- challenge, the amount of thought required
- variety, rotation of assignments
- recognition, the way in which the inidividual learns he or she has done well or poorly
- establishing a client or customer relationship that puts the employee in contact with those who benefit from the end result

SUMMARY

Managing change is one of the prime challenges for the manager and is one way in which the manager can make a measurable impact, create a positive and forward thrust.

Managing change first requires identifying a discomfort or need for change. Next, it requires translating that discomfort into a picture or a story that motivates people to need to change. If this can be considered motivation by pushing, the next step is motivating by pulling or attracting. It is to create an attractive picture, or model, of the new state.

Next, it is important to gain sufficient involvement, whether at group, intermediate, or top-management level, so that the people involved become owners of the problem and of the results of change. Part of this process requires identifying their needs such that they can see some improvement for themselves in the proposed change.

The elements of the organization or the job which should be considered for change in the human resource context are those that improve work quality for the individual. These aspects are generally in the eye of the beholder. Quality work for one person does not necessarily meet the next person's requirements. Aspects of the job which affect quality have to do primarily with:

- · the match of the individual to the job
- · the benefits the employee receives from work
- · the openness of communications and respect for the individual
- · the opportunity for personal development
- · the feeling of power associated with a position of adulthood with respect to the organization

Management of Change Checkup

1. How would you assess your organization's sense of urgency for changed methods, introduction of new equipment, new facilities, and improved relations between people and processes? Pick the most descriptive statement.   (   )

    a. In our organization change is the only constant. If one is away for a short period it is like returning to a new organization.
    b. Compared to most organizations ours is one with a lot of changes, and those who work in the organization learn to expect it and live with it.
    c. Our organization has some aspects that change relatively frequently and others that stay fixed. It is an organization of contrasts and of mixed signals on change.
    d. There are few significant changes in our organization, but those we have are dramatic and we all experience trouble with them.
    e. Most things in our organization stay the same. There seems to be little pressure for change.

2. What is your personal outlook toward change?

		yes	partially	no
a.	I enjoy personal change	( )	( )	( )
b.	Generally change must be forced	( )	( )	( )
c.	My outlook toward change represents an adaptation to organizational norms	( )	( )	( )
d.	Process or organizational change is generally for the better	( )	( )	( )
e.	I tend to lose through organizational change	( )	( )	( )

3. Which of the following styles of introducing organizational and process change is most descriptive of how you introduce change?   (   )
    a. Generally I go to the group with the need for changed methods and enlist their aid in planning a solution.
    b. I'm mixed in my style, sometimes participative, sometimes directive, sometimes avoiding change as I sense what is right.
    c. I generally tell the group that a change is necessary, define the change, and expect them to go along with my direction.
    d. Generally I rely on others to introduce change, but I work to aid in the process.
    e. I simply avoid making changes.

4. What is your score card on introducing change? Pick the most applicable statement.   (   )

    a. I regularly and successfully introduce change.
    b. I have recently successfully introduced change.
    c. I can identify changes in the distant past which I was responsible for implementing.
    d. I've not impeded change; I've worked with it when someone else initiated it.
    e. I am resistive to change. I generally cannot bring myself to manage a situation even if it requires change in organization or process.

5. Which of the following statements best reflects your mode of sensing when a change is needed?   ( )

   a. I determine that a change is needed when measures of activity and productivity or measures of friction and problems demonstrate to me that we are becoming less successful and the usual corrections don't seem to work.
   b. My sense of when to make a change is primarily based on facts and measures, but there is some measure or feel which finally causes me to take action.
   c. I'm not sure and seem to have no clear pattern of sensing when change is needed.
   d. My sense of when to make a change is more related to feel than facts, but I believe I take both into account.
   e. My sense of when to make a change comes from some sixth sense, some gut feel, and does not seem to relate to specific measures that I can put my finger on.

6. There are several types of change that can improve operations in an organization. In thinking about your organization, rank the following from a high of 1 to a low of 5 as you feel they might be needed and effective in causing improvement.

   a. Invest in capital equipment and new facilities and services to amplify the energies of the people and increase their power.   ( )
   b. Invest in training, expanded work experiences, and rotation to increase the capabilities of the human resources.   ( )
   c. Change the organizational boundaries and responsibilities such that work is made more whole (forms more natural work units), provides feedback and possibilities for departmental control, and expands the impact of my group.   ( )
   d. Change the level and characteristics of participation in management to include greater delegation of responsibility and decision making to the group, even to the extent of eliminating a layer of management.   ( )
   e. Change the nature and character of person-to-person communication, especially about goals and process, moving the organization toward more open, adult, and less defensive communication.   ( )

7. Values motivate; therefore, a method of introducing change is to deal with values. Think about the ways your organization and you attempt to establish values, and consider whether the following are candidates for change and a basis for motivating organizational change.

	candidate for improvement	don't know	generally good
a. Values can be established by policy and practice.	( )	( )	( )
b. Values can be established by the nature and communication of organizational goals.	( )	( )	( )
c. Values can be established by educational programs where employees gain new goals and understandings.	( )	( )	)

d. Values can be established through reward and recognition systems.   (   )   (   )   (   )

e. Values can be established by the beliefs and actions of a dynamic effective leader.   (   )   (   )   (   )

8. Which of the following statements most nearly represents your experience with, and feelings about, job design, job enlargement, and job enrichment?   (   )

a. I feel job design is a powerful way to introduce change, and I've been successful in enlarging and enriching jobs and gained significant improvements.

b. I feel job design and redesign is a powerful technique, and I've been successful in selected areas.

c. I feel job design and redesign is a powerful technique, but I've not tried it and know little about how to do so.

d. I believe there may be some value for some people in job redesign, but my attempts have been limited.

e. I don't feel job design is particularly useful in my type of activity, or I've tried it and been quite unsuccessful.

Ideas for Action: Improving Your Ability to Manage Change

something
to try

1. Start by improving your personal management of change. First try a *small* personal change and keep track of your feelings, the reactions of others, and all the techniques that seem to help. See my book, *Personal Vitality* (Addison-Wesley, 1977) for suggestions.   (   )

2. Talk with your manager to jointly identify a need for change or an aspect of organizational discomfort. Work together to devise a way of creating an understanding of the need and motivation for participation on the part of the involved parties. Assess the effectiveness of your plan by periodic review.   (   )

3. Work with the organization human resource professionals to devise a measurement or survey device such as an attitude survey to be used as a base for opening up a discussion and consideration of change which will improve work conditions and employee satisfaction.   (   )

4. Hold a group meeting with the purpose of listing, without negative comment, all the problems everyone can identify. Then use the group to sort through the problems and pick those of highest priority for action which can be addressed by the group. Work with the group to develop an action plan. Implement the change and then convene the group to analyze how it's going and what might make it go better.   (   )

5. Invite a consultant, internal or external, to make a review and help you identify aspects of inadequate functions which are candidates for change. Devise and sell a program for introducing the necessary changes.   (   )

6. Try working with an employee or an employee group on the redesign of a job or jobs using the job redesign worksheet below.   (   )

7. Change in some cases is not permanent but represents variety. Variety can provide stimulation for the individual who needs variety. Make a survey in your organization about how people feel about the amount of variety of activities. Work with the group and individuals to achieve a better match on variety.   (   )

8. An important aspect of improvement is outlook and expectations. That is, we set the stage for improvement. Try a deliberate plan of expecting improvement and announcing your expectations in a variety of ways.   (   )

9. The next time you need to sell or introduce a change, try creating a model or picture of the new situation as a means of aiding in communication.   (   )

10. Consider trading positions with another manager for a short time as a means of forcing yourself to take a look at the organization from a different perspective. Use this changed perspective as a way of identifying needed change.   (   )

231

Job Redesign Worksheet

It may be useful to modify the following aspects of a job. Changing these aspects may improve effectiveness, psychic income, and personal growth. Not all aspects will be equally important to different individuals or to the same individual at different times or different phases of life. Also, some jobs are not amenable to redesign because of technical and interface requirements. Use this as a checklist and a way of discovering some of the aspects which can and need to be changed. Use it as a basis for discussion with the employee in the job.

1. Discretion, or the ability to make decisions about one's work, includes setting work goals, schedules, and priorities and having the freedom to determine how and when to do parts of the job. Does the employee feel he or she now has freedom to control the job? Does the employee feel he or she would be motivated by increased freedom to control the job? If not, what changes would improve it? Can we make these changes?

2. Learning, the requirement to gain new knowledge and skills, has been identified as an important aspect of a job. Does this job require continual learning? What would have to change to increase the learning requirement? Does the employee feel additional need to learn would be positive?

3. Social purpose, or whether or not the job and the organization contribute positively to the quality of life, may be an important aspect of a job. Is this issue important to the employee? If it is, is it satisfactory? If not, is there a way to improve the sense of social purpose?

4. Wholeness is another aspect of a job which is important and sometimes amenable to change. That is, a good job is one which is large enough to be identifiable and provide the individual with identity. How does this job rate on this aspect? How does the employee feel about it? Can and should it be changed?

5. Closure and cycle time to feedback are important aspects of a job. Closure means being able to bring the task to a definable end. Cycle time is the time from beginning the task to feedback (evidence) that something has been accomplished. One's personal sense of accomplishment, of doing something, is related both to the nature and timing of feedback. For example, some jobs provide physical evidence of accomplishment, such as seeing paint on a wall; others provide subjective or diffuse evidence. How does the employee feel about these aspects? Does he or she find satisfaction with the nature of accomplishment which is possible? Should we and can we consider change?

6. Growth and leading somewhere for many are important aspects of a job. Growth is being able to do something tomorrow you cannot do today. Leading somewhere means providing a base for greater challenge and responsibility. How does the employee feel about this job and his or her growth with respect to it? Is there something which can or should be done to change this aspect of the job?

7. Social support defines the relations with other people which contribute to the feeling of belonging and of having stimulating, pleasant relationships. Is there social support of quality on this job? How does the employee feel about it? Is there a way to change this aspect of the job?

8. Challenge, or the aspect of a job which stretches and demands application of one's capabilities and energy, is important. Does this job provide the right kinds and amount of challenge for the employee? Should this factor be changed? If so, how?

9. Variety, or the change in kinds of activity, can be important in stimulating personal growth and keeping one interested and involved. Does this job provide sufficient variety for the employee? Can the character and amount of variety be changed?

10. Enrichment is the vertical loading of a job. That is, enrichment adds higher level responsibilities and activities. It can be considered as the depth of a job. How does the employee feel about the depth of the job? Can and should this aspect be improved?

11. Enlargement of a job can be considered the horizontal loading of a job. It is equivalent to breadth. How does the employee feel about the span of the job? Can the span of activities be changed to improve this job? Should it?

12. Recognition, or the way in which one gains positive feedback for accomplishment, is important. How does the employee feel about recognition? How and by whom is accomplishment recognized on this job? Can and should the form and amount of recognition be modified?

13. Matching the individual to the job is important. The individual's interests, skills, and knowledge, for example, should be matched to the requirements of the job. Good matching is transitory, and perfect matching might stifle growth. However, poor matching is frustrating and provides stress. How are the individual and the job matched on all the needs and capabilities which are important to this individual and important to the organization? Can it be improved? Should it? How?

CHAPTER
15

Elements of The Career Management Process

The Manager's Role

Career Counseling Interview

Rocks and Shoals

Family Careers

Career Management and
Planning

Until the late sixties, the general belief was that career decisions were made early in life and cemented by education and experience. The one life, one career imperative held sway over our thinking. Now the era of multiple careers is upon us. With it comes the need to develop techniques and devices to aid us in career management and planning. With it comes the need to teach and train people in techniques that make career transitions easier and fruitful. With it comes the need for the individual to assume career management responsibility and for the manager to assume career counseling and assistance responsibility.

Career planning includes all of the processes necessary to decide on a direction, a theme, for one's career and on the many jobs that make up the career. Unlike the popular impression, it does not generally mean choosing a particular job or position but rather a general direction that can be useful, growth oriented, and fulfilling for a period of time. The processes of career planning include some form of self-assessment of interests, skills, goals, and values and how one is doing. Planning also includes the assessment of opportunities and the establishment of goals and action plans. Career management includes career planning, often thought of as a one-time event, and the making of the multiple decisions about direction, personal change, and the relevance of opportunities. Career management is a constant process while career planning is best done periodically when some change makes reassessment desirable.

The purposes behind the increasing interest in our times in career management are both personal and organizational. From a personal perspective using some of the career management processes has the potential for improving your fit with your career and your job. Improved fit should mean greater opportunity to pursue your goals, utilize your capabilities, enhance your growth, and develop and improve your sense of satisfaction from work. Since our values, interests, and needs change with our phase of life, the advent of adult career management has made it more acceptable for individuals to change, to be responsive to their needs, and thus increase fulfillment. From the organization's perspective, adult career planning and management has the potential for improving the use and effectiveness of human resources, thus improving attitudes about work and the general work environment. All these factors should contribute positively to the achievement of organization goals.

This is a difficult chapter because you must read it at two levels. First, because you have a career, it is necessary to read it in the first person. You and your career are what we are talking about. Because this book is written for managers, you need to read it on a second level—as a manager. When we suggest, that the individual should engage in self-assessment, it is therefore appropriate to think about your own self-assessment and how you as a manager can help someone else in the self-assessment process.

Elements of The Career Management Process

Asking yourself tough questions about values, needs, and interests is not easy. Career planning and management is work. Facing up to what you do well and what you do not do well is not easy. Career planning and management is a personal process, and implementing it should be a voluntary and personal choice. For many people it is tough and has some aspects of discomfort. This is true because assessment of self means asking difficult questions, questions we find it easier not to address or easier to be slightly untruthful about. Part of this discomfort comes from a feeling that self-interest is somehow bad or at least not socially acceptable. Part comes from the understanding that if we come up with different answers we will be faced with making changes, and change can be uncomfortable. Another part comes from the fact that most of our experiences and training teach us to answer questions as we believe someone else wants them to be answered. The early recipient of the answers was a parent. Later it was a teacher and still later a boss. All you have to think about to verify this expectation is to think of the teacher, parent, or manager asking, "What is it you want to do?" Most often in your experience, I suspect, this has meant that the teacher, parent, or manager had an agenda to suggest and you felt you should come up with or agree with that agenda rather than really express your desire. Now, the person who needs the answer is you. And you and I as managers need both to face this question ourselves and to help the individual employee face this reality. A manager must have faced these hard questions himself or herself in order to help someone else.

The first element of the career management and planning process is sensing the need to engage in the process. Some people literally believe careers take care of themselves. They don't. Managing a career requires becoming sensitive to your feelings, inner drums, and sensitive to feedback from your environment that may suggest that all is not well or some change may be necessary. Some of the kinds of feelings that suggest reassessment are boredom, vague feelings of uneasiness with the job or work environment, a sense that you are having to put out more energy to do the job than you used to, a feeling of falling behind or increased job pressure, an actual failure or a vague sense of impending need to change. These are but a few of the internal or personal signals. External signals may be new organizational plans that portend the end of your assignment, changes in family that bring about changed need for income, changes in technology that create the need for new knowledge and new skills, changes in your performance as appraised by your manager, and changes in the organization of work. Again these are but some of the events that may precipitate the need to reassess career. Unfortunately, it is relatively easy for the individual to deny or miss these signals. The status quo is usually comfortable; and change, threatening. For the manager the challenge of signals for change is multifaceted. First, he or she may be getting these signals relative to his or her own career. This can affect the manager's ability to be helpful and supportive to the employee receiving career change signals, and it can also affect the quality of the manager's general management ability. Second, for the employee the manager is often the creator or transmitter of the signal that establishes the need for reassessment. Third, part of the manager's human resource function is to counsel and assist the employee. And last, these signals for change may literally run counter to the pressures for production, for meeting schedules, and for getting the things done, all of which are counted and measured as performance.

After sensing the need for assessment, next comes the actual assessment process. What is there to be assessed? The signal, the input, the feeling, or the feedback must first be assessed. What is the quality and reliability of the signal? What does it mean? The same signal, for example, having to work harder to perform at the same level, could mean that something in the work has changed, and the change was missed, that the person has failed to grow in job capability, that the individual's interest and motivation is declining, or that there is some real change in physical capability such as a normal change in eyesight. Assessment then means finding out what the signal means. Assessment also means looking at one's interests, values, needs, goals, rate of growth, satisfaction from work, level of utilization, and other aspects of how life and career are measuring up. Assessment also means an outward look at the world of work, at alternatives and opportunities. This can be thought of as a sort of radar search of the organization to determine whether one's job can be redesigned, modified, to increase satisfaction, or whether new organizational needs provide an opportunity for personal job change, growth, and increased satisfaction. If the organization context does not seem to provide sufficient opportunity, then the outward opportunity search should expand beyond the organization.

The manager has several roles in assessment. These roles include acting as a catalyst to help the individual face the tough questions as an inquisitor to assure the questions are asked, as a mirror to reflect back for a more thorough review, and as a reality tester to question whether the thoughts represent a "pie in the sky." In these ways the manager can enhance the quality, depth, and thoroughness of the self-assessment process. It is important that the manager supplement, not take over, the process. The individual must be responsible for the choices; if the manager takes over the process, the individual will find it easy to place responsibility on the manager's shoulders. The manager, through providing feedback on job performance and a different perspective of the organization and its needs, may also provide new data for the assessment process.

The next element in career management is giving oneself permission to change, based on the new direction determined by assessment. We set limits, we establish rules, and, in response to society's values, we establish a range of acceptable actions. If as a result of our assessment it appears that some change in ourselves, in our job, in our organizational role, or even in career or work organization might bring increased rewards, we have to step up to make it acceptable to change. Sometimes, for example, these changes mean giving up status or position or even apparent acceptability among our friends. Sometimes these changes mean costs in energy devoted to study, in reduced or loss of income, and in apparent loss of security. Giving ourselves permission is personal and private. The major contribution of friends, family, and managers is their acceptance of change in us. No one can give us our own permission to change. There is an important message here for us as managers. We can help in providing an environment where it is OK to change. We cannot and should not allow ourselves to be put in the position of authorizing the change for someone else.

Setting or establishing a new goal is the next step in the process. If the reassessment ends in a need to change and we give ourselves permission, then we must establish a new goal. This is a dual process of giving up, letting go of old goals, and establishing new ones. Goals should be at two levels. They should provide a general direction or theme for the distant future and specific steps in the near future. The most powerful and useful goals are ones we can realize within at most a year or two. Too distant goals have a characteristic of changing in value and character by the time we can arrive there. A useful goal is specific, next step oriented, and time oriented. A useful goal has action steps that we can talk about now. The goal may be to redesign the job we are on so that it creates more positive return on our investment of energy, time, and interest. It may be to prepare ourselves with further education or experience for the next step. It may be to change our experience and increase our learning rate by actual change of job or roles. Goal setting is again a personal process. But here the manager can be of more help. He or she can provide interpretation of the framework and the organization in which it can be achieved. While the manager can help, however, he or she should never take over; the goals must be owned by the individual.

The next element of career management is matching the person with the assignment or job. A perfect match, which is both undesirable and probably unachievable, is not what we are after. There is something in the imperfection of the match that adds to excitement and striving. Matching is the iterative changing process of fitting our needs and capabilities with the opportunities or the needs and capabilities of the organization. Good jobs, and thus good careers, are designed, not found, because matching requires change both on the part of the individual and the job. That good jobs are designed can be confirmed by asking any group of people about their best assignments or jobs. What you will find is that they believe and feel they influenced them, they designed them. Matching, therefore, is the creative process of fitting and adjusting yourself and the organizational opportunity. If you can achieve a situation where the pursuit of the organizational goals brings you closer to your goals you have achieved a good fit. If you can achieve a situation where using your skills meets the skill requirements of the organization, you have achieved a good fit. If you can achieve the situation where the capabilities of the organization for recognition and reward meet your needs for recognition and reward, then you have achieved a good fit. The manager's role in achieving job/person fit was covered in chapter seven; however, a brief recapitulation may be helpful.

In matching, the manager has the power and the responsibility to vary the nature and requirements of the assignment. He or she has the responsibility to elicit and listen to the goals, needs, and capabilities of the employee and to work with the individual for the best fit. In working to achieve job/person fit the manager is motivated both by the interests of the organization for productivity and his or her human resource management responsibilities. The manager can improve the match between employee and organization and thus increase the rewards for both individual and organization. In doing so the manager gains a reward, too—a sense of accomplishment, of contributing to the employee's growth and satisfaction.

Last, an element of career management is action. It is well and good to do self-assessment, to give oneself permission to change, and to establish new goals, but this is not enough. One must step off the diving board. Nothing will happen unless we take action. Taking action requires guts; it requires taking a risk. Taking action occurs when we feel that the risk is worth the payoff. Taking action requires support from the manager, even though the initiative must come from the individual.

Understanding of the overall process for both the individual and the manager may be improved by reference to Figure 10. The steps taken by the individual are shown progressing down the middle. Note that three points have been designated where the process can be aborted if the individual does not feel the cost or risk is worth the projected improvement. The manager's points of influence and involvement in the process are shown down the right-hand side of the diagram. The career counseling session is voluntary. Although it should be available, the employee should choose to use it.

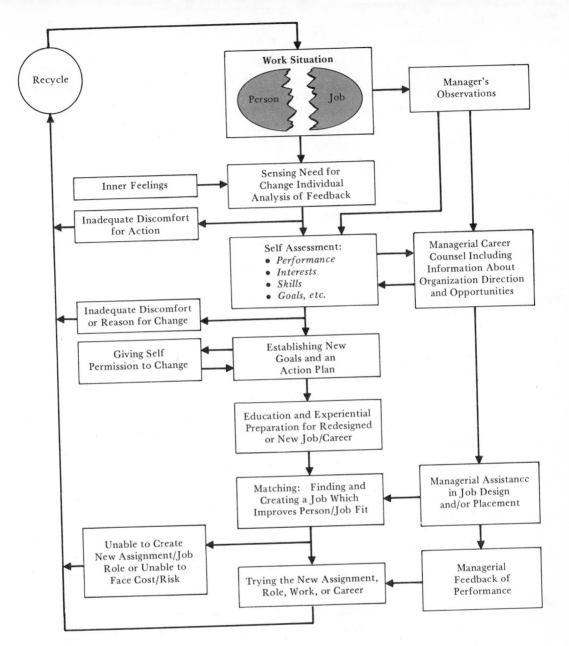

Figure 10. *The career management process.*
The diagram illustrates the career management process with the individual's responsibilities in the center. The steps are: sensing the need for change, self-assessment, establishing new goals, giving self permission, gaining educational and experiential preparation for change, matching, and trying the new assignment, role, or career. There are three points where the person may abort the process if the risks and costs do not seem to be warranted by the improvement expected. The manager's functions are defined on the right side of the diagram; of the four managerial functions only one is voluntary, by choice of the individual, and that is to ask for career counsel.

The manager's involvement in the career management process is one of reducing the risk and providing support and comfort. All change is threatening, but the manager can reduce the threat. All change involves risk, but the manager can reduce the risk. All change requires accepting new values, but the manager can help the employee to see these new values. The manager's role is not to push the person off the diving board but rather to reassure the individual that if something untoward happens in the new change he or she will be there to help. It is with respect to increasing the feeling of safety in taking actions for change that the manager has the greatest value.

The Manager's Role

Although we have emphasized the roles as we went along, it is worthwhile to recapitulate. The individual must supply the energy. The manager can make the process seem safer and more rewarding. The individual must sense the need for reassessment and change. The manager can accentuate and highlight the need. The individual must do the reassessment. The manager can be an aid in the process. The individual must give self permission to change. The manager can set an environment where change is acceptable and provide support in the change process. The individual must set new goals. The manager can provide both a realistic test of these goals and help set up the conditions for achieving these goals. The individual must actually initiate the action. The manager can create the opportunity for action and provide support and safety as the individual steps off the known and tried path into the open space of the unknown and change.

In summary, the manager's role in career management consists of:

· being an exemplar, a model
· establishing a supportive environment for personal development and change
· providing opportunity for career discussions
· providing information about the organization
· assisting in job design and redesign
· providing support for experiential and educational preparation
· providing feedback, reality testing
· letting the employee move on

Career Counseling Interview

An important vehicle for the manager in assisting the employee in career management and planning is the counseling interview. This may range from informal chats about job and career to a formal interview of several sessions. The manager should make it available. The employee should make the choice as to whether to use the manager's help.

The criteria for a good interview are as follows:

- The interviewer-counselor (manager) has a plan.
- The interviewee (employee) is invited in advance and plans for the interview.
- There is a clear purpose (objective) for the interview, and it is shared by both parties.
- The session is uninterrupted; the manager is able to give full attention and is unhurried.
- There is a frank, open, adult exchange of views and mutual trust and respect.
- The manager is a good listener, reflecting the feelings expressed by the employee.
- The manager fulfills the role of catalyst for enhanced employee understanding and does not prescribe answers.
- Sensitive personal topics, if discussed, are initiated by the employee, thus protecting employee privacy.
- The interview closes with agreement and an action plan.

Typical goals for the career interview are as follows:

- communicating organizational and managerial interest in the employee's development
- assisting the employee in taking personal responsibility for career management
- gaining an improved employee understanding of what he or she does well and gains satisfaction from doing
- exploring interests, capabilities, needs, goals, and alternatives
- establishing a basis for improving the current job or deciding upon the next step in an employee growth and development plan
- establishing an action plan as appropriate

For further discussion of the career management process and its elements from a somewhat different perspective, read my book, *Personal Vitality*

243

Workbook (Addison-Wesley, 1977), which discusses personal assessment, career management, managing change, and redesigning your job.

Rocks and Shoals

Every change that we make as individuals is not always for the better. Change involves risks for the individual and special risks for the manager. For the manager the first risk is that he or she will become the cause, the initiator, the responsible party. When as individuals we make mistakes we often try to pass off the responsibility to someone else. The manager is a prime target for this shift of responsibility in career management because he or she represents the organization. It is easy and sometimes comfortable, though not particularly useful, to blame our failure to gain positive results from change on the organization. In this case the manager is the organization. Managers can avoid being the scapegoat in all but the chronic cases by studiously putting the responsibility for choice on the shoulders of the employee. This is not easy because the employee is often trying to place the responsibility on the manager and because the clear, open, frank communication necessary for properly executed career change is more often the exception than the rule.

The second risk comes about because of the rapid rate of change and the manager's inability to control the future. In a high-technology organization, for example, often the time required to execute a career change is longer than the time cycle in which the organization can make changes in direction. For example, I have seen employees and managers commit to a three-month training program, both in good faith, only to see the organization change direction before the training program is completed. This leaves the employees feeling misled and prepared for a new opportunity that no longer exists. The result is a loss of management credibility. The employee loses faith in management.

The third risk is the difference between expectations and reality. Try as we will as managers, what the employee hears is often different from what we try to transmit. More than one of the employee grievances I have investigated and adjudicated have revolved around an employee assumption of organizational and managerial commitment that did not really exist. One of the most normal and frequent of these miscommunications has to do with the employee assumption about further education or training. Organizations are willing to invest in broadening or general education of employees for many and varied potential needs. Some employees tend to believe that education should always pay off in an improved job with increased status and pay. Thus, the employee frequently expects an organizational and managerial commitment to immediately and specifically use additional education. This is not always the case.

Still another rock or shoal has to do with possible inaccuracy, or in effect lack of realism, in the employee's reassessment process. This might be called the grass-is-greener phenomenon. Because the assessment process can be painful and inaccurate judgments are possible, the employee may come up with a plan for change that does not represent his or her true interests, needs, and motivations. When the employee executes the change, there is a big let down. The change does not meet expectations. Caught in this situation, it is easier for the employee to blame the organization then himself or herself.

Closely related to the last problem is the fact that the employee's change may be predicated on an ability to learn new skills or change activities that is not actually there. For example, an employee who is not receiving sufficient rewards from current work activity often seeks reward in craft activities. Craft activities are favorite new goals because they provide a strong sense of personal achievement. Yet, the percentage of the population that has the ability, the interest, and the commitment to achieve success in craft enterprise is considerably smaller than the percentage who believe they can.

These are but a few examples of the rocks and shoals of career management and planning. The responsibility for choices must clearly rest on the shoulders of the employee. At best the manager can be an interpreter, a translator of the organization's needs, and a catalyst or aid in the career management process.

Family Careers

As managers we must be sensitive to cultural and social changes that can affect the conduct of our roles in organizations. One of these changes is the emergence of the family career in a new form. Just as careers are becoming multiple, careers are shifting from being something most often attributed to the male to something everyone is entitled to and wishes to gain achievement through. The career of a woman as a wife and mother is not alone satisfying or enough. Even the career of the child, not historically seen as a career, is taking on new form. Thus we enter the era of family careers.

What is a family career? A family career is the blending of support of individual careers through the family unit. In a historic sense the farm was a family career. All members contributed to one enterprise. One modern aspect is what has been called the dual-career family. In such a family both husband and wife pursue separate careers and manage their careers in such a way that each person has the opportunity to achieve. One family I know has devised a system that, although not rigidly, provides each partner with a season of fruition. Thus for a period, the husband deliberately engineers his career to be secondary to his wife's and makes decisions that may not be the best for his career in order to give his wife a clear field to respond to her career directions. For another period, the wife does the same and deliberately makes it possible for her husband to respond to career changes and needs dictated by his career. On the surface this looks merely like self-sacrifice for the other. In the sense of the emerging family career, it need not be so. It is possible for each to gain a sense of accomplishment through the other's success as well as through their own. Certainly the pairing of some professions makes this easier than others. Professions that have short cycle times, like teaching for a year, make these shifts easier. When the husband's and wife's careers interests are related, it is easier than when they are distinctly different. This is primarily true because of the improved communication and understanding that is thus possible.

Just as husband and wife may share careers, so too can the family share a child's career. For example, a family may forego a career move in order to let their teenager finish high school in one school. This happens also when the teenager is supported in some sport or other interest by family contribution of time and energy. It may carry on into later life when the family provides the money or the actual energy and contribution to make a new business venture a success, or to support extensive graduate training.

For the manager the family career may affect what happens in the organization because he or she is personally involved. It may affect the ability to manage the work group or to provide career counsel and assistance because the employee is involved. The primary impact is that we as managers can no longer operate on the assumption that the individual we have in the group, the employee we manage, is *the* person with the career. We cannot make the assumption that our employee is the prime wage earner. We cannot make the assumption that status and salary alone will motivate change. We cannot make the assumption that the call, the need, of the organization will receive cheerful response. Gone are the days when you can call the employee in and say he or she has fifteen minutes to call his or her spouse to announce a change that involves increased pay, status, and responsibility, and relocation. The emergence of family careers in the context of our current working world has increased the complexity of human resource management.

SUMMARY

Career management and planning is a necessary part of our lives today because of the rapid and pervasive change of our times, and because we have entered the exciting era of multiple and family careers. The responsibilities of career management are shared between the employee and the manager. But there may be an unseen third party in the family. The tough part, facing up to the difficult questions of changing values, interests, and needs, and managing these in the context of the organization and the family, falls on the individual. The supportive part of being a catalyst, a mirror, and a reality tester falls on the manager.

For the individual the payoff of redesigning the job, replanning the career, and managing change can be increased growth, improved satisfaction, and a better life. For the organization the payoff can be increased employee commitment, improved effectiveness, and better use of the human resource. A better match between organization and individual should benefit both the individual and the organization.

Career Management Checkup

1. How are you doing in managing your own career? In order to be helpful to the employee, the manager should have his or her own career under control and should have experienced the pains and rewards of self-assessment and personal change. Choose the most appropriate response.   ( )

    a. I periodically reassess my career, create new goals, and take actions to create change and improvement.

    b. I have reassessed my career several times and been reasonably successful in taking charge and making change.

    c. I have sensed the need for reassessment and change but have been reluctant to invest the effort in reassessment and take the risks of change.

    d. I have not been sensitive to the need for change and feel quite comfortable in my job, career, and role. I have changed when required by the organization but with some minor sense of discomfort.

    e. I have responded to the call of the organization on demand without expressing myself or my needs. I have not taken personal responsibility for managing my career and life.

2. Which statement best expresses your understanding of what the organization expects of you?   ( )

    a. The manager carries the major role for career counsel and we should regularly have career-oriented discussions with employees and help them to grow to greater challenges and responsibility. This need is supported by forms and procedures.

    b. The manager is generally expected to provide career counsel for the employee, but it is not explicitly supported by a requirement or forms.

    c. Although I've never been told so directly, I believe I am supposed to provide career assistance to the employee.

    d. I don't believe the organization expects me to assist employees with their careers.

    e. The organization has no real interest in career development.

3. Which statement best expresses how you see your role in helping your employees in career management?   ( )

    a. I am an active participant in aiding them in their iterative process of reassessment, choice, and change.

    b. I have provided assistance in the matching of person and job in the context of my department or group but have generally not extended myself to help beyond that.

    c. I have been of assistance in reality testing, opportunity search, and counsel when the employee has taken the initiative.

    d.   I am reluctant to enter into the career management process because of the risks and feel unsure of my role, although I do try to help.

    e.   I deliberately avoid involvement and consider that this is a personal process in which I should take no active part.

4.   Which statement best expresses your feeling about your preparation for the role of the manager in career management?   (   )

    a.   I feel I have the information, the understanding, and the outlook necessary to be helpful.

    b.   I feel I have much of the information and the positive outlook necessary but desire greater support from the staff professionals and some additional training.

    c.   I feel inadequately prepared and experience a need for organizational support, training, and assistance.

    d.   I am at sea with regard to the manager's role in this process and need extensive help and support, including training.

    e.   I don't feel that the manager has a role as a career counselor and feel it should be left to professionals.

5.   Which statement best reflects your actual performance as a counselor and catalyst for career management with your group?   (   )

    a.   At least once a year I have a career-oriented interview with each of my employees, they make the choices for change, and we jointly create an action program where appropriate.

    b.   I have fairly regularly had career-oriented discussions with employees, but I have too little time because the timing is most often dependent on their request. Those we have are generally worthwhile.

    c.   I have had few career discussions and only at the insistence of the employee, but those I have had I consider reasonably successful.

    d.   I feel uncomfortable in the career-counseling role and so generally avoid it when possible. I have, however, had a few career discussions with employees, but consider them of limited value.

    e.   I have not had career discussions with employees becuase it is not a requirement and I don't feel prepared for the role.

6.   What areas do you need to improve in your career management assistance to your employees? (Rank in order of priority.)

    a. _____   training in career counsel and interviewing

    b. _____   a clear statement from management as to what is expected of me

    c. _____   a better understanding of the direction and goals of the organization

    d. _____   improved understanding and training in career management techniques

    e. _____   to get my own career and goals decided

    f. _____   counsel from my manager

g. ____ educational information for my employees
h. ____ opportunity information for my employees
i. ____ a career planning device or workbook for use by employees
j. ____ more time to deal with human resource issues
k. ____ career planning workshops and professional counseling assistance for my employees
l. ____ better, more challenging, growth-oriented work for my employees
m. ____ training in job redesign and work motivation

7. What is your greatest challenge in being helpful in careers? (Rank in order of priority.):

a. ____ to motivate the young employee to be interested in developing a career in our organization
b. ____ to deal with the obsolete, turned off, and overpromoted employee
c. ____ to find opportunities for growth in a no-growth organization
d. ____ to deal with the employee in the mid-life crisis or other major transition
e. ____ to deal with the ambitious, assertive person who wants more responsibility and challenge now
f. ____ to deal with the employee who is perfectly satisfied with the status quo
g. ____ to deal with the issues surrounding retirement
h. ____ to find opportunities and help employees get out of a shrinking organization
i. ____ to help employees cross almost impossible barriers between divisions or parts of the organization
j. ____ to keep from making career decisions for my employees

Ideas For Action: Improvements In Career Management

something
to try

1. Search out and use some career/life workbook to analyze your own career/life planning and management so that you become more familiar with the process and the feeling and stresses it creates. My *Personal Vitality Workbook* (Addison-Wesley, 1977) is a possibility. ( )

2. Enroll in a career workshop where you explore your own career goals and plans with a group of people. ( )

3. Hold a group or department meeting to encourage your employees to discuss needs, fears, and issues in career management. Out of this discussion experiment with some new actions in support of your employees' individual development. ( )

4. Read more on the topic of career planning and management so that you are more cognizant of current thinking and techniques. *Careers '79* (Vitality Associates) has a good annotated bibliography of career readings. ( )

5. Seek out the personnel professionals in your organization who have some understanding of the processes of career planning and management and explore with them what new initiatives you may take in your organization. ( )

6. Have a career interview with each of your employees and jointly prepare an action program where appropriate. ( )

7. Enroll in either an internal or an external educational program on career planning and management where you can learn the processes and prepare to be more helpful to your employees. ( )

8. For those of your employees who seem to be at career crossroads and need more assistance than you can provide find additional counsel or educational programs. ( )

9. Talk with other managers about the possibility of providing temporary assignments or at a minimum descriptive talks and visits to broaden your employees' understanding of other parts of the organization. ( )

10. Work with your management to clarify the organization's statements about its goals and future so you can provide a better picture of the context in which to plan a career. ( )

CHAPTER
16

Elements of a Strategy

Tactics

The Style That Is In You

The Style You Can Create

Developing Your Own Managerial
Strategy and Style

Your impact depends on you. Not only is it important to know who you are and what you believe; it is also important to have a strategy, a master plan. Your strategy represents your overall theme, your long-range goals, and your game plan. For example, do you see yourself primarily as an innovator, a controller of work flows, a counselor of employees, or as a decision maker? Your image of yourself represents your strategy and molds your style. Your strategy should reflect who you want to be and what you wish to achieve. It will also reflect your beliefs about people. Your strategy reflects your education, your experience, and the mission of the organization of which you are a part. Most of all, your strategy is your leadership outlook. The first secret about your managerial strategy is that you have one even if you have not thought it out or planned it. One you've thought out and chosen, however, is superior because it helps you to come across as sincere, credible, consistent, and aware of where you want to go and why. Even if an individual disagrees with the thrust, it is better to work with and for someone who has a considered strategy.

What do I mean by saying you have a strategy even if you have not consciously chosen it? In default, your strategy becomes what others interpret as your guiding theme. If the image you project is confusing, then they see your strategy as blurred. I suggest you turn right now to the checkup at the end of this chapter. This checkup will help you to look at yourself and see what the evidence is of your theme, your overall plan, your strategy.

Your strategy is a contributor to your tactics and style. That is, we usually choose action plans and management styles, interpersonal styles, and even dress styles that we believe support and enhance our overall goals. Our goals form the base for our strategy. Thus developing styles that support your strategy is necessary to improve the probability of achieving your overall goals, and to clarify the messages you send to your associates and subordinates. Style is important in successful management; it sets mood, the climate for acceptance or rejection. It is your interpretation of your strategy and represents your interpretation of your many roles. Your style is created not only by your goals but also by an interaction of your personalities, your self-images, and your images of the world. Your style is affected by the priorities and values you assign to your several roles. For example, a manager who views the teaching role as important will tend to act in accord with that image and develop a style that supports it. Style is also a product of experience, of being at home with yourself and your mode, and an ability to sense and get in touch with the environment. Above all your style should be yours because authenticity is a key input to successful management.

Although your style should be yours, other people play an important role in developing it. Modeling, trying out an approach used by a friend or associate, is a normal and ongoing approach to style development. We see this especially in children when we can tell who they were playing with just by their tone of voice or attitude. It is much harder to identify style modeling in ourselves. People vary significantly on their ability and desire to model. It is also probable that we do less of it as we grow in experience and assurance of who we are.

A primary element of style is interpersonal exchange. A secondary element is the way we interpret and transmit the goals of the organization. For example, one who has a game plan for increased power may bias organizational objectives in ways which increase his or her power. A third element is decison-making style. For example, the style associated with making decisions with a mathematical model is considerably different from that based on "gut" feelings. And a fourth element of style is how you implement action. This includes styles of delegation and participation, timing of action, and tactics.

Elements of A Strategy

A strategy is an overall plan, an all-encompassing plan, to achieve a broad future objective. As managers we have several objectives. Some may represent needs for personal achievement; others, our share of organizational achievement; and still others, our goals for the groups of employees we supervise. Both personal goals and organizational goals can set the tone or outlook for our relationships with our employees. So although this is a book about human resource management, the management of others, we must first examine personal and organizational goals to understand strategy and style.

Since personal goals are an input to our human resource management strategy we need some technique for categorizing personal goals and determining how they may influence the strategy. If your personal goal is to achieve a high income, you might adopt a strategy which maximizes the output from your employees. If your personal goal is to become known for your contribution to technological knowledge, you might adopt a strategy which maximizes the creative technical innovation in your group. If your personal goal is increased status and power in the organization, you might adopt a strategy of deploying your employees to increase your power and influence. These examples should demonstrate the relationship between your goals and your strategy in dealing with your employees.

Organizational goals also affect your human resource strategy and your managerial style. For example, an organizational goal which sets forth a positive human resource policy such as treating every employee as an individual and in a fair manner sets conditions which limit your degrees of freedom. Or an organizational goal of minimal manufacturing cost in a human intensive process will probably establish an environment of relatively low pay and high incentives for increased output. Such an environment puts brackets around, or limits, your personal human resource strategy if you are to be in tune with the organization. How to assess the organization climate is discussed in chapter two. Here, therefore, we will emphasize the design, execution, and measure of your impact.

After examining these inputs, your personal goals, and the organization's goals and policies as reflected in the H/R environment, you are ready to begin constructing your human resource strategy. A personal strategy should have as a minimum some of the following elements:*

Element	*Examples*
Work motivation: What beliefs about work motivation will I use as my operating strategy?	· People are achievement oriented. · People want to work because of interest in work. · People don't want to work but put in their time to get pay. · People want to grow through their work.

---

*It is probable that you may expect a combination of these and other examples. You may wish to add to the list and rank the examples in importance.

Element	*Examples*
Recruitment criteria: Where will I recruit for my group and what types of people will I seek?	· I will seek highly educated people because of their versatility. · I will seek only the qualifications needed for the specific job. · I will generally recruit outside the organization. · I will generally seek only those who have proven capability in the organization.
Training, education, and coaching: What will be my role in the growth and development of employees?	· I will utilize organizational programs but take no personal role in training. · I will try to teach through every assignment and every action. · I will create an environment where the individual takes personal responsibility for planning and executing his or her own training. · I plan to take no active role in education of employees but will focus on applying their current capabilities.
Group output goal: What do I want to create as the primary output of my group?	· I want us to be known for maximum quantity. · I want us to be known for the best quality. · I want the group to be outstanding and have a top reputation in the organization as measured by some organizational goal.

Element	*Examples*
Employee income goal (psychic and monetary): What satisfactions do I see as primary gains for the people in my group?	· I want them to gain in knowledge and skill. · I want them to earn the maximum income. · I want them to graduate quickly from the group. · I want them to work loyally and hard to support our group and feel satisfaction in the group accomplishment.
Operational style: What do I want to be the operational pattern and style of my group?	· Team self-management with sharing and mutual help. · Independent work with individual self-management. · Primary relationship to me as leader and director of work. · Interpersonal competition within the group as a primary aspect of the work environment.
Group/organization interface: How do I want my group to relate to the organization as a whole?	· I want it to be a strong team with primary loyalty to me and our group. · I want it to relate more strongly to the organization than to the department or subgroup. · This is not important, and I'll take what happens.

These elements and examples of types of answers are intended to be illustrative and are not presented with any value judgments. That is, although my underlying bias for work as rewarding, growth oriented, and vitality oriented and for climate as adult, open in communication, and participative must be clear by now, it is not my intent to impose a strategy, but rather to encourage each manager to deliberately and thoughtfully create one.

Creating a strategy means thinking through in some orderly fashion what you want to happen. The advantage gained is consistency and authenticity. Employees are sensitive to the manager who has a broad plan and a set of principles. Employees generally prefer such a manager to one whose decisions and actions do not fall into a definable pattern. In fact, from discussions and my own feelings I suspect that most of us would rather work for a predictable, definable manager with a strategy, even if we don't agree with all elements, than to work for a manager who has no central theme.

Tactics

Tactics can be understood best as your implementation actions. Tactics stand between your strategy and your style. Tactics are the game plan. Tactics are less affected by who you are and your image than either strategy or style. But they are not independent of strategy and style. Most importantly, your tactical approach reflects your understanding of what works for you in the organization.

In one organization where I have experience, the tactical approach often used is to create a crisis and then appear as the one who can save the organization. In that organization I was once counseled by my manager to create some crisis. His feeling was that my approach was not gaining recognition because I appeared to manage on an even keel. From his perspective I never had problems. I was not making a sufficient issue of the actions I was taking.

Effective tactics are a reflection of organizational expectations. Effective tactics are often dependent on one's organizational position and status. Thus a manager in a line operation which represents the central purpose of the organization will often find success through different tactics from the manager in a supportive role. Tactics are also dependent on your team's capabilities. Tactics which are dependent on technical expertise and acceptance of that expertise cannot, for example, be used by the manager with a team perceived to be weak in technology. Tactics which require a loyal team are inappropriate for the manager whose team is independent. Strategy, tactics, and style must fit the person, the organization, and the team.

The Style That Is In You

Early in my career I ran across an executive whose style caused others to fear him because he was so blustery. He literally shouted people out of his office. Somehow instinctively when I was caught in this blast I shouted back. My action was not a rationally conceived analytical response. I reacted intuitively. From then on we respected each other and had a good working relationship. He respected someone with the guts to shout back. Right after my encounter but before I really knew the outcome, my manager sat me down and counseled me about the serious error I had made. The style within me happened to work, but it was not the style of my manager. We need to develop a sense of when to let ourselves, our emotions, our brain's right hemisphere govern actions.

Interpersonal style is established in part by events in early life, long before we enter the working world. Interpersonal style is based on our view of ourselves, on our assessment of feedback from our actions. Do we feel dependent or independent? Do we have a need to control or can we be rather free and shift style with changing conditions? Do we feel a need to tell or are we comfortable in asking? Do we tend to be quick, even too quick, and thus conclusion jumpers who don't give our fellow employees enough air time? Each of us needs a kind of balance between giving and taking, listening and talking. Do we tend to the dramatic or are we relatively quiet and unassertive? These are but a few examples of interpersonal behavioral dimensions.

Your goals, your aspirations, also shape your style in many ways. The measure of your achievement motivation, for example, can cause a severe impact on style and behavior. Richard III had a style, killing off those who were in his way in order to achieve the position of king. True, he found his success hollow and of short duration when he got there. His style was shaped by his deformity and his ambition. Though less dramatic, there are Richards in today's organizational world. Their style is to arrange events so that the blame for failures falls on others and the glory of success falls on them. Modern understanding of the different functions of the brain hemispheres demonstrates another aspect of the style within us. Left-hemisphere thinking modes tend to be linear, analytical, and mathematical. Right-hemisphere thinking modes tend to be intuitive, nonlinear, subjective, and imaginative. Each of us has a unique balance and mode of using these brain hemispheres. Our style may be first to look at events in a linear, scientific, left-hemisphere mode. Our style may be intuitive, pattern oriented, and right-hemisphere dominated. These outlooks or dominances also affect our career choice and our education and thus affect our success as managers. Management is a role which requires right-hemisphere capability. In fact, this book although attempting to present a balanced view, is right-hemisphere influenced, stressing as it does the environment and many of the subjective and feeling parts of people management. This chapter has as its companion chapter five where we stressed the necessity of your determining who you are. Who you are, who you see yourself as being, and who you want to be shape your style.

The Style You Can Create

If your style is in a sense predetermined by brain pattern, your self-image, your personality, your goals and early training, then why write a chapter suggesting you create your own style? First, some aspects of style are modifiable. You can change what becomes important to you to change. Second, you can learn to use your style to best advantage. Third, there are aspects of managerial style, behavior in the context of the organization, that are new and unique to organizational cultures. These aspects of style can be learned and understood only in the context of the organization. These styles are not something you bring to work as a predetermined base. Some of these aspects of style are often called the politics of the organization. They represent behavior patterns which seem to be successful, seem to be rewarded by the organization. They tend to reflect the style of the leader or leaders, the type of activity or mission of the organization, and the cultural context in which the organization exists. For example, an organization in the Arab world and one in the United States would reflect the cultures in which they exist. Behavioral or action style, like style in clothing, should fit both the wearer and the context. A blustery style does not fit the mild mannered conservative person. But a blustery or aggressive style may be required in certain organizations. A quiet and patient style does not fit the aggressive and loud person. Yet the quiet style may be required in certain organizations, for example, a hospital. Thus, choosing a style or maximizing the effectiveness of a style, brings us back to the fundamental fact that the quality of management starts with self-knowledge. This means you may or may not try to change or modify your style, but you must do so from a base of knowledge. The basic need is to develop a range of style. Some of these will fit you better than others, but all will work better with practice. Your search should be to identify the styles which seem most effective for you and the contexts in which they work.

I once knew of a near-genius mathematician. He often drove to work without shifting gears in his car. His interest and attention was somewhere else. A manager without a range, a repertoire of styles, is like the man who drives under all conditions in one gear. Early in my middle-management experience, one of my subordinate managers tried to teach me this lesson. He came into my office and said, "When was the last time you lost your temper?" My response was I couldn't remember because I prided myself in not losing my temper. He then suggested gently that I should occasionally let myself blow up for three reasons. First, it might just be the secret to motivating action under certain conditions. Second, it would allow me to relieve internal stress and thus contribute to a better life. Third, I would probably be more real to my subordinates since normal people occasionally lose their temper. I was so controlled I was not coming across as authentic.

It is important in these examples to understand that I am suggesting a choice of approach which fits both the person and the environment. I am not suggesting shifting gears for the sake of shifting. I am not suggesting there is one right way or that we all develop the same style. I am not suggesting that we all regularly and frequently lose our temper. I am not even suggesting there is one right style. I am suggesting that we each need to develop the ability to use different approaches. This is in keeping with understanding that people are different and respond to different stimuli. It also reflects the understanding that the environment or climate of the organization may make some approaches significantly more effective than others.

In thinking about how the organizational climate and the context affect style let us look at how we might break bad news to our superior. Incidentally, no one likes surprises. Our managers don't, we generally don't, and our employees don't. For our example let us consider only three styles or techniques. They are the direct, blunt revelation, the piecemeal revelation to prepare the recipient, and the indirect revelation with which we try to avoid the sting. The first could be represented by just going in to the superior's office and telling him or her in a straightforward fashion. The second could be represented by revealing but a piece or part of the news, getting a response, and perhaps giving further information in response to a question. The third approach might be represented by arranging to have other people reveal pieces and parts of the news. This might cause the superior to probe and find out and not directly identify you as the carrier of the news. Any one of these approaches might work and be appropriate.

Starting with the basic premise that managers don't like surprises and that negative news is seldom comfortable but often necessary, how would you choose an approach? What influences your choice? Or perhaps rather than making a conscious choice, would you respond to a gut feeling and act in keeping with that feeling? A brief review of your own real-life experiences should reveal cases where each of the alternatives might be the right one. Some determinants of your choice might be:

- the magnitude of the problem and its seriousness or necessity for action
- the openness and stability of your relationship with your superior
- the level of trust you have in your manager and the organization
- the potential impact on your manager's evaluation of your performance
- the general state of the organization (that is, overall success, growth, decline)
- the impact on other parts of the organization
- the risks and costs, both organizational and personal, of delay in revealing the problem
- the impact of the problem on your manager's career and position
- the norms of successful behavior in the organization

This may sound overly political or manipulative. That is one of the dangers of discussing this aspect of behavior in an organization. Nevertheless, experience suggests that successful managers are conscious of their style, work to develop a range of effective approaches, and are conscious of the politics of the organization. Like any other approach carried to excess it diverts you from the real meaning of work. This means it is wrong to spend all your time or energy analyzing and managing style. However, being oblivious to your style can turn a potentially effective manager into an average or poor manager. Being unconscious of how your style may affect what happens may create problems for you and can severely limit your success.

SUMMARY

It is not enough to know the functions of the manager. It is not enough to be skilled at activities like screening applicants and appraisal and counseling. To be a good manager one must have a strategy, be a student of tactics, and develop a style which is successful in one's organization. Although this seems like a tall order, we come by some of these things normally. This chapter proposes that you work consciously at the design of your strategy and style using tactics consistent with both strategy and style within your organizational climate.

A useful strategy is built on our personal goals as interpreted by us in the context of the organization. It becomes a guiding theme. Strategies are by their nature long term. In the short term they are converted to action plans, tactics, and style. A positive human resource strategy for a manager might grow out of a goal to have his or her employees grow and become the leaders of the organization. Translated into action this might mean that all activities, all tasks which can be, should be designed to cause those who do them to learn and increase capabilities. Tactics which would implement such a strategy mght include redesign of jobs so that they provide learning and growth opportunities as well as the psychic reward appropriate for the individuals involved. Pursuit of this strategy might or might not provide growth for the manager, for this would be dependent on organizational culture. Such strategy should provide growth for the employees, again dependent on the norms and culture of the organization.

With strategy and tactics in place you must next address style. Style has primarily to do with how you relate to other people, although there can also be an organizational style. Style, then, has to do with how you talk about the process. Style has to do with whether you tell or ask, with whether you push or pull, with whether you exhort or set an example, and so on. Your style must fit you as a person, and be one in which you come across as authentic. Your style should be compatible with the expectations and needs of your employees and it should generally be compatible with the norms of the organization.

Creating a forward thrust as a manager is important to your own progress, to your feeling of impact and contribution, and to the success of the organization. Developing your own strategy and style is important in creating your forward thrust.

Personal Managerial Strategy and Style Checkup

1. On another piece of paper list the last ten decisions you made, directions you gave, statements you transmitted, or actions you took. If these decisions and actions were all the data about you that you had, what would you conclude is your belief about people?

    People are:

    ____ inherently good   ____ inherently bad
    ____ generally need detailed direction   ____ able to be self-directing
    ____ threatening to your position   ____ desirous of learning and growth
    ____ agents you use to help you gain your ends ____ creative and ingenious
    ____ highly competitive   ____ participants, sharing in responsibility for
    ____ generally achievement oriented   organization goals
    ____ working only to gain money   ____ other _____

2. Your strategy, overall plan, and prevailing thrust should also be evident in the ten decisions or actions you listed for question 1. Looking back at these, pick the statement which best reflects the theme expressed by those observations.   ( )

    a. This person is driving to get to the top of the organization, to be the leader, to have more power.
    b. This person believes work should be fun and a rewarding growth-oriented activity and demonstrates his or her interest in the people of the organization.
    c. This person believes that the mission of the organization represents a calling, an important contribution to humanity above and beyond the materialistic profit motive for success.
    d. This person expresses a win/win strategy in his or her actions and decisions and definitely does not wish to be successful at the expense of others.
    e. This person is most interested in improving the process including interpersonal relations and seems to give results a somewhat lower priority.
    f. This person believes everything can be measured in monetary terms.
    g. Other _____
        _____
        _____

3. Your strategy reflects both your goals and your acceptance or agreement with the goals of the organization. Goals will come through in your decisions and style. Which statement best represents your feelings?   ( )

    a. My goals and those of the organization merge and are almost totally congruent.
    b. Many of my goals and those of the organization overlap, and I can support the organization easily and wholeheartedly.

c.   I am confused with many fluctuations of feeling about being part of and being separate from the organization.

d.   I am frequently at odds with the organization but still able to put up an appearance of conformity and belief in organization goals.

e.   My goal is to use the organization to achieve my goals, which are nearly totally separate from the organization.

4.   Which statement best describes your interpersonal style? (Check the appropriate point on the range.)

	very much	very little
My tendency is to tell employees what to do.	⌊___⌊___⌊___⌊___⌊	
My tendency is to ask questions so the employee figures out what to do.	⌊___⌊___⌊___⌊___⌊	
My tendency is to try to control the results of the group.	⌊___⌊___⌊___⌊___⌊	
My tendency is, after I've done what I can, to accept what happens.	⌊___⌊___⌊___⌊___⌊	
My tendency is to be outgoing, talkative, and socially gregarious.	⌊___⌊___⌊___⌊___⌊	
My tendency is to be withdrawn, speak minimally and avoid interpersonal relationships.	⌊___⌊___⌊___⌊___⌊	
My tendency is to base judgments on an analytical and problem-solving orientation.	⌊___⌊___⌊___⌊___⌊	
My tendency is to base judgments on caring and feeling.	⌊___⌊___⌊___⌊___⌊	
My tendency is to base my actions on a thorough understanding of the facts.	⌊___⌊___⌊___⌊___⌊	
My tendency is to base my actions on intuition.	⌊___⌊___⌊___⌊___⌊	

5.   How well thought out is your strategy? Are you conscious of having one? Pick the most appropriate statement.   (   )

a.   I have been conscious of an overall strategy or thrust and have or can write it down in a rather explicit form. Most, nearly 100 percent, of my actions and decisions reflect that plan.

b.   I have been conscious of an overall strategy and consider that fully 80 percent of my decisions or actions reflect that thrust.

c.   I have a theme or thrust that I've thought about, but I've never been explicit about it. I feel that about 60 percent of my decisions and actions represent this consistent theme.

d.   I have a feeling of a central theme but it is vague and undefined. Probably no more than 30 percent of my decisions and actions reflect this strategy.

e.   I am not conscious of having an overall strategy since I look at each incident as a separate, unrelated event.

6. We implement our strategy in decisions and actions. Often it is not so much the content or explicit action which transmits our theme but rather our style, including tone of voice, nonverbal signals, and apparent sincerity. Which of the following best reflects your feeling about your consistency of strategy and style?   (   )

    a. My style totally supports my strategy and I'm very consistent.
    b. My style supports my strategy and gives clear signals 80 percent of the time.
    c. My style supports my strategy and gives clear signals 50 percent of the time.
    d. My style supports my strategy and gives clear signals 30 percent of the time.
    e. My style probably confuses people about my strategy, which is not all that consistent either.

7. Strategy and style reflect values. Out of the following possible approaches, pick the one which feels right.   (   )

    a. I take a commanding position and fight hard for what I believe to be right. It is a personal challenge to win and to cause others to follow by the strength of my position.
    b. I work hard to create a consensus and gain support in the right places. My strategy is much like that of a member of Congress, actively giving support to others in order to gain support for my position.
    c. I survey the field and give my support to the several I feel have a chance of winning. I'm content to be just outside the limelight.
    d. I'm primarily loyal to one leader, and I'm betting that he or she will win by supporting their position.
    e. I simply don't play games, and I am not part of any power group. My strategy is to do what is right and not play politics.

8. Your human resource strategy reflects the way you gain the support and following of those who work for you. Pick the most appropriate statements.

    Generally I expect them to respect my position of power and authority and follow without question.   (   )
    Generally I expect to have to sell them my position, but I expect them to buy.   (   )
    Generally I discuss the issues and give the group the impression that they are participating, but it is really my decision.   (   )
    Generally I expect to have to discuss my position and let them contribute to forming a group position before they will buy.   (   )
    Generally I expect to contribute to the group position as an equal member, and all actions result from consensus.   (   )

9. Which statement best reflects how you made your reputation in the organization?   (   )

    a. The high productivity (measurable output) of my group both in quality and quantity.
    b. What I say and do and how I manage to promote a good image of myself in the organization.

c. The way in which I size up and play the politics of the organization.

d. Being responsive to the requests and needs of the management above me.

e. The good morale of my group and the lack of employee or industrial relations problems.

10. Which statement best reflects your feelings about competition in the organization?   (   )

a. Competition is essentially person to person, and winning is based on creating ideas and concepts which are put into practice.

b. Competition is essentially person to person, and winning is based on demonstrating that I can get more out for less money, time, and personnel.

c. Competition is essentially individual. Those who win are those who demonstrate they are getting the most out of themselves.

d. Competition is essentially group to group. To win it is necessary to demonstrate that my group is more valuable, contributes most to the organization.

e. There is no real competition in the organization.

Ideas for Action: Improving Your Strategy and Style

something
to try

1. Analyze your personal goals and translate them into the appropriate supportive strategy and style in dealing with your employees. The following analysis may help. Parenthetical statements are merely examples to assist you.   (   )

    a. One of my goals is to (example: get promoted): _____
        _____

    b. To achieve that goal the following achievements in the organization would be helpful (example: to build a better relationship with upper management, to increase the productivity of my department): _____
        _____
        _____

    c. Some of the achievements under (b) are by their nature personal but some can be enhanced by the support and assistance of those you supervise. Mark those under (b) which can be enhanced by the people you direct with an asterisk.

    d. Now translate those identified under (c) into strategies (example: work to increase group participation in planning and work design as a way to increase productivity.
        _____
        _____

    e. Identify those elements of management style, ways of dealing with your employees, which will best carry out the strategies identified under (d) (example: become more open and approachable).
        _____
        _____
        _____
        _____
        _____
        _____
        _____
        _____

2. Discuss strategy and style with your fellow managers and share ways of creating useful strategies and style.   (   )

3. Take a course internal to the organization, if available, or at a nearby college on leadership and motivation.   (   )

4. Read a book or books on leadership and motivation. Biographies of organizational leaders are especially good for examining this aspect of strategy and style.   (   )

5. Create the practice of reviewing what happened at the end of each day and asking:
What was my strategy today? How was it evident?
Would a change in strategy or style have improved results?
What experiment or change should I try tomorrow?   (   )

6. At the end of a meeting in your office, take time to ask the group to identify the strategy or theme within which they would place the discussion, type of problem or decision.   (   )

7. Try making your strategy more explicit and stating it as a means of improving communication and effectiveness.   (   )

8. Discuss strategy and style openly with your manager. Seek advice on ways he or she sees that you might be more effective.   (   )

9. Adopt a strategy of personal achievement through the growth and development of other people. Choose several of your employees whom you believe are worthy of development and begin specific plans to accelerate their growth.   (   )

10. Adopt a strategy which makes an increase in the adult as opposed to the dependent behavior in the organization a desired goal. Actively look for ways to carry that out and especially to reflect it in your managerial style.   (   )

CHAPTER
17

The Manager's Role

Vitality and Renewal

My first book about human resources was entitled *Personal Vitality*. Because I feel deeply that personal and organizational vitality must be outputs of work, it is appropriate to close this book with a chapter on vitality. Vitality is what human resource management is about. If we are successful in managing people, we create vitality, we don't use up people. A negative idea prevalent in our culture is that people should deteriorate with use and increasing age. This concept sets up expectations which waste human potential and encourage premature decline.

Vitality can be thought of as adaptability and performance power. Vitality is the power to be successful in what we do and to adjust to changing conditions. It is a quality of aliveness and desire to commit ourselves to something. An increase in vitality is the result of well-chosen quality work, work that is meaningful to us, uses our capabilities, and thus causes us to gain in capability and energy. Vital people make a vital organization. More than ever we need vital people and vital organizations. We are demanding greater adaptability, the competition is increasing, and we are just beginning to understand that some of our past progress has been bought at costs we now question. Some of these costs are a deterioration in quality or an ecological impact which is negative.

Vitality is an important topic too because we have just recently eliminated arbitrary retirement on the basis of age. This means that the human and organizational costs of expecting or allowing decline in interest, growth, and effectiveness can no longer be tolerated. We must learn to build both organizations and a society which expect, support, and create continued learning, human and organizational renewal, and growth in capability. Now is the time for exploring human ecology as it is the time for emphasis on environmental ecology. It is as appropriate to put behind us the misuse of human beings as the misuse of our natural resources.

Vitality is created through a cycle which is both normal and natural (Figure 11). However, many of our ways of life, designs of our organizations, and work designs have impeded or interfered with this cycle. The

271

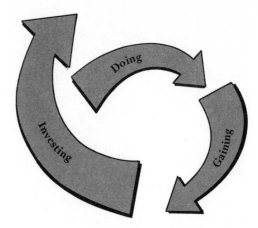

Figure 11.   *The vitality cycle*

challenge of human resource management is, therefore, to remove some of the interferences and to support the normal renewal and growth process.

In order to grow in capability, we must use the capabilities we have. Like an atrophied muscle, our skills and knowledge decline in usefulness when unused. *Doing* — choosing an activity of importance to us, which uses our capabilities and causes us to stretch — is the first element of the vitality cycle. This first step sounds deceptively simple but every day we do things which use us up rather than challenge and stretch us to create development and improve satisfaction. Why do we do things which don't add to our vitality? Sometimes we choose devitalizing activity simply because we are caught in a routine. Sometimes we do the wrong things because we have denied or failed to heed the feedback which tells us they fail to produce development and satisfaction, or that they produce negative stress and lead to stress-related disorders. Sometimes we choose the wrong activities because we believe we are trapped, forced by others to do so. Sometimes we stay with the unrewarding activities because we have denied ourselves the permission to change and grow. Sometimes we choose wrong activities because we believe we are responding to the expectations of the organization, our manager, friends, or our family.

I am not suggesting that every single thing we do must contribute to our vitality; I am suggesting that we need to change the proportions so that we do more things which contribute to vitality. Each one of us is entitled to some activities every day which add to our learning, growth, and capability. For many people these activities should occur at work, for this is a central and major endeavor in life. I feel this entitlement, like the freedoms guaranteed by our Constitution, should be considered a basic human right. Each of us—mother, father, citizen, manager, worker—should work to preserve and enhance this right. We should do this because our very existence, the length of our life, and the existence of future generations depends on our ability to build renewal, growth, and vitality into our culture. This need has become far more imperative because of our technological culture with rapid paced and pervasive change. The complexity of our lives has made it necessary for us to create, to manage a process which probably occurred more naturally in a simple life.

If we choose to do something that stretches us, uses our capabilities and causes us to strive for growth, then the second part of the vitality cycle comes into being. The second element is *gaining*. The gains we should achieve are psychological, physical, and monetary. They are gains in our sense of personal worth and in satisfaction with life and work. They are gains in our sense of accomplishment. They are gains in our sense of creation. They are gains in skills and knowledge. They are gains in our respect for our own capability. They are gains in recognition from others. They are gains in our ability to relate to, work with, and assist other people. The gains are many and varied. What is important is that the gains we achieve by applying ourselves should have meaning to us. The gains should be intrinsic in the activity. The gains should fit with our values and goals. The gains should represent a return on our investment, our investment of our energies, interests, and skills. The gains should provide us with new strengths and power.

As with any other return on an investment we now have something more to invest. *Investing* is the third element of the vitality cycle. Because we chose to do things of importance to us, things which caused us to reap a benefit, we have gains to invest. It is possible, then, to invest in ways which assure we have more vitality, more aliveness, more capability, more thrust, more power as we come around the next time. If we gained a new sense of capability, we can apply this new capability to doing more, doing better, doing something of greater value. If we gained a new sense of wonder and curiosity, we can invest this in study and enhancement of understanding and capability. If we gained a new sense of energy, we have more energy to apply to doing something of importance.

The Manager's Role

This book has been about the many things the manager can do to enhance the match between the employee and work. Enhancing the match is contributing to vitality. Even small improvements in the employee's sense of achieving personal goals in the context of the organization's goals contribute to vitality. The increase in vitality is both personal and organizational. If we can improve the learning that takes place in doing the tasks and assignments, we enhance vitality. If we, as managers, can provide the support that makes personal change and development both desirable and supportable, we enhance vitality. It is in this sense that vitality is what human resource management is all about.

If, as managers we can adopt a strategy which makes enhancing individual and organizational vitality our goal, we have created a positive human resource strategy. If we can adopt techniques and processes which enhance rather than use up human capability, we are implementing our strategy. If we can personally choose to do the things which represent broad gains or income for us, then we too, as managers, can invest in greater power, increased adaptability, greater thrust the next time around. Greater vitality benefits us as individuals, the employee, the organization, and the nation.

Ideas for Action: Creating A Vital Organization

Something to try

1. Choose a mission or purpose that is exciting and attracts people. Define and aggressively communicate organizational goals.   ( )
2. Pick leader-managers who radiate their acceptance of and interest in the challenge, and thus create a stimulating, exciting environment.   ( )
3. Establish organizational policies supportive of a good human resource environment. Create ways of matching employee needs and capabilities with organizational needs and capabilities. Provide pervasive support for personal development and growth through work and career changes.   ( )
4. Motivate managers to design jobs and tasks that motivate through identification with organizational goals, utilization of capabilities, and psychic rewards.   ( )
5. Establish educational and training programs that provide necessary cognitive and technical knowledge, management development, and life-career management skills.   ( )
6. Engage in organizational and work design to improve the quality of work life with special emphasis on creating an adult environment.   ( )
7. Establish management systems to motivate the employees to take personal responsibility for their own career-life management.   ( )
8. Establish reward and recognition systems to reward those who maintain and enhance their personal vitality and effectiveness.   ( )
9. Motivate managers to examine their management practices, processes, and styles to eliminate activities which deplete vitality and enhance those which aid in creating vitality.   ( )
10. Establish performance expectations that make increasing age an unacceptable excuse for decline, turning off, and giving up.   ( )

INDEX